READING MICAH IN NIGERIA

INTERNATIONAL VOICES IN BIBLICAL STUDIES

Jione Havea, General Editor

Editorial Board
Jin Young Choi
Gerald O. West

Number 15

READING MICAH IN NIGERIA
Ethics, Wealth, and Corruption

by
Blessing Onoriode Boloje

Atlanta

Copyright © 2023 by Blessing Onoriode Boloje

All rights reserved. No part of this work may be reproduced or transmitted in any form or by any means, electronic or mechanical, including photocopying and recording, or by means of any information storage or retrieval system, except as may be expressly permitted by the 1976 Copyright Act or in writing from the publisher. Requests for permission should be addressed in writing to the Rights and Permissions Office, SBL Press, 825 Houston Mill Road, Atlanta, GA 30329 USA.

Library of Congress Control Number: 2023937134

Contents

Foreword vii
Acknowledgments ix
Abbreviations xi

1. Introduction 1
   1.1. Background and General Orientation   1
   1.2. Driving Questions and Intended Orientation   4
   1.3. Methodology, Scope, and Structure   6

2. Micah: Character, Location, Context, Book 17
   2.1. Micah's Character   17
   2.2. Location of Micah   20
   2.3. Context of Micah's Oracles   23
   2.4. Preliminary Remarks on the Book of Micah   35

3. Socioeconomic Transgressions and Power Relations
   in Micah's Oracles 47
   3.1. Economic Piracy and Land Confiscation (2:1–5)   47
   3.2. Distorted Theological Rationalization and Condemnation
        of Injustice (2:6–11)   55
   3.3. Corrupt Economic, Political, and Religious System (3:1–12)   66

4. Religious Unfaithfulness and Community Moral Depravity
   in Micah's Oracle 77
   4.1. Israel's Religious Sins (6:1–8)   77
   4.2. Cheating and Violence (6:9–16)   92
   4.3. Total Corruption of the People (7:1–6)   102

5. Ethical Burdens in Micah's Oracles 111
   5.1. Yahweh's Sovereignty and the Concern for Justice   115
   5.2. Responsible Leadership and Accountability   119

    5.3. Community Relationship and Social Solidarity   128
    5.4. Worship and Dedicated Lifestyle   134

6. Micah's Ethical Thrust for Contemporary Socioeconomic
   and Religious Engagement 139
    6.1. Contemporary Christian Communities and Religious Leaders   140
    6.2. The Wider Society and Socioeconomic Realities   161
    6.3. Injustice and National Development   167

7. Conclusion 169

Bibliography 173

Modern Authors Index 189

Ancient Sources Index 195

Foreword

There is hardly a biblical prophet who calls for ethical action as directly as Micah, whose prophecy is dated to the eighth century BCE by the superscription in Mic 1:1. Micah's prophetic accusation is highly poetic and yet always very concrete. The announced punishments are repeatedly reciprocal: those who have caused injustice by exploiting the land will suffer injustice through redistribution of land without compensation; those who accumulated wealth in palace like houses will experience homelessness and loss; and those who squeezed the poor by seizure will become needy themselves. The ruthless greed of the possessing few could not be more violent: They "strip the robe from the peaceful," they "tear the skin off my people," and they "eat the flesh of God's people." It is a relentless reckoning with the institutions—prophets and priests have failed—that allowed it to come to this acutely immoral situation. A prophet in this situation does not have an easy task: he has to find solid, authoritative, yet also common ground. This challenge has driven the tradents of the book of Micah seriously, which is why they have supplemented, expanded, amended, and edited it over several centuries. On what basis can one condemn the behavior which is obviously damaging to the community? The theological tradents sought their way between natural law and revelation. They linked the argument of accusation to the torah and thus substantiated it. The intertextual entanglement with the social laws of the torah and the rereading of Micah's straightforward analysis allowed them to coin the simple yet enigmatic basic ethical principle: "He has told you, man, what is good; and what does the Lord require of you but to do justice, and to love kindness, and to walk humbly with your God?" (Mic 6:8).

Because the description of the wickedness is so dense and at the same time so immediately comprehensible, and because the necessity of a social change towards an economic and social order based on justice is so pressing, this prophetic book—like no other—seems to be suitable for a transfer to the unrighteousness of the present. The task of exegesis is not to simply skip the inconvenient (or problematic / awkward / bothersome / etc.) gap of historical distance, but to thoroughly unfold the discourses that have been reflected in the multi-layered book. Exegesis does not simply comprise a direct application of a biblical text for one's own community or communities of readers, but rather the exposure of structural parallels, such as, for instance, accountability of leadership or morality as a base of convenience and economic development, the necessity of community building as a means of survival, et cetera. Here, exegesis of Micah has a great deal to offer, and the current book of Blessing Boloje does so. He argues carefully and applies masterfully the appropriate exegetical methods to the text, which unfolds its urgent relevance for today's readers. Although the author is as sensitive as possible to the parallels in African societies, especially to twenty-first century Nigeria, and although he is quite open to the necessary critical analysis of actual leadership, and although he is of the firm conviction that Micah is God's word, he does not simply read the current challenges into the text. Rather, he points out what the text in its historical context can mean for a community that is based on the Bible and finds hope and perspective in it. Hence, this balanced study becomes extremely valuable in two ways: for its exegetical discussion, because it offers further approaches to the explanation of Micah's prophecy, and for its social discussion regarding contemporary Africa-Nigerian context, because it shows structural parallels that make it possible to search for alternative courses of action.

Prof. Dr. Christian Frevel
Lehrstuhl für Altes Testament
Katholisch-Theologische Fakultät
Universität Bochum

ACKNOWLEDGMENTS

This project was conceptualized towards the end of my one-year postdoctoral fellowship at the Department of Old Testament and Hebrew Scriptures, Faculty of Theology and Religion, University of Pretoria in 2015. The project reflects my passionate desire for reading and applying biblical texts through the lens of ethics, to the context and culture that I am most familiar with—the African-Nigerian context. I wish, therefore, to acknowledge the tremendous supports and insights of many Institutions and people who read and contributed through discussions and comments, from the time of writing the proposal for funding to its culmination in this volume. I am delighted to use this medium to express my profound gratitude to the Baptist Theological Seminary, Eku, for supporting my research leave.

I am extremely grateful to the Alexander von Humboldt Foundation for awarding me its prestigious fellowship (Georg Forster Fellowship), that has allowed me to do this study in Germany. I am especially appreciative of my host, Prof. Dr. Christian Frevel, Lehrstuhl für AltesTestament, Katholisch-Theologische Fakultät, Universität Bochum for creating the space in his department to host, support, and motivate me to complete this study for publication. He made time out of his very busy schedules, to meet with me for discussion, reading the draft chapters and making well-informed comments that helped me to articulate the workings of my ethical positions and for graciously and generously contributing an insightful foreword to this volume. I appreciate the supportive roles of the staff of the department during this period especially, Johannes Bremer, Jordan Davis, Katharina Pyschny, and Katharina Werbeck.

I am sincerely thankful to Prof. Dr. Rainer Kessler (Phillips Universität Marburg), Prof. Dr. Dr. Willie J. Wessels (University of South Africa), for agreeing to read the manuscript, making their critical comments, offering suggestions, and making recommendations. In the same vein, I appreciate the duo of Prof. John E. Goldingay (Fuller Theological Seminary, California) and Prof Heather A. McKay (Edge Hill University, Lancashire, UK) for their proofreading and copyediting. The chair and staff of the Department of Old Testament and Hebrew Scriptures, Faculty of Theology and Religion, University of Pretoria have been very supportive of my research ventures. Since the completion of my doctoral research, I have spent a very fruitful research time with the department as a postdoctoral fellow (2015) and research associate (since 2016). My thanks are warmly offered to Professors Dirk Human, Alphonso Groenewald, Sias Meyer, Jurie Le Roux. I am also very grateful to Prof. Dr. Aaron Schart (University of Essen-Duisburg, Germany) for inviting me to his Institute to give lectures and seminars, before and during my research stay in Germany.

Some of the ideas in this work were presented orally in conferences and previous publications, in particular: "Micah's Theory of the Justice of Judgement (Micah 3:1–12)" *Journal for Semitics* 26.2 (2017): 689–710; "Trading Yahweh's Word for a Price: Ethical Implications of the Collusion of Prophets and Priests in Micah 3:5–7, 11," *Old Testament Essays* 31.3 (2018): 630–50; "Economic Piracy and Land Confiscation (Micah 2:1–5): A Portrayal of Evildoers, Evildoing and Yahweh's Action," *Journal for Semitics* 28.1(2019): 1–15; "Extravagant Rituals or Ethical Religion (Micah 6:6–8)? Ritual Interface with Social Responsibility in Micah" *Old Testament Essays* 32.3 (2019): 800–20; "Micah 2:9 and the Traumatic Effects of Depriving Children of Their Parents," *HTS Teologiese Studies/Theological Studies* (2020):76.1, a5960; "'The Godly Person Has Perished from the Land" (Mi 7:1–6): Micah's Lamentation of Judah's Corruption and Its Ethical Imperatives for a Healthy Community Living," *HTS Teologiese Studies/ Theological Studies* (2021):774, a6757. These articles are, however, not presented as chapters in this book.

I appreciate most sincerely, the editor and members of the board of International Voices in Biblical Studies (IVBS), Jione Havea, Jin Young Choi, Emily Colgan, Musa Dube, Julián Andrés González, David Joy, and Gerald O. West, for the review process, meetings, and approval of this project for publication. My deepest gratitude goes to my wife and to our Children, for their patience during my absence from home. Finally, I heartily appreciate the love, encouragement, prayers, and enthusiasm of a galaxy of others too numerous to mention, or even to remember, who in some small ways have contributed to the successful completion of this project. To one and all, I say thank you.

ABBREVIATIONS

AB	Anchor Bible
ABD	Freedman, D. N., ed. *Anchor Bible Dictionary*. 6 vols. New York, 1992.
AJBS	*African Journal of Biblical Studies*
AJET	*African Journal of Evangelical Theology*
AOTC	Abingdon Old Testament Commentaries
ATR	*Anglican Theological Review*
BASOR	*Bulletin of the American Schools of Oriental Research*
BDB	Brown, F. Driver, S. R. and Briggs, C. *Hebrew and English Lexicon of the Old Testament*. Oxford: Clarendon.
BibInt	Biblical Interpretation
BSac	*Bibliotheca Sacra*
BT	*Bible Translator*
BTB	*Biblical Theology Bulletin*
BZAW	Beihefte zur Zeitschrift für die Alttestamentliche Wissenschaft
CPI	Corruption Perceptions Index
CurTM	*Currents in Theology and Mission*
ECWA	Evangelical Church Winning All
EJT	*Evangelical Journal of Theology*
ESJ	*European Scientific Journal*
ExAud	*Ex auditu*
FOTL	Forms of the Old Testament Literature
GNB	Good News Bible
HALOT	Koehler, Ludwig, Walter Baumgartner, and Johann J. Stamm, eds. *The Hebrew and Aramaic Lexicon of the Old Testament*. 5 vols. Leiden: Brill, 1994–1999.
HTR	*Harvard Theological Review*
HvTSt	*Harvormde teologiese studies*
IJHSS	*International Journal of Humanities and Social Science*
IJSRSSMS	*International Journal of Scientific Research in Social Sciences and Management Studies*

Int	*Interpretation*
JPC	*Journal of Psychology and Christianity*
JBL	*Journal of Biblical Literature*
JBT	*Journal of Black Theology*
JBQ	*Jewish Bible Quarterly*
JNSL	*Journal of Northwest Semitic Languages*
JORIND	*Journal of Research in National Development*
JP	*Journal for Preachers*
JPAPR	*Journal of Public Administration and Policy Research*
JPE	*Journal of Political Economy*
JRSSupp	Journal of Religion and Society Supplement Series
JSDA	*Journal of Sustainable Development in Africa*
JSem	*Journal for Semitics*
JSOT	*Journal for the Study of Old Testament*
JSOTSup	Journal for the Study of Old Testament Supplement Series
JSSS	*Journal of Studies in Social Sciences*
LHBOTS	Library of Hebrew Bible/Old Testament Studies
LXX	Septuagint
MT	Masoretic Text
NASB	New American Standard Bible
NICOT	New International Commentary on the Old Testament
NIV	New International Version
NJB	The New Jerusalem Bible
NJPS	New Jewish Population Society
NRSV	New Revised Standard Version
OTE	Old Testament Essays
OTL	Old Testament Library
PJ	*Perkins Journal*
PSt	*Political Studies*
REB	Revised English Bible
RevExp	*Review and Expositor*
RQ	*Restoration Quarterly*
SBJT	*Southern Baptist Journal of Theology*
SemeiaSt	Semeia Studies
Scrip	*Scriptura*
SJER	*Sky Journal of Educational Research*
SJT	*Scottish Journal of Theology*
SWJT	*South-western Journal of Theology*
StRel	*Studies in Religion*
TDOT	Botterweck, G. Johannes, and Helmer Ringgren, eds. *Theological Dictionary of the Old Testament*. Translated by John T. Willis et al. 8 vols. Grand Rapids: Eerdmans, 1974–2006.

THOTC	Two Horizons Old Testament Commentary
TI	Transparency International
TOTC	Tyndale Old Testament Commentaries
TWOT	Harris, R. L., and G. L. Archer Jr., eds. *Theological Wordbook of the Old Testament*. 2 Vols. Chicago: Moody Press, 1980.
TynBul	*Tyndale Bulletin*
UNDP	United Nations Development Programme
VE	*Verbum et Ecclesia*
VE	*Vox Evangelica*
VT	*Vetus Testamentum*
VTSup	Vetus Testamentum Supplement
WBC	*Word Biblical Commentary*
WCC	World Council of Churches

1

INTRODUCTION

The effects of our actions may be postponed but they are never lost. There is an inevitable reward for good deeds and an inescapable punishment for bad.
—Wu Ming Fu

1.1. Background and General Orientation

This project developed from reflections on the perennial issues of injustice, poverty, wealth, and oppression especially of marginalized majority prevalent in many parts of the world but practically ubiquitous in Nigeria (and Africa in general).[1] In Nigeria, there is generally an obvious manifestation of socioeconomic and religious contrast between affluent lifestyle of leaders (and those connected to them) and the destitution of marginalized majority who have become perpetual economic hostages. Nigeria as a country is generally referred to as the "Giant of Africa" due essentially to its huge population and economy. But sadly, it remains a country with untapped and underdeveloped resources, neglected projects and shattered hopes. The situation is compounded largely by unproductive, greedy, irresponsible, and unaccountable leadership and citizens who are unpatriotic and/or corrupt.

A report by *The World Poverty Clock* noted that "Nigeria has become the poverty capital of the world."[2] Samuel Abogunrin notes that poverty in Nigeria is "the inevitable consequence of a process in which a few economically powerful Nigerians wield political power to control institutions for their own private

---

[1] On the one hand, the description of Nigeria bears the stamp of my personal experience. My description may not be entirely comprehensive but an obvious reflection of the day-to-day realities in the country. On the other hand, these descriptive realities also find expression in various narratives about Nigerians and Nigeria.

[2] Yomi Kazeem, "Nigeria has become the poverty capital of the world," June 25, 2018, https://qz.com/africa/1313380/nigerias-has-the-highest-rate-of-extreme-poverty-globally/.

profit."³ The so far unsuccessful attempt to lift the country and her citizens out of the labyrinth of poverty has been attributed to the failure of the country's leadership in managing her massive oil wealth and other resources because of corruption. According to Kazeem's 2018 report, there are about 86.9 million Nigerians living in extreme poverty. This estimate represents approximately 50 percent of the country's estimated population of 180 million people. While there is certainly no unanimous definition of poverty, Peter Townsend in relating poverty to income notes that "people can be said to be in poverty when they are deprived of income and other resources needed to obtain the conditions of life—the diets, material goods, amenities, standards and services—that enable them to play the roles, meet the obligations and participate in the relationships and customs of their society."⁴ The massive rate of poverty in the midst of the nation's wealth has been linked to the scourge of corruption in the country. This description is however not different from the rest of Africa.⁵ The report of *ActionAid Nigeria* on "corruption and poverty in Nigeria" associates corruption with "the massive stealing of public resources that would have been invested in providing wealth-creating infrastructure and social services for the citizenry, thus reducing poverty."⁶

In their studies, Staffan Andersson and Paul M. Heywood analyze the pivotal role of the Corruption Perceptions Index (CPI), made available by Transparency International (TI). From the TI report, a working definition of corruption is noted:

> Corruption is operationally defined as the misuse of entrusted power for private gain. TI further differentiates between 'according to rule' corruption and 'against the rule' corruption. Facilitation payments, where a bribe is paid to receive preferential treatment for something that the bribe receiver is required to do by law, constitute the former. The latter, on the other hand, is a bribe paid to obtain services the bribe receiver is prohibited from providing.⁷

---

³ Samuel O. Abogunrin, "The Community of Goods in the Early Church and the Distribution of National Wealth," *AJBS* 1.2 (1986): 85.
⁴ Peter Townsend, "What Is Poverty? An Historical Perspective," in *UNDP: What Is Poverty? Concepts and Measures* (Brasilia: International Poverty Center, 2006): 5. http://www.ipc-undp.org/pub/IPCPovertyInFocus9.pdf.
⁵ Lual A. Deng, *Rethinking African Development: Towards a Framework for Social Integration and Ecological Harmony* (Asmara: Africa World, 1998), 141–46.
⁶ ActionAid Nigeria, "Corruption and Poverty in Nigeria: A Report" (Abuja: Nigeria, 2015), 6. http://www.actionaid.org/nigeria/publications/poverty-and-corruption-nigeria.
⁷ Staffan Andersson and Paul M. Heywood, "The Politics of Perception: Use and Abuse of Transparency International's Approach to Measuring Corruption," *PSt* 57.4 (2009): 748. https://doi.org/10.1111/j.1467-9248.2008.00758.x.

1. Introduction

As an exploitation of entrusted privilege for personal advantage, corruption is seen almost everywhere and thrives in every society in different modes. It is manifested in a nation's politics, socioeconomic relations, and religious spaces with attitudes such as misappropriation of public assets for personal use, exploitation, extortion, bribery, cheating, favoritism, and embezzlement. It is regrettable to observe that those who are entrusted with the responsibility of making sure that equity and justice prevail at all levels of their national life have become increasingly indifferent to the perennial issues of injustice, poverty, and oppression. Exploitation and corruption are seen to be trivial matters and the order of justice is no longer regarded as an outstanding component for corporate regard, not even for self-regulation. Consequently, the nation's inner self is completely fragmented as it has negligibly and shamelessly accepted exploitation and corruption not simply as the standard of social relationships, but it's amplified consequent product, impunity, as a national symbol. As observed, the shadow of impunity is upon the nation; it is overwhelming every social space. Certainly, this situation has created a monumental tragedy in which there is an unimaginable scale of political, socioeconomic, and religious contradictions and transgressions that affect national security, unity, peace, progress and general well-being and prosperity for all citizens. In every department of national life are issues of exploitation and human oppression, hypocrisy, bribery and corruption and an overwhelmingly extravagant and extreme performance of rituals among religious—often Christians—communities, which as those of modern days are, were noticeably the characteristic trademark of Micah's era.[8] As it exists today in Nigeria, there is a growing evangelical quest about God and deep concern for equity and justice as the opulent wealth of the national leadership contrasts with the poverty of the marginalized majority. Micah's oracles present obvious infidelity to injustice in key quarters of his society which becomes a stimulating impetus for this current project. The literary text of Micah's oracles indicates how the less-privileged became victims of oppression (cf. Mic 2:1–11), how traditional moral and social solidarities resulting from the Old Testament Covenant were gradually disregarded or overlooked,[9] and how the authorized religion of the temple at Jerusalem seemed to lack the courage to challenge the blatant and deliberate scope of current injustices.

This project is driven by the moral sensitivity of the prophet Micah as it provides a germane and viable platform for evaluating contemporary ethical and religious issues of faith and life in the Nigerian society. The message of Micah's prophecies underscores the fact that the literary paradigm of preserving Micah's oracles of various forms for the benefit of later readers serves to situate the

---

[8] For examples of religious overdoing in Micah's era see 2:1–5; 2:6–11; 3:1–12; 6:1–8.
[9] Juan I. Alfaro, *Justice and Loyalty: A Commentary on the Book of Micah* (Grand Rapids: Eerdmans, 1989), 6.

book's relevance beyond the original community or communities of readers to transhistorical readers with similar structural socioeconomic and religious ideologies and theology of resistance against oppression. The unfolding chapters and sections of this project will articulate the relevance of the literary text of Micah, of its rhetoric of stern condemnation of corruption and exploitation of the poor and powerless, for contemporary readers of faith communities and larger human society.

1.2. Driving Questions and Intended Orientation

Prophetic discourse responds to specific situations by highlighting the implications or consequences of the current line of action. It is meant to remove or revise the "'actual or potential exigency' by persuading others to modify circumstances and thus avert or minimize the catastrophic consequences foreseen as a result of the trend of events."[10] Every prophetic discourse presents a matrix of factors to which it is providing a response and this, to some extent, is seen in the situation addressed by Micah's discourse. Specifically, this project will address the following fundamental questions as ways of analyzing and assessing Micah's ethos of justice as witness to Yahweh's healing agenda in a covenant community and, nowadays, in any human society:

- What sociopolitical economic and religious circumstances and events called forth Micah's prophetic discourse?
- How did Micah's prophetic discourse deal with socioeconomic injustice, worship, and false security within his community (that is, the relation of social and cult criticism: "Sozialkritik und Kultkritik")?
- What are the essential ethical thrusts of Micah's prophetic discourse?
- Do Micah's prophetic discourse and its ethical concerns provide their readers with normative principles that are acceptable for understanding the Bible in theology and ethics? How can certain ethical principles be drawn from biblical texts?
- What ethical demands do Micah's prophetic discourses make upon an individual's life and ethical responsibility in his or her daily living and in the Christian community, in Nigeria or in wider human society?
- What ethical models and practical demands does reflection on Micah's prophetic discourse present to faith communities and to wider human society—their attitude toward, and use of, their possessions, administration of justice, and to the practice of Christian orthodoxy?

---

[10] Charles S. Shaw, *The Speeches of Micah: A Rhetorical-Historical Analysis*, JSOTSup 145 (Sheffield: JSOT, 1993), 22.

This project holds that the moral uncertainty in Nigeria and corrupt communities elsewhere in Africa and beyond, created by unprecedented problems of socioeconomic and religious contradictions, if honestly and directly faced as well as well-handled, generate practical resourcefulness that starts to make those desiring a more moral culture, more proficient to meet their challenges. The project will analyze how various features of socioeconomic and religious transgressions seem to overwhelm possibilities of moral agency. A biblical theological ethics such as this project proposes begin, then, by analyzing how the challenges of unprecedented socioeconomic relations, threaten to overwhelm people's capacities of theological response, and alienate the practice of Christian life from reality. If the practice of faith within Christian communities and wider human society must overcome unprecedented socioeconomic relations, then as a moral community, Christian believers must generate ways to sustain the meaning of their way of life in changing and challenging situations. What love and justice will come to imply for life in an era of socioeconomic inequalities, true worship and false security depends on the church's innovations that make these concepts work through any unanticipated anomalies and situations. These innovations will become authoritative in as much as adherents recognize them as coherent interpretations of traditions, and in as much as they adopt them as authentic ways of speaking faith and addressing the challenges posed by the sociocultural climate of her age.[11] This project will underscore Micah's ethical thrust for contemporary engagement in a socioeconomically and religiously challenging context of the Nigerian society.

The project will highlight the significance of a well-informed social solidarity for considerable appreciation of the biblical text of Micah and for modeling faith and commitment in one's contemporary world of socioeconomic and religious contradictions. It will clarify hermeneutically the relevance of Micah's critique for Christian communities in Nigeria and the Nigerian society, and consequently communicate a prophetic vision that can direct society toward a different kind of future. Since a moral society is that in which the rights of the poor, weak, vulnerable (such as widows and the fatherless) and powerless are protected, this project will stimulate stewardship of responsibility and accountability on God's—and the Earth's—available resources at the disposal of all by emphasizing Micah's ethos of justice. The theological nexus of socioeconomic and religious demands in Micah's oracles are paradoxically outstanding and elegant. The project will constantly emphasize the literary prophetic character of Micah along with various rhetorical ways of appropriating his rich theological traditions so as to accomplish his theological and ethical objective of inviting his audience to accede to the urgent and desperate demands for justice and the de-

---

[11] Willis Jenkins, *The Future of Ethics: Sustainability, Social Justice, and Religious Creativity* (Washington, DC: Georgetown University Press, 2013), 23.

velopment of an equitable society. Thus, the relevance of this project rests not only in the identification of the essential ethical drives of Micah's oracles, but more importantly in the relation and application of those theological and ethical thrusts to current and daily life situations of contemporary Nigerian society—in particular—and of other societies that are faced with similar socioeconomic and religious contradictions.

The outcomes of this project will benefit, first, theological and religious studies' students, irrespective of their context, as knowledge gained from it will enhance their teaching on the prophetic literature, as well as on the book of Micah. It will, furthermore, enhance pastors' and leaders' understanding of ethics, leadership and responsibility, and this will in turn contribute to their use of the book of Micah. Study of this book will offer valuable insights into prophetic protest against injustice in ancient Israelite society, but also in contemporary faith communities and human societies.

1.3. Methodology, Scope, and Structure

A multiplicity of methods dominates biblical scholarship and the study of Micah is no exception. The unique setting (historical context) in which a Biblical text was produced and in which it is situated (literary context) are of utmost significance. Since the eighteenth-century enlightenment rationalism, there has been a shift in the interpretive practices. As a period in which texts were interpreted just as secular classical texts, scriptural texts were seen as a response to the historical or social forces of the period. Anthony Mansueto quoted in Itumeleng J. Mosala notes:

> The roots of both historical criticism and the sociological tradition can be traced to the crisis of 19th century liberalism. The tremendous development of the productive forces unleashed by modem industry and in particular steam power, and the great revolutions of the later eighteenth and the nineteenth century *undermined* the older, ideological theories of social life—e.g., natural law doctrines—and sparked a wave of historical studies and theoretical investigations struggling to come to terms with the diversity of human social existence, the dynamics of social change, conflict and integration: i.e. with the new world of bourgeois society, and its manifest difference from the old world of the ancient regime.[12]

---

[12] Anthony Mansueto, "From Historical Criticism to Historical Materialism" (paper presented at Graduate Theological Union, Berkeley, CA, 1983), 3, quoted in Itumeleng J. Mosala, *Biblical Hermeneutics and Black Theology in South Africa* (Grand Rapids, MI: Eerdmans, 1989), 44.

1. Introduction

Arising from this development, certain obvious contradictions and difficult passages in the Biblical text were clarified by comparing their possible meanings in relation to the contemporary context. What is thus generally held is that people at different levels of development will have the privilege of textual interpretation in different ways, as there is no singular method to interpret Biblical texts. According to Mosala, "A new criticism has begun to operate that expresses itself in various ways."[13] While ambiguities and doubts exist among majority of scholars regarding the identification and clarification of what constitutes the interpretative circle; that is, the hermeneutic principle or the interpreter, Grant R. Osborne imagines hermeneutics as a spiral from text to context.[14] In contemporary scholarship, W. Randolph Tate remarks that,

> there are three different groups of theories regarding the locus and actualization of meaning: *author-centered* (with attention directed to the world behind the text), *text-centered* (with the focus on the world within the text, or the textual world), and *reader-centered* (where the spotlight is trained upon the world in front of the text, or the reader's world).[15]

With respect to the world behind the text (author-centered theory), the interpreter would have to make a strong apology for historical research, recognize the significance of language, and establish the historical and ideological backgrounds.[16] Since exegetical questions are prerequisite, it is necessary according to Tate that the interpreter demonstrates, "a knowledge of background studies, which is an indispensable prerequisite for the explication of plausible textual meaning; that is, historical, cultural, generic, grammatical, ideological, and even geographical studies are prerequisites for a successful interpretation of a text."[17] Tate continues with an impressive analysis of the author-centered theory when he remarks:

> While an author may imagine a literary world with all sorts of new possibilities, the expression of such an imaginative world is impossible apart from the author's real world. An author can imagine a world and express it textually only through the real historical, cultural, literary, and ideological setting. For this

---

[13] Mosala, *Biblical Hermeneutics and Black Theology in South Africa*, 44.
[14] Grant R. Osborne, *The Hermeneutical Spiral: A Comprehensive Introduction to Biblical Interpretation* (Downers Grove: Inter-Varsity, 1997).
[15] W. Randolph Tate, *Biblical Interpretation: An Integrated Approach* (Grand Rapids: Baker Academic, 2008), 2.
[16] Tate, *Biblical Interpretation*, 11–72.
[17] Tate, *Biblical Interpretation*, 11.

reason, historical considerations are at once validated as an important adjunct to hermeneutics.[18]

This kind of hermeneutical presupposition is supported by A. Berkeley Mickelsen who remarks that:

> The interpreter ... must understand the particular biblical culture which influenced the original source, message, and receptors. He must note both how it differs and how it resembles his own. Only then can [s]he effectively communicate[s] the message from one culture pattern to another.[19]

Similarly, Hans Snoek remarks that, "context plays an important role in the reflection on exegesis and actualization. Indeed, explanation and interpretation of the Bible do not occur in a vacuum but are partially determined by tradition and culture."[20] However, the difficulty of associating with the social, economic, and cultural context when reading the Bible through the approach of the contextualization is reflected in Mosala's grand-breaking work, *Biblical Hermeneutics and Black Theology in South Africa*. Mosala argues that

> An approach to the study or appropriation of the Bible that begins with the theological notion of the Bible as the Word of God, therefore, presupposes a hermeneutical epistemology for which truth is not historical, cultural, or economic. For such an epistemology the Word of God is pre-established. The political, cultural, economic, or historical relevance of this Word of God comes out of its capacity to be applied to the various facets of human life, and in this case of black human life. Its relevance does not issue out of its very character as a historical, cultural, political, or economic product.[21]

The world within the text approach sees the text as a literary creation. Accordingly, "this literary quality requires interpretation, and of central importance in interpretation are the concepts of genre and sub-genre."[22] The essential focus of a text-centered criticism is its spotlight on artistic strategies, literary forms, and textual coherence. Practitioners of methods that may be called text-centered assume that the text must be viewed spatially, as a whole.[23] Though these approaches, adopted by various interpreters of the biblical text, pose varied and

---

[18] Tate, *Biblical Interpretation*, 15.
[19] A. Berkeley Mickelsen, *Interpreting the Bible* (Grand Rapids: Eerdmans, 1963), 170.
[20] Hans Snoek, "Key Concepts in the Dialogue between African and European Biblical Scholars," in *African and European Readers of the Bible in Dialogue*, Studies of Religion in Africa 32 (Leiden: Brill, 2008), 86.
[21] Mosala, *Biblical Hermeneutics and Black Theology in South Africa*, 19–20.
[22] Tate, *Biblical Interpretation*, 90.
[23] Tate, *Biblical Interpretation*, 180.

complex questions, they are inextricably intertwined and linked to one another.[24] According to P. Chatelion Counet and Ulrich Berges, "one can speak either of synchronic oriented diachronics (question: how come the final text to its present form), or diachronic oriented synchronics (question: what is the meaning and function of the final text)."[25]

The world in front of the text approach (the world of the reader) reflects on the complex process of reading the text, by observing the role of the reader's presuppositions and preunderstanding. Tate remarks that, "Without an author, there is no text; without a reader, a text does not communicate. In a real sense, an unread text carries no meaning, because it can mean nothing until there is a mutual engagement between reader and text. Meaning involves a process of signification in the act of reading."[26] He notes further:

> If written discourse is communication between author, text, and reader, then what role does the reader play in determining meaning at the receiving end of the process? Communication has not occurred until the message (text) has reached its final destination. For this reason, the reception of a text by the reader should be a primary consideration in any hermeneutic.[27]

A simple, illustrative, and straight-forward study approach to the world in front of the text would be the existential approach.[28] Existential methods are 'instrumental methods' that allow the text to be read as a means to an end, not as an end in itself. The goal of this kind of reading is often an encounter with reality beyond the text to which the text bears witness. It may be described as self-involving. Readers do not treat the text as a historical or literary artifact but as something to engage experientially, something that could or should affect their lives. As an embodiment or actualization technique of interpretation, it consists of advocacy criticism, liberation exegesis and ideological criticism, especially in the context of the struggle for justice or liberation.[29]

Since the Bible is accepted by Christians as "the word of God" (a basic and primary evangelical notion of this study), its interpretation is influenced by a variety of worldviews. In the global North the dominant tendency is a liberal and contemporaneous reading of the Bible (with the use of the historical-critical

---

[24] Alphonso Groenewald, *Psalm 69: Its Structure, Redaction and Composition* (Munster: LIT Verlag, 2003), 9.
[25] P. Chatelion Counet and Ulrich Berges, *One Text, A Thousand Methods: Studies in Memory of Sjef van Tilborg*, BibInt 71 (Leiden: Brill, 2005), 6.
[26] Tate, *Biblical Interpretation*, 189.
[27] Tate, *Biblical Interpretation*, 190.
[28] Michael J. Gorman, *Elements of Biblical Exegesis: A Basic Guide for Students and Ministers* (Peabody, MA: Hendrickson, 2008), 16.
[29] Gorman, *Elements of Biblical* Exegesis, 16–20.

method), but most churches in the global South are very conservative. Philip Jerkins makes a clear illustration of the difference in the reading of the Bible in Asia and Africa compared to reading it in Europe and North America, when he notes:

> These include a much greater respect for the authority of scripture, especially in matter of morality; a willingness to the Bible as an inspired text and a tendency to literalism; a special interest in supernatural elements of scripture, such as miracles, vision and healings; a belief in the continuing power of prophecy; and a veneration of the Old Testament, which is considered as authoritative as the New.[30]

Given that this project is undertaken within an African context of socioeconomic and religious contradictions, a description of African Biblical Hermeneutics (ABH) and models, and how certain models of ABH are related to this project, is vital in this methodology section. ABH is scholarship initiative that addresses methods of contextual interpretation of the Bible in such a way that is respectful of the various dimensions of African life and thought. To define and explain ABH, David T. Adamo says,

> African Biblical Hermeneutics is vital to the wellbeing of African society. African Biblical Hermeneutics is a methodological resource that makes African social cultural contexts the subject of interpretation. This is a methodology that reappraises ancient biblical tradition and African world-views, cultures and life experiences, with the purpose of correcting the effect of the cultural, ideological conditioning to which Africa and Africans have been subjected in the business of biblical interpretation.[31]

In his stimulating work *The Task and Distinctiveness of African Biblical Hermeneutics*, Adamo defines African Biblical Hermeneutics as "the principle of interpretation of the Bible for transformation in Africa. It can also be called African cultural hermeneutics and African Biblical transformational hermeneutics."[32] Similarly, regarding what constitute ABH, Gerald O. West remarks that, "African biblical hermeneutics is a reflective discipline, analysing what African biblical scholars do. Though often cast in a prescriptive mood, it is properly a descriptive project. Of course, identifying, describing and analysing what scholars are up to when they do their work can take on normative or even imperative

---

[30] Philip Jenkins, *The New Faces of Christianity: Believing the Bible in the Global South* (Oxford: Oxford University Press, 2008), 4.
[31] David T. Adamo, "What Is African Biblical Hermeneutics?," *JBT* 13.1 (2015): 59.
[32] David T. Adamo, "The Task and Distinctiveness of African Biblical Hermeneutics," *OTE* 28.1 (2015): 31. http://dx.doi.org/10.17159/2312-3621/2015/v28n1a4.

force."³³ The most significant factors in this reflective scholarship, is the contextual forms of biblical interpretation. West notes, "Whilst we have not always been as meticulous and rigorous in our use of social scientific forms of analysis with respect to context as we have with the textual forms of analysis, we aspire to a careful and critical analysis of context, moving beyond the anecdotal."³⁴

In a chapter on the use of the Bible in black theology, Mosala deduced certain features of black theology that represent an ideological captivity to the hermeneutical principles of a theology of oppression and advanced the urgent need for the Bible to "become a viable theoretical weapon of struggle in the hands of the exploited masses themselves."³⁵ Mosala recognized as problematic the "contextualization approach" of the Bible that conceals hermeneutically important fact in spite of its crammed harmonizing perspectives. Stated more clearly, he remarks that the biblical texts "are products of complex and problematical histories and societies." Consequently,

> as products, records, and sites of social, historical, cultural, gender, racial, and ideological struggles, they radically and indelibly bear the marks of their origins and history. The ideological aura of the Bible as the Word of God conceals this reality. A black biblical hermeneutics of liberation must battle to recover precisely that history and those origins of struggle in the text and engage them anew in the service of ongoing human struggles.³⁶

Although Mosala does accept with reservation "existentialist uses of the Bible in the struggle for liberation" as a substitute for a theoretically well-grounded biblical hermeneutics of liberation, he gave his reason for his reserved acceptance:

> while texts that are against oppressed people may be coopted by the interlocutors of the liberation struggle, the fact that these texts have their ideological roots in oppressive practices means that the texts are capable of undergirding the interests of the oppressors even when used by the oppressed. In other words, oppressive texts cannot be totally tamed or subverted into liberating texts.³⁷

---

³³ Gerald O. West, "Exegesis Seeking Appropriation; Appropriation Seeking Exegesis: Re-reading 2 Samuel 13:1–22 in Search of Redemptive Masculinities," *VE* 34.2 (2013):1, art. #761, 6 pages. http://dx.doi. org/10.4102/ve.v34i2.761.
³⁴ West, "Exegesis Seeking Appropriation," 2.
³⁵ Mosala, *Biblical Hermeneutics and Black Theology in South Africa*, 13.
³⁶ Mosala, *Biblical Hermeneutics and Black Theology in South Africa*, 20.
³⁷ Mosala, *Biblical Hermeneutics and Black Theology in South Africa*, 30.

He developed a materialist black biblical hermeneutics of liberation that takes its cue from an understanding of the existence of various ways of reading, with an initial criticism of recent sociological approaches that have not taken seriously the materialist framework of analysis. Although he appreciates the significant advancement sociological approach has brought to bear on biblical study based on its objects of analysis, his contrary objection is an apology,

> for an open acknowledgment of the class interests that are being represented and thus an acknowledgment of at least the social limitation of the methods. More importantly, like the historical-critical methods before it, biblical sociology tries to be scientific by identifying with the intellectual projects of secular methods on the one side. On the other, it maintains the social and political agenda of the ruling class by not taking seriously the issues of class, ideology, and political economy of not only the societies of the Bible but the societies of the biblical sociologists themselves.[38]

In his South African black liberation, Mosala categorized the struggle into three stages: the communal, the tributary, and the capitalist. These modes of production formed a basis for his development of a biblical hermeneutics of liberation method that is grounded in his South African black struggle against oppression and exploitation. These materialist modes of reading of the biblical texts constitute an integral part of the process of using the Bible in the black struggle for liberation.[39] Clearly, Mosala's historical-materialist exegetical considerations of the text of Micah served his purpose of black liberation struggle in South Africa. However, the argument that "the social-ideological location and commitment of the reader must be accorded *methodological* priority"[40] provides my study with a hermeneutical lens that prioritizes the literary-theological analysis of the text of Micah for a community of readers with socioeconomic and religious ambiguities.

While different comparative approaches have been developed in ABH,[41] West's Contextual Bible Study approach—which depends on the Bible and thus

---

[38] Mosala, *Biblical Hermeneutics and Black Theology in South Africa*, 65.
[39] Mosala, *Biblical Hermeneutics and Black Theology in South Africa*, 69–99.
[40] Mosala, *Biblical Hermeneutics and Black Theology in South Africa*, 123.
[41] Justin S. Ukpong analyses different stages of African Biblical interpretation and notes: first, a reactive and apologetic stage that focuses on the legitimization of African religion and culture and dominated by the comparative method; second, a reactive-proactive stage that uses African context as resource for biblical interpretation, and dominated by Africa-in-the Bible approach, inculturation-evaluative method and liberation hermeneutics; and third, a proactive stage that recognizes the ordinary reader, the African context as subject of biblical interpretation and its domination by liberation and holistic inculturation methodologies. Justin S. Ukpong, "Developments in Biblical Interpretation in Modern Africa:

provides a reflective surface of interpretation—is very stimulating for this project. According to West, "Contextual Bible Study is a South African contribution to the trajectory of biblical liberation hermeneutics."[42] In an earlier write-up, West notes:

> A Contextual Bible Study is an act of faith. So Contextual Bible Study is always immersed and saturated with prayer and singing; nothing happens among African Christians without spontaneous prayer and singing! Not only does every Bible study begin with prayer and singing, but nobody takes a position in the front of the group without being 'escorted' to the front with singing. Ordinary African Christians believe that God is with them, always, and that the Bible is a resource through which God speaks into their lives and contexts.[43]

Since the African context influences the African reading and application of the Bible, the essential commitment of Contextual Bible Study must be that of an acknowledgement and recognition of the environmental factors that have shaped and re-shapes development in Africa. Considered as one of the basic sources of African and black theology, a Contextual Bible Study according to West "belongs to the local community, and so this component is crucial, for the participants are asked to appropriate and act on what they have discerned from their re-reading of Scripture."[44] It is within this kind of contextual reading that a hermeneutic of appropriation in which relative ethical questions and concerns are drawn for an African-Nigerian reading audience of the book of Micah in this study.

This study will provide a theological-ethical-interpretation of Micah's oracles.[45] As a rhetorical-literary production, there are noteworthy ideological and theological intentions in the book of Micah that require cautious attention to presentation and style. As an ancient book, the production and subsequent transmission of Micah involved several activities, such as writing and composition, which in turn required social and economic resources.[46] While interpreters and readers pay attention and respond to the particular structures and techniques

---

Historical and Hermeneutical Directions," in *The Bible in Africa: Transactions, Trajectories, and Trends*, ed. Gerald O. West and Musa W. Dube (Leiden: Brill, 2000), 12.

[42] Gerald O. West, "Locating 'Contextual Bible Study' within Biblical Liberation Hermeneutics and Intercultural Biblical Hermeneutics," *HvTSt* 70.1 (2014): 1, art. #2641, 10 pages. http://dx.doi.org/10.4102/ hts.v70i1.2641.

[43] Gerald O. West, "Do Two Walk Together? Walking with the Other through Contextual Bible Study," *Anglican Theological Review* 93.3 (2011): 434.

[44] West, "Do Two Walk Together?," 448.

[45] Ehud Ben Zvi, *Micah*, FOTL 21B (Grand Rapids: Eerdmans, 2000), 4.

[46] I realize that this means the élite of that society, which had a significant role in the production of the text.

in a number of ways, the theological and aesthetic beauty of the text on pressing social and ethical issues are viable components of the process of conveying its life-giving and instructive power for contemporary reflection and application.

The chain of tradition from the eighth-century prophetic character (Micah) that is shaped, reflected and reinforced in the final form of the text situates the book as an important text for Christian and Jewish faith communities' self-understanding, their understanding of the divine economy and their place in it, their understanding of Yahweh's past and future actions and a hope of greater and glorious future in their resistance against oppression.[47] Consequently, these preserved ideological and theological socioeconomic situations and paradigms in the literary text of Micah constitute, in particular, a viable basis for mediating ethical relevance for contemporary readers who are confronted with socioeconomic and religious contradictions in multidirectional paths.

This project acknowledges the essential significance of the historical-critical methodology but focuses more on the synchronic and theological interpretations of Scripture with canonical connections that allow for theological-ethical implications for contemporary audiences and (re)readers of the book of Micah who are faced with pressing socioeconomic, religious and ethical issues. This synchronic and theological approach seeks to understand as much as possible the context of a given text, by attempting to focus on syntactical, stylistic, semantic components rather than determining specific historical situation or the different stages of the history and development of the text.[48] The primary objective of this model of analysis is to determine the structural relations and moral intentions that are found in the text.[49] The process for discovering as much as possible the anticipated meaning of the text is to study and assess its literary features, stylistic and semantic structure and coherence, as well as the canonical and/or theological meanings.[50] While the procedure attempts to distinguish the anticipated meaning from the importance of the text, the significance of the text is found only when its essential principles are appropriately applied or contextualised within a given context. To effect this outcome, the principal task of interpretation is to determine as much as possible the meaning of the text for

---

[47] Ben Zvi, *Micah*, 5.
[48] It is important to note that there are distinctions between the oracles' historical context (*Sitz im Leben*) and their literary context (*Sitz im Buch*). The *Sitz im Buch* also needs to be extended to the larger literary context of the biblical canon (*Sitz im Kanon*). The exegetical approach seeks to locate the book of Micah in a broader theological context in view of the implications of the book's message for contemporary reflection.
[49] Groenewald, *Psalm 69*, 11–12.
[50] Elliott E. Johnson, *Expository Hermeneutics: An Introduction* (Grand Rapids: Academic, 1990), 35.

1. Introduction

his/her community (of readers), thereby obtaining a message for contemporary reflection.

The scope of this project is limited to the distinctiveness of socioeconomic and religious transgressions in Micah's oracles and how these chains of preserved traditions equip contemporary readers and communities of readers in their struggle and resistance against socioeconomic and religious contradictions. Granted that the book of Micah is a literary document that was meant to be heard and reheard by an ancient audience, the project will begin by addressing the issues related to the book of Micah, the literary character of the prophet (Micah), location and context. While giving attention to contextual and historical matters, the project shall extensively focus on the textual subunits of oracles that deal with socioeconomic and religious matters. This exegetical procedure will help to place the message of the book in a larger theological context that allows contemporary readers glimpses of insights into the past, stimulating images of the future and instructive reflection on the applicability of both of those to the realities of contemporary audiences in their quests for justice and transformation.

The first chapter (introduction) begins with general orientation, driving questions and intended orientation, methodology, scope, and structure. The second chapter addresses the character of the prophet Micah, his location and context and preliminary exploration on the book of Micah as a literary document that presents Yahweh's word to a community or communities of readers. Consequently, attention is given to various studies that address the book of Micah as a prophetic book with significant literary and theological features.

In view of the fact that Micah's rhetoric challenges behaviour and attitudes of leaders and people on issues of oppression and justice, the third and fourth chapters focus on various units of socioeconomic transgressions, power relations, and religious unfaithfulness and community moral depravity in Micah's oracles. The following literary units and subunits, are selected for consideration: 2:1–5; 2:6–11; 3:1–4; 3:5–7; 3:9–12; 6:6–8; 6:9–16; and 7:1–6. The units address issues of greed and corruption of the influential, distorted theological justification and condemnation of social evils, leadership and ritual failure, cheating and violence, and societal disintegration on account of gross corruption. The exegetical process involves the translation of the verses from the MT, an explanation of the setting, literary contexts, form, and structure of the passage(s), as well as analysis of the basic ideas of such passages where necessary.

Canonical synthesis and theological analysis provides the platform and opportunity for assessing the experience and affirmation of the primary readership and community or communities of readers from one generation to the other, within the overall context of the Old Testament/Hebrew Bible canon.[51] From this insider Christian perspective, the fifth chapter examines the essential ethical burdens in the various exegetical units and subunits of Micah's oracles. This canonical synthesis demonstrates that Micah's oracles cohere with other Old Testament texts through intertextual connections.[52] Consequently, such coherence equips contemporary exegetes to give appropriate contextual interpretation of the texts. The exegetical foundations of the selected oracle units and their ethical concerns provide the opportunity for the contextual application of its message in the sixth chapter. As a biblical and theological interpretation, the application does not focus on any church or particular denomination or faith community in Nigeria since socioeconomic issues affect all Christians notwithstanding their denominations.

The project appeals to existing literatures that throw light on current socioeconomic and religious developments in Nigeria. Although contemporary Nigerian's socioeconomic and religious problems are distanced and separated by time from those of ancient Israelites' prophets like Micah (in terms of audience and other variables), the similarities (oppression and exploitation of the poor, injustice, leadership failure, economic abuse of the marginalized and underprivileged, unethical lifestyle and hypocritical worship) are painfully close to the realities of life for many today. While contextualizing or appropriating an ancient text like Micah may be subjectively challenging, the challenge is relatively minimized when the principle of contemporaneity of prophetic text is followed; that is when the biblical text is approached not only as God's Word, but as a single continuum.[53] By this understanding and approach, this project allows the message of Micah to enter and find expression in various socioeconomic and religious spheres in Nigeria. Thus, the ethical and theological traditions of Micah are interpreted and animated in a manner in which the prophetic concerns of the past are creatively linked with the present so that the word of God becomes relevant for today. The final chapter (7) brings the project to close with summaries and recommendations that reflect the potential relevance of the ethical message of Micah for a modern-day Nigerian context of diverse faith communities and societal orientation.

---

[51] Although I write from the perspective of a Christian reader with the choice of the term Old Testament, I do not exclude Jewish faith community readership, and thus the term Hebrew Bible is used together here.
[52] Paul R. House, *Old Testament Theology* (Downers Grove: InterVarsity, 1998), 8.
[53] Michael U. Udoekpo, *Rethinking the Prophetic Critique of Amos 5 for Contemporary Nigeria and the USA* (Eugene, OR: Wipf & Stock, 2017), xxvi; cf. Roy L. Honeycutt, "Amos and Contemporary Issues," *RevExp* 63 (1966): 441.

2

MICAH: CHARACTER, LOCATION, CONTEXT, BOOK

> History has demonstrated that the most notable winners usually encountered heartbreaking obstacles before they triumphed. They won because they refused to become discouraged by their defeats.
> —B. C. Forbes

An ethical analysis of the interrelatedness and connection of socioeconomic realities in eighth-century BCE provides the backdrop for understanding the character of Micah, the location and circumstances of his ministry. There was obviously a preliterary stage in which Micah's oracles were first spoken before they were transmitted in writing and became part of a literary document. The book's superscription, which functions as the initial part of the prophet's curriculum vitae, provides information about the prophetic character, location, authority, historical context, and audience of his messages (1:1; cf. 3:1). Thus, this chapter identifies the prophetic character, location and context of his oracles.

2.1. Micah's Character

The name Micah is a shortened form[1] whose meaning is a rhetorical question: "who is like Yahweh?" The name stresses the wonderment, transcendence and incomparability of Yahweh, the God of Israel rather than Micah's piousness and godliness.[2] The rhetorical question put forward by Micah's name reflects Yahweh's transcendence that finds theological expression and has evocative power throughout the book. Yahweh's transcendence according to Micah's name was not an abstraction. The name communicates important information about his

---

[1] Jeremiah 26:28 has both the short form (מִיכָה) in Mic 1:1 and the long form (מִיכָיה) in 2 Chr 13:2.
[2] James L. Mays, *Micah: A Commentary* (London: SCM, 1976), 1.

message and allows his audience, whether ancient or contemporary, to discover important information about Yahweh.

Micah's speeches indicate that, "He is a God who takes his covenant with his people seriously (1:5), who will brook no rivals to transcendence (1:6–7), and who controls the nations—even the dreaded Assyrian army (1:6–16)."[3] At the same time, Micah is concerned with existential matters like exploitation of the poor, made weak and helpless by the covetous rich (2:1–3, 8–9; 3:1–3); he is committed to honesty, equity and fairness (2:6–11; 3:5–8), the necessity of justice and the importance of human rights (6:6–8), and he is furious with oppression (7:18).[4] Throughout the collection of speeches, one can observe Micah's lamentation regarding the scarcity of those who are like Yahweh; those who are committed to the practice of justice and love of חסד (mercy, fidelity, loyalty, loving-kindness, covenant love).[5] From Micah's perspective, such persons have disappeared from the land (7:1–2).

Micah's name heralds significant information about his message, but little is known about his character. Like the rest of the prophetic figures in the Hebrew Bible, this is not so surprising since the details of the lives of the prophets were not as significant as their invitation to the prophetic office and their submission as vehicles for the transmission of Yahweh's word in history.[6] Thus, "What holds true for all the prophets holds true for Micah: His life has disappeared behind the word which he was sent to proclaim."[7] Therefore, primary and significant information about Micah can only be gathered from the document bearing his name as well as other secondary documents.

Micah's genealogy or parentage and original occupation are unknown. Consequently, the spectrum of speculation becomes inevitable.[8] He must have been from the tribe of Judah since his hometown is situated in the territory of Judah. His identification with his hometown rather than his parentage, in the opening verses, suggests that he was regarded as an outsider by his contemporaries with

---

[3] Stephen G. Dempster, *Micah*, THOTC (Grand Rapids: Eerdmans, 2017), 2.
[4] Dempster, *Micah*, 2.
[5] חסד is mostly considered as a responsibility expected of covenant members, especially those who are strong, to help in situation of need. It carries the elements of grace and benevolence extended to the weaker party, much more than a call to duty. See Gordon R. Clark, *The Word Hesed in the Hebrew Bible*, JSOTSup 157 (Sheffield: Sheffield Academic, 1993), 20.
[6] Dempster, *Micah*, 4.
[7] Hans W. Wolff, *Micah the Prophet*, trans. Ralph Gehrke (Philadelphia: Augsburg Fortress, 1981), 4.
[8] Delbert R. Hillers, *Micah: A Commentary on the Book of the Prophet Micah* (Philadelphia: Fortress, 1984), 14; Mays, *Micah*, 15.

whom he ministered in Jerusalem.[9] Some hold that he was not a professional prophet,[10] but a leader of a revolutionary movement,[11] a Levite or dissident priest.[12] He was probably a farmer in the agrarian community of Moresheth, since he is familiar with and utilizes imageries common to farming.[13] According to Stephen G. Dempster, "He certainly identified with the members of his village whose small farms were being swallowed up by wealthy landowners (2:1–4)."[14] Hans Walter Wolff holds that Micah was a leading Moresheth city councilman or elder who served as an advocate of justice for his people, presenting the plights of the peasant farmers and poor to the rich and influential in Jerusalem. This might also account for his literacy (cf. Mic 3:1).[15]

Certainly, Micah is highly persuaded of his calling as a prophet in announcing his qualification, "On the other hand I am filled with power—with the Spirit of the LORD—and with justice and courage to make known to Jacob his rebellious act, even to Israel his sin" (3:8 NAB). The use of the prophetic messenger formulae כה אמר יהוה ("thus says the LORD," 2:3; 3:5) indicates the source of his authority. He received his message, perhaps like Isaiah (1:1; 2:1; 6:1) in a vision (1:1), with the verb חזה suggesting a "general reception of revelation."[16]

---

[9] Bruce K Waltke, "Micah," in *Obadiah, Jonah, and Micah*, ed. Donald J. Wiseman, TOTC (Downers Grove: InterVarsity, 2009), 137; Hans Walter Wolff, "Micah and the Moreshite-The Prophet and His Background," in *Israelite Wisdom: Theological and Literary Essays in Honor of Samuel Terrien*, ed. John Gammie et al. (Missoula: Scholars, 1978), 80.

[10] See Joseph Blenkinsopp, *A History of Prophecy in Israel* (Louisville: Westminster John Knox, 1996), 95; Ralph L. Smith, *Micah-Malachi*, WBC 32 (Waco: Word, 1984), 4; Bruce V. Malchow, "The Rural Prophet: Micah," *CurTM* 7 (1980): 48.

[11] David Pawson, *Unlocking the Bible: A Unique Overview of the Whole Bible* (London: Collins, 2003), 525.

[12] Juan I. Alfaro, *Micah: Justice and Loyalty* (Grand Rapids: Eerdmans, 1996), 4.

[13] His many references to agricultural imageries indicate his familiarity with agricultural economy or personal knowledge of land, farming, crops and animals production: the plantings of a vineyard (1:6), lamenting like the jackals and mourning like the ostriches (1: 8), the baldness of the eagle (1:16), fields and homes (2:2–4), the plowing of a field (3:12), the beating of swords into plowshares and spears into pruninghooks (4:3), fig tree and vine (4:4), the gathering of sheaves to the threshing floor (4:12), the dew and rain on plants (5:7), a lion among sheep (5:8); sowing and reaping (6:15), treading olives and grapes (6:15), the picking of fruit, grapes, and figs (7:1), the briars as hedges (7:4), and the extension of fields' boundary markers (7:11).

[14] Dempster, *Micah*, 6. See also David Pawson, *Unlocking the Bible: A Unique Overview of the Whole Bible* (London: Collins, 2003), 525.

[15] Hans Walter Wolff, *Micah: A Commentary*, trans. Gary Stansell (Minneapolis: Augsburg Fortress, 1990), 6–7. See also, Eric A. Mitchell, "Micah—The Man and His Times," *SWJT* 46 (2003): 67.

[16] Wolff, *Micah*, 37.

Micah appears to have no political and religious association,[17] but he was familiar with the history and religious tradition of his nation.[18] Having experienced the sting of oppression and being provoked by it, he was moved with profound sympathy for those he considered his people (1:9; 2:9; 3:3) and he was courageous in proclaiming Yahweh's judgement with bitter condemnation to a nation with a well-structured and corrupt economic, political, and religious system.[19] According to him, the Judean society has become a nation ruled by those who "devise troubles and work evil" (2:1), "who hate good and love evil" (3:2), and who "abhor justice and twist everything that is straight" (3:9). He was the first prophet to announce the unconditional judgement of Yahweh upon Jerusalem and the sacred temple, the sign of God's presence and blessing among his people (3:12).[20]

His social critique consists of a denouncement of the economic aristocratic group (the opportunistic and heartless social class), whose greed for property and homes had no limits. He had no fear for those who were responsible for the massive injustice but wrestled with the nature of contemporary prophecy and condemned civil, charismatic, and cultic leadership who worked for things that symbolized wealth (3:5–6, 9).

2.2. Location of Micah

The circumstances and situations of the period of his prophetic ministry are indicated in the opening verse. His hometown was called Moresheth, which is most probably identified with Moresheth-Gath[21] (1:1, 14; cf. Jer 26:17–18). It is linked with the Philistine city of Gath to its northwest. It is situated at the contemporary site of Tel el-Judeideh, which is about 20 miles southwest of

---

[17] See Carol J. Dempsey, "Micah 2–3: Literary Artistry, Ethical Message, and Some Considerations about the Image of Yahweh and Micah," *JSOT* 85 (1999): 126.

[18] Dempster, *Micah*, 8. For example, he was aware of the motif of a woman having birth pangs and giving birth to a deliverer (4:9–10; cf. Gen 3:15) of a covenant with the patriarchs (7:20), and of the patriarchal blessings of healing for the nations and curses on enemies (5:6–8; cf. Gen 12:1–3). He was aware of the early covenant at Sinai and its requirements such as the prohibition of coveting (2:2), the early Israelite credo (7:18–19), the apportioning of lands to the tribes and clans of Israel (2:4–5), and the theological notion of the land as a place of security and rest (2:10).

[19] Dempster, *Micah*, 7.

[20] Mays, *Micah*, 13.

[21] Francis I. Andersen and David Noel Freedman hold that the name was assigned by people in Jerusalem, probably as a derogatory term employed by the city-dweller to refer to the "rustic." Francis I. Andersen and David N. Freedman, *Micah: A New Translation with Introduction and Commentary*, AB 24E (New York: Doubleday, 2000), 109.

2. Micah: Character, Location, Context, Book

Jerusalem, in the low hills of the shephelah region to the west of Hebron.[22] Some interpreters identify it with the city of Mareshah (see Targum on Mic 1:1; cf. Josh 15:44). However, a distinction is made in Mic 1:14–15.[23]

Moresheth is situated within "ten kilometers' radius of a neighborhood encompassing" several cities that had been fortified by Rehoboam, king of Judah (2 Chr 11:5–12).[24] It was a border town between central Judah and Jerusalem on one side and the Philistine cities and the Via Maris on the other side, and it was thus part of the interface between these major cultures. The surrounding neighboring cities formed a network of protection for Jerusalem and Judah from attackers who might invade from the coastal highway (e.g., from Egypt or Philistia). According to the Chronicler, there was a time during the reign of Asa in which a vast Ethiopian military force was intercepted in its tracks at Mareshah by a small delegation from Judah who relied on Yahweh's help (2 Chr 14:9–12). Consequently, Mareshah along with its surrounding cities (including Moresheth), were historical cities and symbols of divine intervention and aid in moments of national catastrophe.[25] Since Moresheth was located in the rich and fertile region of the shephelah (southern hill country of Judah), it would have been an important farming community, providing not only fruits and vegetables for self-support but also extra produce of commercial purposes, for the markets of neighboring communities.[26]

Archaeological survey indicates that after the Assyrian invasion, the number of villages in this region was reduced from almost 300 to about 50, with less than 15 percent of the population prior to the invasion remaining. The survey also indicates evidence of increase in taxation for peasants in such areas as Moresheth and elsewhere. For instance, the influence, power, and wealth of the elite are reflected in the royal *LMLK* impressions and the ivory towers of Samar-

---

[22] See Philip J. King, *Amos, Hosea, Micah: An Archaeological Commentary* (Philadelphia: Westminster, 1988), 60; John H. Walton, Victor H. Matthews, and Mark W. Chavalas, eds., *The IVP Bible Background Commentary Old Testament* (Downers Grove: InterVarsity, 2000), 780–81.

[23] Dempster, *Micah*, 5.

[24] Yohanan Aharoni, *The Land of the Bible: A Historical Geography* (Philadelphia: Westminster John Knox, 1979), 330–32. It is probable that Gath in 2 Chr 11:8 refers to Moresheth-Gath and that Moresheth has been omitted as a result of the mention of Mareshah. See, for example, Carl S. Ehrlich, *The Philistines in Transition: A History from ca. 1000–730 B.C.E.* (Leiden: Brill, 1996), 62.

[25] Anson F. Rainey, "The Chronicler and His Sources—Historical and Geographical," in *The Chronicler as Historian*, ed. M. Patrick Graham, Kenneth G. Hoglund, and Steven L. McKenzie, JSOTSupp 238 (Sheffield: Sheffield Academic, 1997), 55–58.

[26] Dempster, *Micah*, 6.

ia.[27] Daniel L. Smith-Christopher contends that Micah's dialectic makes him a zealous supporter of a locally based ideology, with allegiance to family, tribe, and region, whose preservationist tendency made him courageously object to exploitation and seizure of communal resources by the wealthy elite of the city for the expansion of the military to the detriment of the poor.[28] It is likely that military and administrative officials would have regularly come into town and brought the attention and interests of the Jerusalem administration to bear on the life of the community. The manner in which Micah identifies his addressees indicates that his speeches were made in Jerusalem. His audience is depicted as those who have power and influence (2:1, 8), and most often, their power is connected to specific office (3:1, 5, 9, 11). Consequently, he would have been called "the Moreshite" in Jerusalem.[29]

Micah is a younger contemporary of Isaiah (Isa 1:1),[30] both of whom prophesied in Jerusalem and Judah, the home of royal and Zion theology.[31] Isaiah resided in Jerusalem, the capital city, while Micah seems to languish in the countryside of Moresheth, a dependency of Gath. This environmental setting is reflected in the writings of the two prophets. On the one hand, Isaiah writes as one who is familiar with the society and patterns of capitals and with passionate interest in political developments of the time. Micah on the other hand speaks as the "man of the people" who cast his fate with the less privileged individuals of his land and become a prophetic theologian and courageous advocate of the rights of the disadvantaged. He appears almost exclusively as an ethical and religious advocate.[32] Micah however does not offer his readers so much information about the Neo-Assyria influence. His mention of the Assyrians is a description that pictured them as an ordinary enemy, not as a power that could influence his compatriots to undertake a dangerous political scheme. He did not

---

[27] John H. Walton, Victor H. Matthews, and Mark W. Chavalas, *The IVP Bible Background Commentary* (Downers Grove, IL: IVP Academic, 2000), 781–82; Oded Lipschits, Omer Sergi, and Ido Koch, "Royal Judahite Jar Handles: Reconsidering the Chronology of the lmlk Stamp Impressions," *Tel Aviv* 37.1 (2010): 3–32, https://doi.org/10.1179/033443510x12632070179306.

[28] Daniel L. Smith-Christopher, *Micah: A Commentary*, OTL (Louisville: Westminster John Knox, 2015), 20–26.

[29] Mays, *Micah*, 16.

[30] See Philip P. Jenson, *Obadiah, Jonah, Micah: A Theological Commentary*, LHBOTS 496 (New York: T&T Clark, 2008), 95; Robert V. Huber, Robert M. Grant, and Tracey Grant-Starter, eds., *Who Is Who in the Bible* (Pleasantville, NY: Reader's Digest, 1994), 295.

[31] David M. Carr, *An Introduction to the Old Testament: Sacred Texts and Imperial Contexts of the Hebrew Bible* (Chichester: John Wiley, 2010), 117.

[32] Samuel R. Driver, *An Introduction to the Literature of the Old Testament* (New York: Scribner's, 1913), 326.

even raise an alarm against the vulnerability to Judah of the influence of the Egyptians.[33]

2.3. Context of Micah's Oracles

The circumstances and situations that shaped Micah's prophetic ministry are set within the literary context of the eighth-century period in which Israel had become fractured, split into two kingdoms, politically dominated by the Assyrians, socially characterized by a widening gap between the wealthy and poor, and religiously cynical as they combined the worship of Yahweh with that of other gods (cf. 1:7). Since the knowledge of these circumstances and situations of Micah's context will contribute to the understanding of his message and its application, the following subsections will examine the nexus of the political, socioeconomic, and religious backdrop of Micah's oracles.

2.3.1. Political Setting

Micah is "notably lacking in 'political' interest, nor is addresses to the king—so central in so many prophetic texts—represented."[34] He addresses a distinctive aspect of society and of political situation and life. It is seen against the background of a community in which the citizens are under authority. Consequently, its political structure can only be examined by paying attention to the events that shaped the life of the community under authority.[35] The book's prologue introduces Micah the Moresthite (1:1, 14; cf. Jer 26:18) whose prophetic ministry spans the period of three Judean kings: Jotham (742–735), Ahaz (735–715), and Hezekiah (715–687).[36] These kings are however, not explicitly mentioned by Micah in his documented oracles. This literary absence is believed to be a result of Micah's lack of interest in politics and it thus might function as a critique of the Davidic kingdom in the interest of highlighting a just Davidide who will one day rule to the "ends of the earth" (5:4).[37]

---

[33] Driver, *Introduction to the Literature of the Old Testament*, 326. However, brief historical mention of Egypt is found in 6:4; while in 7:12, 15, restoration evidences highlight Egyptian presence.

[34] David J. Reimer, "The Prophet Micah and Political Society," in *Thus Speaks Ishtar of Arbela: Prophecy in Israel, Assyria, and Egypt in the Neo-Assyrian* Period, ed. Robert P. Gordon and Hans M. Barstad (Winona Lake: Eisenbrauns, 2013), 211.

[35] Reimer, "Prophet Micah and Political Society," 211.

[36] Devadasan N. Premnath, "Amos and Hosea: Sociohistorical Background and Prophetic Critique," *Word & World* 28.2 (2008): 126; James D. Nogalski, *The Book of the Twelve: Micah-Malachi* (Macon, GA: Smyth & Helwys, 2011), 511.

[37] Dempster, *Micah*, 9.

The major political events that shaped the backdrop to Micah's ministry are found in 2 Kgs 15–19. These texts show that these kings functioned during the eighth-century Neo-Assyrian political and ideological dominance of the ancient Near East.[38] They relate various Assyrian attacks on the region including the capture of Samaria in 722/721 BCE and the siege of Jerusalem in 701 BCE.[39] With much conviction and belief in royal and Zion theology, the Judeans confronted their own version of threats from the Assyrian onslaught, which were at first indirect. Micah lived and prophesied during a time of international fear and uncertainty, especially the rising threat of the Assyrian empire. Although his prophetic ministry was centered in Jerusalem, he prophesied against Samaria, Jerusalem, and their leaders. His prophetic oracle against Samaria (1:2–8) is believed to have been announced in the early period of his ministry before the destruction of Samaria by the Assyrians in 722 BCE.[40] The first king mentioned in the series of kings under whom Micah ministered was Jotham. He ruled with his father for a number of years before assuming solitary leadership in 742 and reigned until 715 BCE. His successor was his son Ahaz, who reigned for twenty-two years and then was succeeded by Hezekiah who ruled for twenty-eight years, until 687.[41]

At the time of Jotham's reign in Judah, the amazing period of peace and stability enjoyed by both the northern and southern kingdoms has ended. There was the dawning consciousness of the rising threat of the Assyrians in the northeast, resulting in political machinations and conspiracy among the various powers in the neighborhood of Israel to obstruct the Assyrian force from satisfying its insatiable quest for control. Jotham fortified Jerusalem as well as Judah's southwestern border (2 Chr 27:3–7), and at least one military success is recorded against Judah's eastern neighbor, the Ammonites (2 Chr 27:5).[42] While there are no compelling evidences in the book to locate the prophetic ministry of Micah as early as the reign of Jotham, the book's superscription, by stretching Micah's ministry to the time of Jotham, "leaves the reader in no doubt that the major part

---

[38] Donald E. Gowan, *Theology of the Prophetic Books: The Death and Resurrection of Israel* (Louisville: Westminster John Knox, 1998), 50; Iain Provan, V. Philips Long, and Tremper Longman III, *A Biblical History of Israel* (Louisville: Westminster John Knox, 2003), 271–73.
[39] Julia M. O'Brien, *Micah*, Wisdom Commentary 37 (Collegeville, MN: Michael Glazier, 2015), 2.
[40] Mays, *Micah*, 25.
[41] Dempster, *Micah*, 9.
[42] The Chronicler records other wars in which Jotham was involved in the summary of his reign (2 Chr 27:7). He paid the price for his resistance in the attempts of Arameans and the northern kingdom to enroll Judah in a coalition to withstand the Assyrians (2 Kgs 15:37). Dempster, *Micah*, 10.

2. Micah: Character, Location, Context, Book

of the prophet's ministry took place in such a time of threat and insecurity. The chickens of the nation's sin were coming home to roost in judgment. Perhaps the purpose was to claim fresh relevance for the book in some later time of similar despair, danger and uncertainty."[43]

Following Jotham's death, there were continued attempts by the various states to enroll his young son Ahaz, in their efforts to terminate the rising Assyrian threat (cf. Isa 7). During the Syro-Ephraimite invasion (735–734), Israel and Syria laid siege to Jerusalem in hopes of forcing King Ahaz to join their anti-Assyrian alliance. Ahaz was confounded by fear and caught between the devil of his northern neighbors who he was familiar with and the deep blue sea of the Assyrians whom he did not know so well (Isa 7:1–2). Ahaz appealed to Tiglath-pileser of Assyria for help (2 Kgs 16:5–9)[44] and apparently obtained it. He became a political vassal of Assyria who eventually helped him to defeat Israel and other allies, and imposed tribute on Judah. From this point onward Judah, along with Israel, was under Assyrian domination. The denunciations of Micah reflect most probably the social situation during the reign of King Ahaz.[45] Micah's prophecy regarding the destruction of Samaria (1:2–7) came during the latter part of the reign of Ahaz and must have followed his northern predecessor, Hosea, in presenting the idolatry of the northern kingdom as an expression of adultery and unfaithfulness (1:7).[46]

A few decades later another king, Hezekiah came to power (715–687).[47] He is well known for his reversal of the pro-Assyrian policies and idolatrous practices of his father. Although religious reform would be held back as long as Judah was under Assyria's control, it is believed that Micah's preaching may have been responsible for Hezekiah's religious reforms (2 Kgs 18:4–5; 2 Chr 31).[48] It is not clear how quickly he made his reversals, but the Chronicler's accounts (2 Chr 29–32) suggest that Hezekiah began his religious reforms incrementally following rebellions against the Assyrian overlords by the Babylonians under prince Merodach-Baladan.[49] Hezekiah's efforts to deliver

---

[43] Rex Mason, *Micah, Nahum, and Obadiah* (New York: T&T Clark International, 2004), 18.

[44] Ahaz's appeal was contrary to Isaiah's encouragement to him not to fear the blazing firebrands from the north, or cast his lots with the Assyrians, but to trust in Yahweh only (Isa 7:3–14). In Ahaz's mindset, the Assyrians armies and chariots that he could see were more factual than the invincible God. In any case, "Isaiah offered words; Assyria had an army." Abraham J. Heschel, *The Prophets* (New York: Perennial, 2001), 80.

[45] See Huber, Grant, and Grant-Starter, *Who Is Who in the Bible*, 295.

[46] Dempster, *Micah*, 12–13.

[47] Carr, *An Introduction to the Old Testament*, 117.

[48] John Bright, *A History of Israel*, 3rd ed. (Philadelphia: Westminster, 1981), 278.

[49] Bright, *History of Israel*, 284.

Jerusalem from the Assyrians invasion in 701 BCE are attested in both biblical and Assyrian records. According to the biblical record, Hezekiah anticipated a strong Assyrian attack and thus enlarged and fortified Jerusalem's wall and defense base (2 Chr 32:5, 28–30; cf. Isa 22:8–11). He built the Siloam tunnel, known as Hezekiah's Tunnel, to supply water within Jerusalem's city walls (2 Kgs 20:20; 2 Chr 32:2–4) and blocked springs from supplying water to the Assyrian army (2 Chr 32:4, 30). The Siloam Inscription (discovered in 1880), is an important archaeological artifact relating to this event.[50] Driven by his conviction that the ancient religion was not conscientiously and faithfully practiced, he reinstituted Temple worship (2 Chr 29:20–36) after the temple's purification (2 Chr 29:3–19) and for the first time since the reign of King Solomon, he celebrated a national Passover (2 Chr 30:26). He went round various cities in the north and Judah and got rid of high places associated with syncretistic and idolatrous worship (2 Chr 31:1).[51]

He equipped Jerusalem most successfully for the warm-up campaigns of the Assyrians under Sargon II. Micah probably saw the Assyrian army under Sargon II invading in response to the rebellion that involved many city-states, including Moab and Edom, centered in the Philistine city-state of Ashdod in which Judah was tempted to be involved.[52] Having already announced the conquest of Samaria by the Assyrians, the encroachment of the Assyrians' armies so close to Judah's southwest doorstep, and more precisely to Moresheth, must have given enough apprehension to all those involved.[53] The Assyrians crushed the rebellion and probably attached Azekah as a warning to Hezekiah to remain loyal and submissive to the Assyrians' rule.

The death of Sargon II (705) and the accession of his son Sennacherib precipitated the campaign of 701 described in Micah's vision (1:8–16) that addresses the coming ravaging of the Judean countryside under Sennacherib. Sennacherib attacked and seized the fortified city of Lachish (not far from Moresheth). Walter Kaiser writes about reliefs describing this event:

---

[50] On the English transliteration and possible translation of the Inscription, the Gihon fountain, map of the tunnel, the pool of Siloam and the lower pool, see Siloam Inscription (http://www.lavia.org/english/archivo/Siloeen.htm). See also, Robert B. Coote, "Siloam Inscription," *ABD* 6:23–24.

[51] According to 2 Kgs 18:4, he destroyed the high places and cut down the idolatrous Asherah poles and the brazen serpent that Moses had made (cf. Num 21:6–9). John Day, "Asherah," *ABD* 1:483–87.

[52] As a prophetic sign and warning of what would happen to rebels, Isaiah himself went naked and barefoot in Jerusalem (Isa 20).

[53] Dempster, *Micah*, 14.

2. Micah: Character, Location, Context, Book

There Sennacherib is presented as sitting on his throne (*nimedu*) while the people of Lachish pass in front of him with their carts and belongings. The scene is filled with pathos, for the people are leaving the city as a spoil for the Assyrians as the populace heads out for deportation. Likewise, the graphic depiction of the capture of the city itself is one filled with violence and enormous energy as the walls are breached and many lives are lost. It is the closest that we come to a photograph of a historical event from antiquity.[54]

Sennacherib besieged and conquered all the fortified cities of Judah, leaving only Jerusalem and a fragment with Hezekiah (2 Kgs 18:13). During the attack on Lachish, Hezekiah offered apology to Sennacherib for what he had done and pleaded to present tribute to him. Sennacherib prescribes a fine of three hundred talents of silver and thirty talents of gold (2 Kgs 18:13–14). Hezekiah gave him all the silver that was found in the temple and removed the gold from the doors and doorposts of the temple to pay these fines (2 Kgs 18:15–16). However, despite Hezekiah's payment of the fine, Sennacherib deceitfully sent his army to Jerusalem (Isa 37:9–13).[55] Significantly, there is no indication of Sennacherib's capture of and destruction of Jerusalem before his death (2 Kgs 19:35–37). Micah's prediction of the destruction of Jerusalem's temple seems best suited to this period (3:9–12), and it is separately confirmed a century later in a reference to Hezekiah's political era found in the narrative account of Jeremiah's "Temple Sermon":

> Then some of the elders of the land rose up and spoke to all the assembly of the people, saying, "Micah of Moresheth prophesied in the days of Hezekiah king of Judah; and he spoke to all the people of Judah, saying, 'Thus the LORD of hosts has said, Zion will be plowed *as* a field, And Jerusalem will become ruins, And the mountain of the house as the high places of a forest.'" Did Hezekiah king of Judah and all Judah put him to death? Did he not fear the LORD and entreat the favor of the LORD, and the LORD changed His mind about the misfortune which He had pronounced against them? But we are committing a great evil against ourselves. (Jer 26:17–19, NASB)

Kristin Weingart, arguing in support of an eighth century historical setting for Micah's prophetic activity posits that,

---

[54] Walter C. Kaiser Jr., *A History of Israel* (Nashville: Broadman & Holman, 1998), 379–80; Nadav Na'aman, "Hezekiah's Fortified Cities and the *LMLK* Stamps," *BASOR* 261 (1986): 5–21.

[55] See Alan R. Millard, "Sennacherib's Attack on Hezekiah," *TynBul* 36 (1985): 61–77; Bustenay Oded, "Judah and the Exiles," in *Israelite and Judean* History, ed. John H. Hayes and J. Maxwell Miller (London: SCM, 1990), 446–51; John A. Motyer, *The Prophecy of Isaiah* (Leicester: Inter-Varsity, 1993), 20.

the literary history of the book of Micah substantiates the assumption of an early Micah composition originating from the late 8th century BCE and discusses the extent, structure, and pragmatics of the composition which comprises Mic 1:5–3:12. Focusing on the situation of the eminent Assyrian threat, Micah uses the fate of Samaria as a rhetorical device in order to persuade his Judean addressees of his message. In doing so, Micah not only displays a familiarity with North Israelite prophetic traditions, the composition also adopts compositional elements and rhetorical strategies found in Hosea and Amos.[56]

Although Micah was seen as an antiestablishment prophet, he became a national hero, who was loved by King Hezekiah for inspiring repentance led by none other than the king himself.[57] Obviously, there is some liberty for establishing the precise time frame for Micah's oracles, considering the general historical constraints indicated in the opening verse. If Micah's prophetic ministry began at the beginning of Jotham's reign immediately after his father's death (742 BCE) and continued to the close of Hezekiah's reign (687 BCE), this would be a maximum period of fifty-five years. The minimum years would be in the last years of Jotham until the first year of the reign of Hezekiah, about twenty-two years. However, the natural context for many of Micah's oracles, especially his judgement oracles (1:8–16; 3:9–12), most likely extend until shortly after the Assyrian crisis around 701 BCE, thus consisting of a period of nearly thirty-five years.[58] The uniqueness of Micah's prophecy is seen in his application of the historical lessons of the fate of Samaria (1:1, 5–7) to the reality of Judah and Jerusalem (1:5, 9; 3:9–12). While the historical superscription indicates the significance of history in understanding the biblical message of Micah, it is very instructive to observe that the book omits reference to the northern kings of Israel in its chronology.[59] The address of Micah's message

---

[56] Kristin Weingart, "Wie Samaria so auch Jerusalem: Umfang und Pragmatik einer frühen Micha-Komposition," *VT* 69.3 (2019): 460. https://doi.org/10.1163/15685330–123413.

[57] Dempster, *Micah*, 14. From the theological perspective of the Deuteronomistic, "1–2 Kgs evaluates rulers on how faithfully they promote exclusive worship of YHWH in Jerusalem: Jotham receives positive marks, even though people worshiped at "high places" (e.g., 1 Kgs 14:22–23); Ahaz is judged as idolatrous (2 Kgs 16); and Hezekiah is praised for destroying worship sites outside Jerusalem (2 Kgs 18:4–5)." Julia M. O'Brien, *Micah*, Wisdom Commentary 37 (Collegeville, MN: Michael Glazier Book, 2015), 2.

[58] Dempster, *Micah*, 61.

[59] Prophetic editors normally omitted reference to the northern kings from the historical superscriptions, especially for the prophets of the southern kingdom. Sometimes a northern king will be mentioned for prophets of the northern kingdom, following a long dynastic reign, but only after the relevant kings of Judah (Hos 1:1; Amos 1:1). The only

clearly states Samaria and Jerusalem (1:1) and the first oracle directly refers to Samaria (1:2–7). Micah's oracle (6:9–16) with reference to the statutes of Omri and the counsels of the house of Ahab is more relevant to the northern kingdom than to the southern. Micah's major concern was Judah and Jerusalem, and the presence of Samaria in the final version of the book serves as a powerful warning to Judah.[60]

2.3.2. Socioeconomic Struggles

From this historical standpoint of the political society, the socioeconomic dynamics of the eighth century will be discussed to provide further basis for understanding Micah's oracles. The socioeconomic situations of the period of Micah point to historical events of late eighth century BCE Judah, which was incessantly under the political and military intimidation and danger of the Assyrian Empire.[61] Although Assyrian rule has been characterized as fear-invoking cruelty, the reality is that such violence, depending on the circumstances, could have diplomatic intention associated with it. Assyria's subjugation and rule was, nonetheless, economically motivated.[62] Assyria's economy was essentially maintained both by the tributes received from subjugated peoples and by the ill-gotten gains of their armies.[63]

The Assyrian campaign orchestrated by Sennacherib inflicted devastating military and economic damage on Judah and led to a dramatic demographic decline, especially in the Shephelah.[64] The pressure of Assyria heightened the advantages that Israel's and Judah's kings, Jeroboam II and Uzziah, had gained through their various sociopolitical policies. The agricultural economies of Israel and Judah that had hitherto functioned at a sustenance level now achieved an administratively large scale and well controlled one.[65] This shift of production control had implications on the social realities as it enhanced large scale production and estates, but disadvantaged traditional methods of agriculture as well as community members' social relation. Societies that were viable to navigate dif-

---

obvious mention of a northern king is Jeroboam II, who completed the dynasty of Jehu that was sanctioned by the prophets. Dempster, *Micah*, 62.

[60] Dempster, *Micah*, 63.

[61] R. Daniel Carroll, "A Passion for Justice and the Conflicted self: Lessons from the Book of Micah," *JPC* 25.2 (2006):173.

[62] Smith-Christopher, *Micah*, 6.

[63] In attempting to pay the imposed tributes and taxes, Ahaz had to empty the temple and its treasury. Bright, *History of Israel*, 277.

[64] Lipschits, Sergi, and Koch, "Royal Judahite Jar Handles," 20.

[65] Marvin L. Chaney, "The Political Economy of Peasant Poverty: What the Eighth-Century Prophets Presumed but Did Not State," *JRSSup* 10 (2014): 36.

ficulties went positively and productively through evolutionary and developmental stages in which agricultural production control was removed from family units and given to large scale administrative groups that could orchestrate and coordinate monopolization and promotion of crop cultivation, protection, storage, and redistribution of goods within communities.[66]

Reasonable claims to eighth century prophetic oracles imagine and refer to the economic structures and dynamics of their day and under the influence of Yahweh interpreted events of their era by looking back at crucial experiences of the past.[67] Interestingly, the initial addressees of these literary compositions of the prophetic texts had direct and pressing understanding of the cultural and social situations that were imagined and addressed, and as such had no need for explanation. No twenty-first century reader, however, can claim such illuminating understanding. Thus careful historical efforts are needed for any contemporary reader to understand and appreciate the socioeconomic context of prophetic addresses on peasant poverty.[68]

Prophetic writings attributed to eighth-century prophets offer a significant matrix of materials on various issues of socioeconomic transgression in ancient Israel and Judah (Isa 5:8–18; 10:1–2; Mic 2:1–2). While the prophetic indictments against injustice in ancient Israel and Judah have attracted the attention of many a reader and interpreter,[69] they have presented contextual complexity and ambiguity.[70] Micah's prophecy confronts contemporary readers and interpreters with ambiguity regarding socioeconomic contexts and variables—the driving force of the prophet's indictment, identity of wrongdoers and victims—in light of the limited amount of evidence offered by the text.[71] Thus in light of the scarce nature of the records, both biblical and archeological, and the difficulty of ascertaining with precision the specific systemic, economic and social focus of Yahweh's anger, many scholars have resorted to sociological theories for direction.

---

[66] Matthew J. M. Coomber, "Caught in the Crossfire? Economic Injustice and Prophetic Motivation in Eighth-Century Judah," *BibInt* 19 (2011): 400.

[67] Bernhard W. Anderson, *The Eighth Century Prophets: Amos, Hosea, Isaiah, Micah* (Philadelphia: Fortress, 1978), 6; Chaney, "Political Economy of Peasant Poverty," 34.

[68] Chaney, "Political Economy of Peasant Poverty," 35.

[69] John Barton, *Understanding Old Testament Ethics: Approaches and Explorations* (Louisville: Westminster John Knox, 2003), 77–144.

[70] Coomber, "Caught in the Crossfire?," 397.

[71] The existence of the poor and victims of oppression are not seen in archaeological records but their memory is preserved in Micah. As it is in human history, their voice was not heard. But in the book of Micah, the poor are considered of value. See Alfaro, *Micah*, 6–7.

2. Micah: Character, Location, Context, Book

Two core issues of concern to ancient Israel and Judah in the eighth century are unprecedented economic growth and greater socioeconomic injustice. While the prophetic texts of this period do not give much attention to economic transformation, they ironically announced the greatest number and the most severe of oracles of judgement. Applying information from archaeological studies, social sciences research, and biblical texts other than the prophetic texts, Premnath identifies the specific pointers to the unparalleled economic growth of ancient Israel and Judah in the eighth century to include "colonization, regional specialization, demographics, and trade and commerce."[72] This territorial and geopolitical expansion benefited Israel and Judah as it enabled them to take advantage of business, trade, and investment.

The gradual and steady growth of the economy of ancient Israel and Judah in the eighth century is reflected in what John Bright refers to as "a dramatic reversal of fortune" and the "heights of power and prosperity."[73] Dominating prophetic indictments of the eighth century and contemporary scholarly discourse is how emerging agrarian societies witnessed speedy economic growth, with neglect of the means of subsistence, consolidation of land for wealth development, and a growing accumulation of its associated benefits by the elites.[74] The socioeconomic incongruity is aggravated by the uncontrollable greed and moral corruption and indifference of individuals.[75] From a sociological point of view, Premnath explores the social reality, namely, "evidences of, and allusions to, the process of land accumulation (*latifundialization*)" of the eighth-century in Israel and Judah through the window of the prophetic oracles of Amos, Hosea, Isaiah, and Micah, in order to ascertain as well as establish the relevance of their messages and prophetic vision for contemporary application. He described *latifundialization* thus: "the process of land accumulation in the hands of a few wealthy elite to the deprivation of the peasantry."[76] The defining factor behind the prophetic indictments against land ownership abuse in the eighth century prophetic texts lay in the relation between landowners and peasants. From a sociological perspective, it is interesting to observe how in eighth-century Judah, "the wealthy" manipulated and unjustly appropriated the rights and privileges of

---

[72] Premnath, "Amos and Hosea: Sociohistorical Background and Prophetic Critique," 126.
[73] Bright, *History of Israel*, 252.
[74] Coomber, "Caught in the Crossfire?," 401.
[75] Norman K. Gottwald, "Social Class as an Analytic and Hermeneutical Category in Biblical Studies," *JBL* 112 (1993): 3.
[76] Devadasan N. Premnath, *Eighth-Century Prophets: A Social Analysis* (Saint Louis: Chalice, 2003), 1.

"the poor" in a legal structure that was otherwise based upon Yahweh's blueprints for covenant community living.[77]

In agrarian societies in Israel and Judah especially in the hill country, before the eighth century economic expansion, most peasants held and worked on small plots of pastureland in diverse subsistence farming, producing the majority of what they ate and the majority of what they produced, across a broad chronological and geographic span. The situation was, however, different in the lowland. Tracts of land in the lowlands, on average, were bigger and concentrated in relatively few hands. Chaney notes that, "Most agricultural labor was done by tenant farmers, day laborers, peasants under corvée or debt obligations, or other workers whose access to land, livelihood, and personal freedom were insecure, attenuated, or under threat."[78] It was thus easy for the social and wealthy elite to navigate their quests to intensify their agricultural enlargements in the lowlands. As the balance of power worked in favor of the elite, shared and communal dependence soon deteriorated into obvious exploitation.[79]

The radical changes in the socioeconomic structure brought inequality, commercialization, and centralization of power in the hands of the influential class. The crashing waves of Micah's accusations indicate the degree to which the changing domestic, socioeconomic, and religious landscape has significantly benefited the wealthy at the expense of the poor.[80] Peasants' indebtedness is associated with several factors: heavy exactions in agricultural produce, increase taxation, fall in price of produce at harvest, dishonest business practice of landowners, and failure of rains. A number of these factors, sometimes, make peasants go into borrowing (to feed their families) and subsequent indebtedness. Consequently, peasants are forced to present an item of value, a piece of their land, or sometimes, a family member as collateral for the loan.[81] In the event of inability to pay back the debt, the result is the foreclosure (i.e., removal of the right to redeem the mortgage) of land and/or entering into debt servitude.[82] The supremacy of the elite over the peasants is obvious in Micah's stunning accusations (2:1–2).

Micah's oracles accentuate the role of moneylenders and creditors in impoverishing the peasants and the failure of the judicial system in establishing justice, namely, establishing what was right and who was in the right upon the

---

[77] Otto Kaiser, *Isaiah 1–12: A Commentary* (London: SCM, 1972), 65; Mays, *Micah*, 64; Smith, *Micah—Malachi*, 24.
[78] Chaney, "Political Economy of Peasant Poverty," 40.
[79] Premnath, "Amos and Hosea," 128.
[80] Malchow, "Rural Prophet," 48.
[81] Henry McKeating, *The Books of Amos, Hosea, Micah* (Cambridge: Cambridge University Press, 1971), 162.
[82] Premnath, "Amos and Hosea," 131.

principle of entitlement. However, the judiciary has become a vehicle for subverting justice. Throughout Micah's oracles, there is clear evidence of the exploitation of the poor/peasants by the rich and powerful (2:2, 8; 3:2–3, 10; 6:12), the disenfranchisement of people from their homes and land by creditors and land magnates (2:2), trafficking in children and women (2:9), and corruption in courts (3:1–4, 9, 11; 7:3). Micah addressed various targeted groups regarding their collusion and collaboration in matters of corruption and injustice as well as highlighting the adverse consequences of their practices and policies that impoverished the disadvantaged sections of their society.

2.3.3. Religious Situation

As already noted, Micah lived at a time of crisis. The critical political times of his prophetic call and ministry coincided not only with profound socioeconomic challenges but also with religious and theological malaise. Micah's oracles contain much theological discussion and comment concerning religious activity (1:5–7; 2:6–11; 6:6–7). The tidal wave of idolatry into Judah during Micah's time is first observed during the reign of Ahaz. Syncretism existed as a result of the Assyrians' subjugation. Following the defeat of Judah by Tiglath-pileser, mighty king of the Assyrians, Ahaz sacrificed to their idols, and being impressed and influenced by the Assyrians' faith and religion, he reproduced an altar made to Assyrian specification and fashion, removed the bronze altar of the temple to a marginal position, and replaced it with the new Assyrian altar (2 Kgs 16:10–18). Chronicle records indicate that Ahaz built high places in every city of Judah and even erected an altar on every street corner in Jerusalem (2 Chr 28:24–25). While he could use the Israelite altar for private religious devotion, the public national faith was evidently that of the Assyrians.[83]

Besides the establishment of Assyrian altar in the temple and high places in Judah, there was also the abundance of Canaanite cults found everywhere in the land. The obvious notorious practice of the cults was that of child sacrifice. This has no doubt left its bloody impression on the kings of Israel and Judah and influenced the greater population of the people (2 Kgs 16:2–4). The Chronicler's narrative noted that Ahaz offered up his children in sacrifice: "Moreover, he burned incense in the valley of Ben-hinnom, and burned his sons in fire, according to the abominations of the nations whom the LORD had driven out before the sons of Israel" (2 Chr 28:3; cf. 2 Kgs 16:3). Micah perhaps refers to the Canaanite practice of using high places as venues of worship as well as human sacrifice (1:5; 5:13–15; 6:7).

---

[83] Dempster, *Micah*, 12.

During Hezekiah's reign, several similar social policies and corrupt religious practices from the time of his father Ahaz remained in place, namely, the oppression of the poor by the wealthy, and religious syncretism. A recent archaeological discovery of a seal at the Temple Mount in Jerusalem with the inscription "the Judean king, the biblical-era Hezekiah, son of Ahaz" in addition to a diagram of a sun with wings and two Egyptian Ankhs symbolism indicates religious syncretism.[84] In addition to idolatrous practices in Micah's community, the dual religious functionaries (the prophetic and the priestly) who ought to have stood in the gap and offer a solution for the situation lived with perverted theological perspectives and unethical religious practices. They preached a positive and optimistic message of immutable and infinite grace (2:6–11). Rather than speaking with the priority and authority of their divine commission and through their common element of prophecy and teaching they combined with the social elites and community leaders and thus traded their sacred commission for symbols of wealth and power. Through their distorted oracles and commercialized teachings (3:3–8, 11), temple worship became an obstacle to genuine religious experience, as sacrifice and rituals without the practice of justice were empty and worthless (6:6–8).

While one can understand and speak about factors responsible for social conflicts in a particular context, Micah emphasizes that the factors responsible for rampant socioeconomic injustice have to do with idolatry and failure to honor God in covenant responsibility.[85] David J. Reimer remarks that, "Judah's failings in the public sphere are consistently conjoined to talk of Judah's God: this is seen in both prospect (public calamity is the result of such failures) and consequence (hoped for, indeed assumed, relations with God are further sundered)."[86] At the foundation, the people of Judah had misguidedly taken covenantal responsibility for covenantal advantage and freedom. This development gave way to a high sense of security that eventually led to self-gratification.[87] Their reprehensible acts were an affront to Yahweh's character and attack on the basic ethical structure of his people in covenant community.[88]

---

[84] See Nir Hasson, "Seal Impression with King Hezekiah's Name Discovered in Jerusalem," *Haaretz* (December 2, 2015), https://www.haaretz.com/archaeology/.premium-king-hezekiah-bulla-found-in-jerusalem-1.5429555.
[85] Dempster, *Micah*, 62.
[86] Reimer, "Prophet Micah and Political Society," 224.
[87] Mignon R. Jacobs, "Micah," in *Theological Interpretation of the Old Testament: A Book-by-Book Survey*, ed. Kevin J. Vanhoozer (Grand Rapids: Baker Academic, 2008), 278; R. Walter. L. Moberly, "In God We Trust? The Challenge of the Prophets," *Ex-Aud* 24 (2008): 24.
[88] M. Daniel Carroll R., "A Passion for Justice and the Conflicted Self: Lessons from the Book of Micah," *JPC* 25.2 (2006): 171; Hillers, *Micah*, 33.

2.4. Preliminary Remarks on the Book of Micah

The study of Israelite prophecy has always been an important component of Old Testament scholarship. However, the historical task of clarifying an understanding of the strong impressions from prophetic writings appears to lack scholarly agreement.[89] In recent years, there has been a flurry of interests in studying the prophets as literature. Their stinging criticisms of society, their defence of the vulnerable, and their vision for the future have fascinated people at different levels.[90] Various scholarly interpretations reveal that the prophetic books are not merely a mountain of words beneath which the individual oracles of the representatives of Yahweh lie hidden like treasures, but that they are literary cathedrals that have been skilfully crafted—or rather composed and revised—for centuries by various literary architects.[91] A prophetic book is a literary document that claims an association with a figure of a prophet of the past, in this project—Micah, with whose utterances are presented as Yahweh's word to its audience and readers.[92] Accordingly Ehud Ben Zvi notes, "There are prophetic books and there are written representations of prophecies uttered by living prophets that were produced not long after their proclamation because they were deemed relevant to the immediate concerns of the political centre, such as those attested in Mari and Neo-Assyrian Empire."[93]

Similarly, Odil Hannes Steck notes that a prophetic book or writing presents a literary image of a prophet. This literary image stands before the visually oriented search for the image of a brilliant, creative, original prophetic character. This brilliant literary figure stands again before a kerygmatically oriented search for the image of a theologically inventive prophetic figure. This image could be different from the original prophetic character.[94] These prophetic books are produced only within a particular ancient Near Eastern society that distinguished itself theologically and ideologically as Israel. Thus they are self-contained books that maintained association with the prophetic figure of the past and are

---

[89] Odil Hannes Steck, *The Prophetic Books and Their Theological Witness*, trans. James D. Nogalski (Saint Louis: Chalice, 2000), 6–7.
[90] Ronald L. Troxel, *Prophetic Literature: From Oracle to Books* (Chichester, West Sussex: Wiley-Blackwell, 2012), 1.
[91] Ulrich Berges, "The Book of Isaiah as Isaiah's Book: The Latest Developments in the Research of the Prophets," *OTE* 23.3 (2010): 551.
[92] Ben Zvi, *Micah*, 4; Troxel, *Prophetic Literature*, 4.
[93] Ehud Ben Zvi, "The Concept of Prophetic Books," in *The Production of Prophecy: Constructing Prophecy and Prophets in Yehud*, ed. Diana V. Edelman and Ehud Ben Zvi (London; Oakville: Equinox, 2009), 73.
[94] Steck, *Prophetic Books and Their Theological Witness*, 9–10.

presented to the intended, primary readerships as Yahweh's word.[95] These books are undoubtedly about hope; they were a strategy for developing, modelling, and most importantly, for co-opting and integrating weighty memories of the past. They interpret memories of a shared past, most importantly the monarchic past and its immediate consequences. Accordingly, they promoted social cohesion and a sense of self-identity among the community or communities of readers since the past was essentially about "them."[96]

These collections are filled with first-person revelations from Yahweh, instructing them about the ethical ways of life and the consequences of failing to follow those instructions. Consequently, the prophetic books provide directives from the deity about the proper way a practitioner of monotheistic Judaism is to comport him/herself and about the consequences of such actions.[97] Such instructive potential is reflected in Ben Zvi's remarks about the prophetic collections:

> The prophetic books emphasize human agency and admonish Israel to learn the didactic lessons shaped by these books, which are presented as YHWH's teachings to Israel, and to follow the latter. At the same time they de-emphasize human agency in the larger context of human–divine relationship, in part to strengthen the sense of unconditional hope for the (long-term) future. They assume and communicate a sense that there is something akin to social entropy, that is, Israel tends to sin, and constant effort is required to teach and socialize Israel at least until utopia is achieved.[98]

Granted that the prophetic collections are filled with symbolic messages, Julia M. O'Brien asserts that the prophetic books furnish some of the Bible's most stimulating metaphors. These metaphors provide a useful and valuable subject of study for biblical scholarship, especially in engagement with questions that are related to the literary confusion within the prophetic texts.[99]

---

[95] Ben Zvi, "Concept of Prophetic Books," 74.
[96] Ben Zvi, "Concept of Prophetic Books," 74–75.
[97] Diana V. Edelman, "From Prophets to Prophetic Books: The Fixing of the Divine Word," in *The Production of Prophecy: Constructing Prophecy and Prophets in Yehud*, ed. Diana V. Edelman and Ehud Ben Zvi (London: Equinox, 2009), 41.
[98] Ehud Ben Zvi, "Reconstructing the Intellectual Discourse of Ancient Yehud," *Studies in Religion* 39.1 (2010): 10.
[99] Julia M. O'Brien, *Challenging Prophetic Metaphors: Theology and Ideology in the Prophets* (Louisville: Westminster John Knox, 2008), xiii.

2.4.1. Critical Scholarship

This section presents an overview of studies on the book of Micah. It highlights the issues that dominate scholarly debate on the book of Micah. Two key questions dominate the debate: the origin and the final shape of the book. Literary, historical and theological study, on the one hand, attempts to determine what was original to the prophet and what came from other and later hands. On the other hand, form and redaction-critical methodology focuses on the final shape of the book. These approaches have led to the search for and evaluation of the traditional points of view in different layers of the book.[100]

Redaction-critical scholars hold that Mic 1–3 (because of the anticipation of judgement) refers to the later part of the eighth century as their setting. Micah 4–7, on the other hand, consists of prophecies of salvation added to the Micah collection in the exilic or postexilic periods.[101] These literary characterizations of additional oracles to Micah's collection and the internal mutual relationships that exist between these sections are addressed quite controversially.[102] Reading the book of Micah against a postexilic background, O'Brien remarks that Micah's criticisms function within a context of occupation. The seizures of lands and houses (2:2), the homelessness of women and children, and the concern for the loss of familial inheritance (2:2–4) would have been direct accusations against the elites within the context of the challenges of the ideal of land division among kinship groups (cf. Ezra 2). Thus, the charges against political and religious leaders of greed and financial gains function alongside those that were directed at the social elites.[103] Similarly, Rex Mason, an advocate of a postexilic setting notes that the book of Micah,

> shows how the words of a preexilic prophet could become the text for a proclamation of the certainty of God's salvation for the people who had suffered, and in many ways were still suffering, the judgments of which the prophet had spoken. The prophet's words furnished the material for preaching and worship in the post-exilic period.[104]

---

[100] Rex Mason, *Micah, Nahum, and Obadiah* (New York: T&T Clark International, 2004), 27.

[101] Burkard M. Zapff, "The Book of Micah—The Theological Center of the Book of the Twelve?," in *Perspectives on the Formation of the Book of the Twelve Methodological Foundations—Redactional Processes—Historical Insights*, ed. Rainer Albertz, James D. Nogalski, and Jakob Wöhrle, BZAW 433 (Berlin: de Gruyter, 2012), 131.

[102] Zapff, "Book of Micah," 131.

[103] O'Brien, *Micah*, 52.

[104] Mason, *Micah, Nahum, and Obadiah*, 53.

Ben Zvi holds that Micah as a whole originates in a postmonarchic era. He believes that the book of Micah mirrors the intents and interest of the well-informed, privileged scribes who were residing in Jerusalem during the postexilic period. The mention of the Babylonian exile and other allusions to exile and loss of land (4:10; cf. 2:4,10), the gathering of exiles (2:12–13; 7:17) as well as salvific speeches from various speakers after exile (4:10; 7:11–13, 18–20),[105] indicate well-crafted literary and theological explanation of the words of past prophets regarding the fall of Judah (exile) and its future restoration (hope) to a postmonarchic community.[106] Ben Zvi contends that these literati were from a group that seeks to define their role as "brokers of knowledge" for the postmonarchic Judahite community.[107] However, as stimulating as his explanations of these literati are, such explanations fail to recognize as well as to appreciate the historical and hermeneutical worth of the superscription for the book.[108] According to Dempster, "there is no substantial historical evidence for a group of literati who were 'brokers of knowledge' for the common people, nor is there evidence of theoretical productions being used in the biblical period."[109] With respect to class interest and mode of production in the book of Micah, Mosala employed a historical-materialist method to reconstruct the social system and practices behind the text of Micah in view of what he considered to be "a result of a theoretical commitment that issues out of a concurrent commitment to the black struggle for liberation from capitalism, racism, sexism, and imperialism in South Africa."[110] His materialist method made inquiry into the material conditions of the book of Micah. The development of the essential forces of production found expression during the eighth century BCE that serves as original sociotemporal context of the book of Micah. In his identification of class origin and interests of the text of Micah, Mosala remarked:

> While the text of Micah offers sufficient indications concerning the nature of the material conditions, the configuration of class forces, and the effects of class rule, it is nevertheless itself cast within an ideological framework that at

---

[105] See James D. Nogalski who identifies Mic 7:8–20 as containing salvific speeches of a postexilic collection. James D. Nogalski, "Micah 7:8–20: Re-evaluating the Identity of the Enemy," in *The Bible as a Human Witness to Divine Revelation: Hearing the Word of God through Historically Dissimilar Traditions*, ed. Randall Heskett and Brian Irwin, LHBOTS 469 (New York: Continuum, 2010), 125–42.
[106] Ben Zvi, *Micah*, 9–10.
[107] Ben Zvi, *Micah*, 172.
[108] Dempster, *Micah*, 26.
[109] Dempster, *Micah*, 26.
[110] Mosala, *Biblical Hermeneutics and Black Theology in South Africa*, 102.

2. Micah: Character, Location, Context, Book

the same time creates contradictions within the book and distorts the usefulness of its text for struggling classes today.[111]

The book establishes a connection with Amos and Hosea[112] in the declaration of judgment oracle against Samaria, the capital of the northern kingdom (1:5), and the prediction of the destruction of Jerusalem with its Temple Mount (3:12). With echoes of Amos in the books of Micah and Isaiah, these dual prophets are seen to be representative of early attempts to interpret the crises of Judah through the literary lens of Amos's judgement oracles against the north. This stream of prophetic tradition is believed to have been preserved as a means of ensuring that their unpopular oracles of doom would survive as a literary deposit for future generations.[113] Accordingly, "the correspondence between Hosea and Micah, which the heading of Micah establishes through its chronological reference to the heading of the book of Hosea, attempts to provide a provisional conclusion to a sequence of YHWH's acting in judgment which extends across several writings in the Book of the Twelve."[114]

The relationship that exists between substantial impression of early material in Mic 1–3 and chapters found in probable early material from Isaiah has accentuated scholarly discussion of potential late eighth-century composition.[115] Evidence of parallels and contrast in these early materials include: conflicts with contemporary prophets (Mic 3:5–8, 11; Isa 3:2; 28:7–13; in coalition with priests Mic 3:11 and Isa 28:7) who are rebuked for their drunkenness (Mic 2:11; Isa 28:7) and whose utterances are quoted and refuted (Mic 3:5,11; Isa 28:9–10); condemnation of Judah's leadership for corruption and manipulation of justice (Mic 3:1, 9; Isa 10:2), bribery (Mic 3:11; Isa 1:23; 5:23), and confiscation of symbolic and material possessions (Mic 2:1–3; Isa 3:14; 5:8–10). A contrast is noticed in the question of Yahweh's investment in Zion/Jerusalem, for example, early Isaiah material that stimulates Jerusalem heads to trust in Yahweh's protection of Zion (Isa 8:18; 14:32; 28:16–17; 29:5–8; 31:4–5); hence, Micah announces the destruction of Zion (3:9–12) because of the corruption of Judah's heads that insist that Yahweh is with them and as such they are indomitable.

---

[111] Mosala, *Biblical Hermeneutics and Black Theology in South Africa*, 118.
[112] From a redactional point of view, Aaron Schart understands Micah as a deliberate addition to an already existing corpus of the dual prophets Amos and Hosea. To him, a completely different Micah was probably never written. Aaron Schart, *Die Entstehung des des Zwölfprophetenbuchs: Neubearbeitungen von Amos im Rahmen schriftenuebergreifender Redaktionsprozesse*, BZAW 260 (Berlin: de Gruyter, 1998), 201.
[113] David M. Carr, *An Introduction to the Old Testament: Sacred Texts and Imperial Contexts of the Hebrew Bible* (Chichester: John Wiley, 2010), 332–33.
[114] Zapff, "Book of Micah," 129.
[115] Francis I. Andersen and David Noel Freedman, *Micah*, AB 24E (New York: Doubleday, 2000), 17–20.

These parallels and contrasts indicate some sort of generic textual dependence and point to the books' origin in a similar prophetic-scribal setting.[116]

2.4.2. Structure, Approaches and Unity of the Book

One of the most debated issues in Micah studies is the structure of, and whether there is consistency in, the book. Regarding this structural challenge Matthieu Richelle writes, "The organization of the book of Micah has for a long time been a source of perplexity for exegetes. Whether it is a question of discerning an overall plan for the book or of finding the structure of each oracle, the proposals are numerous and contradictory."[117] The structural perplexity has given rise to a variety of structural trajectories.[118]

Structurally, the book is arranged along different lines that allow for its description as the "binding together of independent oracles into this coherent book."[119] For example, Kenneth Cuffey seeks coherence within the book's structure around the key idea of the remnant which is seen in four strategic places in the book resulting in a four-fold structural division: 1:2–2:13; 3:1–4:8; 4:9–5:14; and 6:1–7:20.[120] Other variations exist between different proposals such as, a three-fold division with a difference as to whether chapter 3 be grouped along with chapters 1–2 or 4–5, while many agree that chapters 6–7 constitute a separate section, and two distinct two-fold divisions: Micah 1–5 and 6–7; or 1–3 and 4–7.[121] Andersen and Freedman accept a threefold division: the book of doom

---

[116] Carr, *Introduction to the Old Testament*, 330–31.
[117] Matthieu Richelle, "The Structure and Theology of Micah 4–5: A New Approach," *VT* 62 (2012): 232.
[118] Allen, *Books of Joel, Obadiah, Jonah and Micah*, 257.
[119] Thomas Edward McComiskey, *The Minor Prophets*, vol. 2 (Grand Rapids: Baker, 1993), 594.
[120] Kenneth H. Cuffey, "The Coherence of Micah: A review of Proposals and a New Interpretation" (DPhil. Diss., Drew University, 1987), 301–4. Daniel J Simundson highlights four distinctive ways that the book of Micah has been conceived: (1) judgment (1–3), mostly salvation (4–5), mix of judgment and hope (6–7); (2) major seams identified by the word hear or listen (1–2; 3–5; 6–7); (3) twofold structure based on hear or listen (1–5; 6–7); (4) guilt and punishment (1–3 with interpolation 2:12–13), future salvation (4–5); postexilic application (6:1–7:7), liturgical hymn (7:8–20). Daniel J Simundson, *Hosea, Joel, Amos, Obadiah, Jonah, Micah*, AOTC (Nashville: Abingdon, 2005), 291–92.
[121] Daniel L. Smith-Christopher, *Micah: A Commentary*, OTL (Louisville, Kentucky: Westminster John Knox, 2015), 33. See also Mignon Jacobs, *The Conceptual Coherence of the Book of Micah*, JSOTSup 322 (Sheffield: Sheffield Academic, 2001), 62–63; Walter Bruggemann, *An Introduction to the Old Testament: The Canon and Christian Imagination* (Louisville, KY: Westminster John Knox, 2003), 234–35.

2. Micah: Character, Location, Context, Book 41

(1:2–3:12); the book of vision (4:1–5:15); the book of contention and conciliation (6:1–7:20).[122]

The originally separate oracles vary in form and are grouped as oracles of judgement and salvation.[123] Each of the oracles begin with the Hebrew verb שמע (listen, hear, 1:2; 3:1; 6:1), used by Israel's prophets to call attention to their messages (cf. Isa 1:2, 10; Amos 3:1; Joel 1:2; Hos 4:1).[124] The oracles of salvation, all of which connect in part to the theme of remnant (2:12–13; 4:6–7; 5:6–7 (7–8); 7:18), correspond to the messages of judgement and as such resolve the potential conflict.[125]

The oracles are not delivered in one single occasion, but they are a compendium of Micah's prophetic messages. Although reasonable reconstructions can be made on the basis of historical and sociocultural evidence manifested in the various speeches in the book, the specific historical context has been greatly obscured in the literary final form of the book.[126] Thus the specific sociocultural and historical context can no longer be determined precisely. For instance, the specific historical contexts for Micah's three judgement oracles in chapter 3 would most probably have been different as court, charismatic, and cult personnel are all addressed. However, these oracles have been fitted together into one literary unit that serves to announce a comprehensive attack on the judicial and religious leadership of Judah. The original social setting would be that when Micah is addressing judicial personnel, it was at the courts (3:1–4); when addressing the priests, it was at the temple (3:9–12); and the indictment of merchants involves the marketplace (6:9–16).[127]

While the oracles were spoken at different times and various places, they have now been fixed in the final medium of writing and arranged and edited as a literary accomplishment. In this way, there is a strategic design to the overall structure of the book.[128] The structure of these oracles is not chronological but on the basis of alternating emphases of judgement and hope.[129] The structure

---

[122] Andersen and Freedman, *Micah*, 7.
[123] Carl Friedrich Keil, *The Twelve Minor Prophets*, trans. James Martin, Biblical Commentary on the Old Testament, 2 vols. (Grand Rapids: Eerdmans, 1949), 1:424.
[124] Charles F. Pfeiffer and Everett F. Harrison, eds., *The Wycliffe Bible Commentary* (Chicago: Moody, 1990), 851.
[125] Bruce K. Waltke, "Micah," in *The Minor Prophets: An Exegetical and Expositional Commentary*, ed. Thomas Edward McComiskey, 3 vols. (Grand Rapids: Baker, 1998), 594.
[126] Walther Zimmerli, "From Prophetic Word to Prophetic Book," in *The Place is Too Small for Us: The Israelite Prophets in Recent Scholarship*, ed. Robert P. Gordon (Winona Lake: Eisenbrauns, 1995), 433–52.
[127] Dempster, *Micah*, 17, 19.
[128] Dempster, *Micah*, 17.
[129] Longman and Dillard, *Introduction to the Old Testament*, 400.

below indicates the occurrences and places in three cycles in which Micah's oracles of hope and comfort are set in a comparison with oracles of warning and uncompromising doom.

Superscription 1:1	Micah's audience is told about the prophetic דבר־יהוה "word of the LORD," its divine Author
First Cycle	Announcement of Judgement, Lamentation and a Future Remnant (1:2–2:13)
Judgment	1:2–7: Yahweh's warnings and judgement on Samaria
	1:8–16: Lamentation over Judah
	2:1–11: **Denouncement of social injustice**
	2:1–5: Economic Piracy and land confiscation
	2:6–11: Theological and ethical disputes on social justice
Hope	2:12–13: Yahweh preserves a remnant in Zion
Second Cycle	Problematic Leadership and Divine Future Leader (3:1–5:15)
Judgment	3:1–12: **Indictment of the Judean Failed leadership**
	3:1–4: Indictment of the Judean political leadership of economic
	3:5–7: Accusation against corrupt prophetic advisers
	3:9–12: Coming judgement on account of gross sin and crime
Hope	3:8: Micah's consciousness of power from Yahweh's Spirit[130]
	4:1–5:15: **Divine Future Leader**
	4:1–13: The Leader's Kingdom
	5:1–15: The Leader's coming[131]
Third Cycle	Divine Punishment and Future Restoration (6:1–7:20)
	Judgement
Judgment	6:1–8: A divine covenant-lawsuit condemning Israel's religious sins
	6:9–16: Condemnation of Israel's social sins
	7:1–6: Micah's anguish and description of unjust and disintegrating Judah's social structure
Hope	7:7–20: Coming vindication and prayer for deliverance

---

[130] I consider Mic 3:8 a special unit that describes Micah's defense or justification of his prophetic ministry in contrast to his contemporaries. It can as well be made as part of 3:5–7, since it is dependent on this oracle that castigated the charismatic leaders of Judah.
[131] Although this unit also appears with some elements of doom (exhortation to prepare for a coming exile (5:1) and for Israel's deprivation and support), it is in fact a promise that Yahweh will rid Israel of her besetting sins. See Bruce K. Waltke, *A Commentary on Micah* (Grand Rapids: Eerdmans, 2007), 15.

In his "discourse structural overview of the prophecy of Micah," Ernst R. Wendland observes that these cycles are not clearly distinguished in the book of Micah since they are thematically related. However, through their obvious general connection "they create a progressive ideational and hortatory intensification of the prophetic message."[132] Although it may be debated, Wendland presents a concentrically expanded chiastic structure that embraces the entire text of Micah.[133]

The literary structure of the book organizes judgement and salvation oracles into three major circles of escalating intensity whereby the negative aspects of condemnation are drowned out by the positive elements of salvation, in which the final chapter dramatically shifts from lament to a hymn of praise. Thus there is a difference between the presentation of the speeches in the canonical and literary context of the book of Micah (aimed at the primary audience) and their actual historical pronouncements (when they first proceeded from the mouth of Micah, aimed at the original audience).[134] The structure is like a symphony with three major circles, alternating around the same theme but with increase in tempo and intensity that bring them to a resounding crescendo. These circles are clearly marked by linguistic signals of importance, inviting the whole world (1:2), the leadership of Israel (3:1), and all Israel (6:1–2) to hear the word of Yahweh. Each of these circles begins with judgement and ends with a note of hope and grace. In the first cycle one can observe an indictment of both the Northern and Southern Kingdoms in more generalized terms. The second cycle concentrates on the corruption of the entire Judean leadership while the third

---

[132] Ernst R. Wendland, "A Discourse Structural Overview of the Prophecy of Micah," *BT* 69/2 (2018): 280. https://journals.sagepub.com/doi/10.1177/2051677018785213.

[133] Wendland, "A Discourse Structural Overview of the Prophecy of Micah," 291:
  A Judgment pronounced against Samaria (1:1–7)
    B The doom of the cities of Judah (1:8–16)
      C Social evils denounced (2:1–13)
        D Wicked rulers and prophets (3:1–12)
          E Peace and security through obedience (4:1–7)
            F Restoration promised after exile (4:8–14)
              G The ruler from Bethlehem (5:1–8)
            F' The future role of the remnant (5:9–14)
          E' God challenges Israel (6:1–8)
        D' Cheating and violence to be punished (6:9–16)
      C' The total corruption of the people (7:1–8)
    B' Penitence and trust in God (7:9–13)
  A' God's compassion and steadfast love (7:14–20)

[134] Dempster, *Micah*, 18.

cycle denounces the entire population for blatant social and moral violations of their covenant obligation with Yahweh.[135]

The interruption of a preponderance of judgement oracles with salvation oracles has made a number of scholars interpret the latter as an insertion and accommodation by later redactors so as to reduce the harsh and negative indictment in the book. In the minds of readers and interpreters, such differences reflect difference in authorship and perhaps a difference in time as well.[136] Scholars who accept the canon of literary-historical criticism think that only the first three chapters contain genuine oracles from the historical Micah,[137] while the rest are confined to anonymous disciples spanning the exilic and postexilic periods.[138] In the mind of such historical-critical scholars, "Salvation oracles, whose predictions transcended the historical horizon of Micah, simply could not be attributed to him."[139] From a grammatical point of view, the grammar of Micah is preexilic; none of the characteristic grammatical features of post-exilic Hebrew are played and many of the religious traditions in Micah that are seen as late are found in preexilic Jeremiah (cf. 23:1–6; 26:18).[140]

In line with John T. Willis's identification of different possibilities, the sequences of the written oracles abound in catchwords and phrases that may have provided a way to preserve their original oral qualities before placing them in the final medium of writing.[141] The literary form of the oracles indicates Micah's use of a variety of genres to communicate his message: warning prophecy, lament song (1:8–16), funeral lament (2:1–5; 7:1–6), prophetic judgement oracle (theophany or epiphany, 1:2–7); judgement speech (3:1–4, 5–8, 9–12; 6:9–16), salvation oracle (2:12–13; 4:1–15), disputation (2:6–11), covenant-lawsuit

---

[135] Wendland, "Discourse Structural Overview of the Prophecy of Micah," 280.

[136] Smith-Christopher, *Micah*, 34. See also, Jeppesen, "New Aspects of Micah Research," 8; Wolff, *Micah*, 17–27; Andersen and Freedman, *Micah*, 18; Jan A. Wagenaar, *Judgement and Salvation: The Composition and Redaction of Micah 2–5*, VTSup 85 (Leiden: Brill, 2001), 6–15; Waltke, *Commentary on Micah*, 13–16.

[137] See, for example, the consensus among studies such as Knud Jeppesen, "New Aspects of Micah Research," *JSOT* 8 (1978): 3–32; Waltke, "Micah," 593.

[138] Allen has questioned the genuineness of Mic 4:1–4, 4:6–8; 7:8–20. Allen, *Books of Joel, Obadiah, Jonah and Micah*, 251. Adam S. Van der Woude regards 1–5 as authentic but consigns 6–7 to an anonymous author whom he regards as Second (Deutero)-Micah. Adam S. Van der Woude, *Micaha*, De Prediking van het Oude Testament (Nijkerk: Callenbach, 1976), 10–11.

[139] Dempster, *Micah*, 27.

[140] Waltke, *Commentary on Micah*, 10–11.

[141] John T. Willis, "Fundamental Issues in Contemporary Micah Studies," *RQ* 13 (1970): 77–90.

speech (6:1–5), entrance liturgy (6:6–8), futility curse (6:15–16), and hymn (7:18–20).[142]

The book's curve moves from punishment to exaltation, from destruction to rebuilding. Smith-Christopher remarks that if a theme has emerged in these various proposed divisions of the book of Micah, it is surely the importance of judgement and salvation as contrasting subjects addressed by the book.[143] A striking feature is the concept of remnant, "which appears in four strategic places in the book: 1:2–2:13; 3:1–4:8; 4:9–5:14 and 6:1–7:20. Each of these sections consists of a negative part followed by a positive section which contains the idea of a remnant (cf. 2:12–13; 4:1–8; 5:1–14; 7:7–20)."[144] Thomas Edward McComiskey makes these remarks about the motif of remnant:

> Micah's doctrine of the remnant is unique among the Prophets and is perhaps his most significant contribution to the prophetic theology of hope. The remnant is a force in the world, not simply a residue of people, as the word 'remnant' (*she'erit*) may seem to imply. It is a force that will ultimately conquer the world (4:11–13). This triumph, while presented in apparently militaristic terminology (4:13; 5:5–6), is actually accomplished by other than physical force [cf. Matt. 5:3–12]. By removing everything that robs his people of complete trust in him (5:10–15), the Ruler from Bethlehem will effect the deliverance of his people. The source of power for God's people in the world is their absolute trust in him and his resources.[145]

Oral rhetorical style[146] and dramatic reading[147] have also been adopted as ways of understanding the various stylistic variations and unanticipated grammatical forms. All of these approaches raise methodological questions since advocates regard the texts from a different or particular perspective which they consider to be important, be it thematic, structural or rhetorical.[148] Since an original stone (speech) thrown into the water can cause an ever widening wave in a

---

[142] For a list of literary genres, see Smith-Christopher, *Micah*, 35; Kenneth L. Barker, "A Literary Analysis of the Book of Micah," *BSac* 155 (1998): 437–48; Timothy M. Pierce, "Micah as a Case Study for Preaching and Teaching the Prophets," *SWJT* 46.1 (2003): 83–85.

[143] Smith-Christopher, *Micah*, 34.

[144] Wilhelm Wessels, "YHWH, the God of New Beginnings: Micah's Testimony," *HvTSt* 69.1(2013):2. art. #1960, 8 pages. http://dx.doi.org/10.4102/ hts.v69i1.1960.

[145] Thomas Edward McComiskey, "Micah," in *Daniel-Minor Prophets*, ed. Frank E. Gaebelein and Richard P. Polcyn, The Expositor's Bible Commentary, 12 vols. (Grand Rapids: Zondervan, 1985), 7:399.

[146] Andersen and Freedman, *Micah*, 24–27.

[147] "Micah is an intentionally dramatic text, 'dramatic' not in the sense of being deeply impressive but in the *technical* sense: Micah is a drama reflecting many of the accepted definitions of ancient dramatic texts." Smith-Christopher, *Micah*, 37.

[148] Wessels, "YHWH, the God of New Beginnings," 3.

lake, a series of contexts could reasonably be imagined: oracle < Book of Micah < Book of the Twelve < Prophetic Books. Consequently, it might be difficult to attempt to differentiate clearly the prophetic voice from the divine voice since the two were seen to be one and the same.[149] Thus from a synchronic point of reference, the literary text is presented as a complete unity from Micah's era that has been integrated into a collection of other prophetic writings and placed into a larger collection of sacred books, which form the Jewish Tanakh or the Christian Bible. These prophetic writings are regarded as the Word of God spoken through the prophets, for all time.[150]

The book has gone through various editorial stages and reached a final form in the exilic period or in the postexilic period in Judah.[151] Thus in terms of its final form, the book reinforces patterns of judgement oracles followed by oracles of restoration, comfort and salvation. The basic horizon of Yahweh's restoration and comfort which normally follows the strictest of prophetic indictment comes into practical focus at the close of the book of Micah (7:18).[152] If one takes the titular superscription (1:1) that identifies Micah as the author of all its prophecies and the editorial observation at 3:1 that suggests editorial hints in the book, no linguistic or literary explanations give grounds for hesitation regarding the book's unity and authenticity.[153] Micah represents a composite unity. The various units of prophetic oracles or collections grew in stages, but each stage was conscious of the primary prophetic voice reflecting its message from the perspective of the eighth century prophet, though exilic and postexilic modifications may have shaped Micah's theological reflection on events.[154] In the next chapter, attempt is made at analyzing various literary units of oracles in the book of Micah that addressed socioeconomic and religious matters.

---

[149] Shaw, *Speeches of Micah*, 221–25.
[150] Dempster, *Micah*, 18.
[151] Nogalski, *Book of the Twelve*, 513–14.
[152] Tremper Longman III and Raymond B. Dillard, *An Introduction to the Old Testament* (Grand Rapids: Zondervan, 2006), 451–52; James L. Mays, *Micah: A Commentary*, OTL (Philadelphia: Westminster, 1976), 21–33; Leslie C. Allen, *The Books of Joel, Obadiah, Jonah and Micah*, NICOT (Grand Rapids: Eerdmans, 1976), 241–52.
[153] Waltke, "Micah," 593; Waltke, *Commentary on Micah*, 13.
[154] Nogalski, *Book of the Twelve*, 516.

3

SOCIOECONOMIC TRANSGRESSIONS AND POWER RELATIONS IN MICAH'S ORACLES

> The problem of socio-economic contradiction in biblical text has been interpreted by biblical scholars to be the result either of random idiosyncratic personal differences of ability or industry, on the one hand, or the inordinate greed and moral corruption of particular individuals, on the other.
> —Norman K. Gottwald

This chapter focuses on socioeconomic and power relations in Micah's oracles. The pre-literary form of the oracles addressed the original addressees while the written, final form of the oracles addresses varying audiences and readers of the book. This chapter takes an exegetical approach to analyzing the various units of oracles dealing with socioeconomic and religious violations with the ultimate intention of connecting Micah's oracles to contemporary reality. The following sections focus on socioeconomic and power relations.

3.1. Economic Piracy and Land Confiscation (2:1–5)

The unit 2:1–5 is part of Mic 2:1–11 that originally comprised of two oracles (2:1–5 and 2:6–11). These two oracles were integrated into one in the book of Micah. The first basic part announced judgements with more general discussion of the sins of the nation (1:2–16) and with less identification of its causes. In this new section (2:1–11), Micah turns from warning of external threat to the people, to internal transgressions that lead to destruction. It essentially deals with more specific identification of crimes of the leader with tough judgements (2:1–5), followed by distorted theological justification and condemnation of social evils (2:6–11).[1]

---

[1] Dempster, *Micah*, 80.

Micah 2:1–5 is a follow up to Micah's sentence of an impending destruction and exile on Samaria (1:3–7) and Judah (1:8–16), as a result of their rebellion and sin against Yahweh.[2] It is difficult to reconstruct the original setting of the oracle, but according to Philip P. Jenson, it "might have been given in Moresheth and aimed at the royal officials who occupied the fortified cities and used their powers to make life comfortable for themselves at the expense of citizens."[3] Considering the third person reference in verse 3, the description of judgment is constructed in more general terms that allow for multiple referents with a view to suggesting a generalized condemnation of such evils.[4] The frame of the text and its particular characterization of evil-doers indicate a power struggle linked to the control of fields and houses. The socioeconomic processes in the background of the characterization of evil-doing in Mic 2:2 are not common in agrarian societies. They mirror the concentration of property through land foreclosure.[5] Imaginably, one could imagine Micah pronouncing the oracle at one of the farms, where the wealthy land magnates were coming to take possession as the owners was evicted due to failure to pay back a loan. An example of this situation is Elijah's encounter with Ahab at Naboth's vineyard (1 Kgs 21:16–20).[6] While it is clear that Micah is confronting the rich oppressors of Yahweh's people, the text does not allow readers to easily contextualize these oracles in terms of any particular historical narrative about an event or events that occurred in particular situations and in which the prophet said such-and-such to a specifically defined group. Ben Zvi remarks that, "On the surface level, the text seems to communicate to its readers a position consistent with a widely accepted ideal of social ethics ... and with a trust in divine retribution against those who violate these ethics."[7]

In its literary structure, Mic 2:1–5 is the first subunit of Micah's second lament oracle (2:1–13), which takes hold of those responsible for the misfortune and downfall of Judah. It is usually regarded as a prophetic announcement of judgement against a group of individuals who violate ethical standards in the covenant community.[8] The characterization of evildoers is sustained by linguis-

---

[2] Marvin Sweeney, *The Twelve Prophets*: *Micah, Nahum, Habakkuk, Zephaniah, Haggai, Zechariah, Malachi*, Berit Olam (Collegeville: Liturgical, 2000), 357.
[3] Philip Peter Jenson, *Obadiah, Jonah, Micah: A Theological Commentary* (New York: T&T Clark, 2008), 119.
[4] Ben Zvi, *Micah*, 54.
[5] Ben Zvi, *Micah*, 44.
[6] Dempster, *Micah*, 93.
[7] Ben Zvi, *Micah*, 52.
[8] Claus Westermann, *Basic Forms of Prophetic Speech*, trans. Hugh C. White (Louisville, KY: Westminster John Knox, 1991), 142; Marvin A. Sweeney, *Isaiah 1–39 with Introduction to Prophetic Literature*, FOTL XVI (Grand Rapids: Eerdmans, 1996), 529.

3. Socioeconomic Transgressions and Power Relations 49

tic and syntactical markers, such as שדה (field) and בית (house, household); בית and נחלה (inheritance); גבר (man) and איש (man); גזל (seize, snatch) and עשק (extort, defraud, oppress). Such characterization is devoid of unequivocal markers pointing to any specific historical situation.[9] The passage describes the situation by employing different denunciation techniques, followed with condemnation of the social transgressions of greed and violence (2:2). The announcement of Yahweh's judgement is introduced by the adverbial particle לכן (therefore) and the messenger formula כה אמר יהוה (thus says the Lord) in 2:3. The internal layers of the oracle indicate varying speakers: the prophet accusing unidentified group (2:1–2), the divine first-person speech (2:3), and third-person references to Yahweh (2:4–5).[10] The following analysis examines this unit in terms of the structure of the woe-cry and its targets (2:1), the social transgressions of the greedy (2:2), and the announcement of Yahweh's judgement (2:3–5).

3.1.1. The Woe-Cry and Its Targets (Micah 2:1)

> Woe to those devising troubles,
>   and working evil on their beds.
> They put it into execution with the daylight;
>   because it is in the power of their hand.

Micah 2:1 begins with a signal of lamentation marked characteristically by the interjection particle הוי (ah, alas, woe) that is used to convey woe-cry or lamentation of distress (Isa 5:9, 13; 28:2–4; 30:3–5; Hab 2:16; Zeph 3:5 cf. 1 Kgs 13:30; Jer 22:18). The interjection is linked with participles that indicate the unnamed group to whom the oracle is addressed. According to Erhard Gerstenberger, "The normal prophetic woe-form contains general and timeless indictments of historically unspecified evildoers."[11] In the present prophetic context, the combination of introductory woe-cry followed by indictment and threats serves as a kerygmatic entity in which the second part is an independent unit of threat and messenger-formula (2:3; cf. Isa 5:24; 28:2–4).[12] Thus the entity functions as a prophetic judgment or woe oracle.[13]

---

[9] Ben Zvi, *Micah*, 44.
[10] Nogalski, *Book of the Twelve*, 535.
[11] Erhard Gerstenberger, "The Woe Oracle of the Prophets," *JBL* 81 (1962): 252.
[12] Gerstenberger, "Woe Oracle of the Prophets," 253.
[13] For a discussion of forms and elements of woe-oracles of the prophets, see W. Eugene March, "Prophecy," in *Old Testament Form Criticism*, ed. John H. Hayes (San Antonio: Trinity University Press, 1974), 164–65; Westermann, *Basic Forms of Prophetic Speech*, 190–94; Gerstenberger, "Woe Oracle of the Prophets," 252–54.

The woe-cry or lamentation is followed by an identification of a group whose scheme and actions the prophet brands as mischievous. As the participles indicate, they have made a habit of "devising troubles, and working evil" (חשבי־און ופעלי רע). These participles are modified by the prepositional phrase, על־משכבותם (upon their beds). Thus Micah's graphic characterization of their scheme as און (troubles, harms, misdeed, injustice) intentionally distinguished from אֹן (generative power, physical strength, riches) and רע (evil, bad; in the absolute, ethical sense),[14] the location of their schemes (on their beds—during the night), and the time of execution (they put it into execution with the daylight), indicate that he is not addressing arbitrary transgressions but well-organized schemes with evil objectives.[15] These perpetrators carefully plan their mischievous actions and move on with execution at every slightest opportunity, believing that with their status—wealth, authority and interest—no one can challenge them: כי יש־לאל ידם (because it is in the power of their hand). The idea of the time of execution of their action associated with daylight indicates supposedly the time when the courts gathered for the defense and protection of people. In the ancient Near East, it was a time for the anticipation of divine help and justice after thieves and evildoers shielded their atrocities under the darkness of the night.[16] It does appear that while the Judean citizens expected justice, they experienced the opposite.

3.1.2. The Socioeconomic Transgressions of the Greedy (Micah 2:2)

> And they covet fields and violently take them;
>   and houses and take them away.
> And they oppress a man and his household,
>   even a man and his inheritance.

Micah 2:2 proceeds with specific elaboration of the "troubles and evil deeds" of the wealthy landowners addressed in 2:1. He identifies the root of their mischief as covetousness; these tyrants covert (המד) the possessions of others and their uncontrollable desire drive them to commit the various transgressions described in 2:2. Helped by the grammatical structure of the verse, the *Qal* consecutive perfect aptly describes the habitual or customary actions of the group. The evils

---

[14] William L. Holladay, *A Concise Hebrew and Aramaic Lexicon of the Old Testament* (Leiden: Brill, 2000), 7.
[15] Nogalski, *Book of the Twelve*, 513.
[16] Waltke, *Commentary on Micah*, 62. The LXX explains the success of the people's schemes and execution by this rendering, "Because they have not lifted up their hands to God" (διοτι ουκ ήραν προς τον θεον τας χειρας αυτων), a setting in which lifting up of hands implies worship and loyalty to God. This apparently due to the lack of understanding of אל (strength, power) to mean God. Waltke, *Commentary on Micah*, 94.

3. Socioeconomic Transgressions and Power Relations

of covetousness (המד) manifest in other heinous violations: גזל (seize, take away by force), נשא (take, grab) and עשק (extort, defraud, oppress). This group covets fields and houses and violently takes them. They exploit property-owners, defrauding them of their homes and legitimate inheritance.[17] Whatever was the means they adopted in taking advantage of the symbolic and material possessions of others, it was in blatant violation of the essential blueprint that established them as a covenant community. Covetousness is an unethical behavior and spiritual malaise that is prohibited in the Decalogue (Exod 20:17; Deut 5:21).[18] Thus at the center of the Micah's indictment is the condemnation of the abuse of position and influence, the greed and thirst for power, possession and wealth that motivate these ungodly individuals in society.[19]

The victims of exploitation in the text are not the poor as much as landowners and famers. They have access to landed property and houses, and they occupy an essential position in Israelite society. Their symbolic and material possessions may have come from inheritance. They could not be traded or substituted for other property (cf. 1 Kgs 21:1–3). In the Old Testament and especially for Israel, God is presented as the supreme landowner who grants families some degree of ownership.[20] The intricate association of Yahweh, Israel and land is most obvious in the language of "inheritance" (נחלה) in connection with Yahweh's gift of land to Israel. This is reflected in Moses' distribution of the land (Num 26:52–57; 27:7) and the enactment of law for the protection of its inheritance (Lev 25:10; Num 36:1–12). For individuals and families, it was not just an asset but a sacred entitlement of trust. If it were lost, at best, a person might reduce himself to a short-term employee or at worst, a slave. When this happens, the individual loses his independence and freedom before Yahweh and lives at the mercy of the land-magnates.[21] While Micah does not specify the methods the land-magnates adopted to exploit and defraud their victims, the corresponding reference in Amos 5:7, 10–17, indicates that it might have been through the court system.[22]

---

[17] Nogalski, *Book of the Twelve*, 536.
[18] Waltke, *Commentary on Micah*, 95.
[19] Nogalski, *Book of the Twelve*, 536; Alfaro, *Micah*, 7–8; cf. Joseph Blenkinsopp, *A History of Prophecy in Israel* (Louisville: Westminster John Knox, 1996), 95.
[20] James McKeown, "Land," *Dictionary of the Old Testament: Pentateuch*, ed. T. Desmond Alexander and David W. Baker (Downers Grove: Inter-Varsity, 2003), 487.
[21] Waltke, *Commentary on Micah*, 106.
[22] Dishonest scales (Hos 12:7) and extortion by force (Isa 52:4) are other possibilities. See Waltke, *Commentary on Micah*, 96.

3.1.3. Announcement of Yahweh's Judgement (Micah 2:3–5)

> Therefore, thus says the LORD,
> Behold, I am planning against
>   this (group, clan, family), calamity
>   from which you cannot remove your necks;
> And you will not walk haughtily,
>   for it is an evil time.
> On that day, they shall take up a parable against you,
>   and a plaintive (sorrowful) lamentation shall be uttered,
> Saying, we are thoroughly miserable,
>   the portion of my people has been exchanged.
> How he removed what is mine
>   Our fields have been given to the apostate.
> Therefore, you will have no one
>   stretching a measuring line for you by lot
>   in the assembly of the LORD.

Micah 2:3 signals a threatening note as it moves from indictment of the land-magnates (2:1–2) to the announcement of judgment. The verse is headed by the transitional particle לכן (therefore). The text imagines a cause-and-effect theology. Based on the principle of just recompense, the judgement sentences are appropriate for the transgressions of the powerful group. Just as they are devising "wickedness and evil on their beds," Yahweh is also "planning evil against this family" (חשב על־המשפחה הזאת רעה) (2:3). Since the transgressions of the powerful group were directed against the possessions and persons of the victims, Yahweh's judgement sentences will be executed against the possessions and persons of the powerful.[23] While in 2:1 the powerful used their power and influence to take advantage of the possessions of the weak and helpless, in 2:3 the powerful are made powerless because they have violated Yahweh's requirement.

The targets of Yahweh's plan "against this family" most probably refers to Judah as a whole (cf. Amos 3:1, 12). The relative pronoun אשר (which, from which) points back to רעה (evil things), from which this family/clan cannot remove its neck (לא־תמישו משם צואריכם). The reference to משפחה (family, clan, tribe) reinforces the community frame. Thus, in accordance with the principle of community responsibility and solidarity, the whole nation (pictured as family or tribe) will suffer the adverse effects of the transgressions of the powerful and oppressive elites. Truly, when Jerusalem fell in 586 BCE both the wicked and the righteous suffered.[24] The burden of these evils will be on their necks, such

---

[23] Waltke, *Commentary on Micah*, 107.
[24] Waltke, *Commentary on Micah*, 97–98.

3. Socioeconomic Transgressions and Power Relations 53

that they cannot escape their effects. Like yokes, the effects of their transgressions will compel, subjugate, and humiliate them. Because they have acted out of greed and the lust for power and have not walked humbly with God (cf. Mic 6:8), Yahweh's yoke upon them will make them walk without self-importance (ולא תלכו רומה); they will be humbled. The final phrase in 2:3 indicates that Yahweh's judgement will not be delayed, and they cannot escape the humiliating punishment of their transgressions, "for the time is evil" (כי עת רעה היא).

Micah 2:4 continues Yahweh's judgement sentences against Judah for the transgressions of the wealthy and powerful with the transitional formula, "on that day." The phrase ביום ההוא (on that day) refers back to the "time of evil" in 2:3 and imagines a special moment of Yahweh's intervention to right evildoing. Most often in the Book of the Twelve, the formula brings revival of hope and restoration of fortunes, but the reverse is the case in 2:4. James D. Nogalski notes that, "this verse adds insult to injury by citing a taunt song placed in the mouths of unnamed enemies. This taunt adds a second stage to the punishment of 2:3 since the cries of those being punished consist of lamentation in response to disaster, calamity, and death."[25] Although it is difficult to determine the scope of this lament, the taunt song is the modification of the words and quote of the wealthy tyrants in Judah; that is "we are thoroughly miserable" (שדוד נשדנו) considering the destruction, the alteration of relationship with Yahweh, and the loss of land.

In the expression חלק עמי (portion of my people), "my people" is a possessive genitive while the noun חלק (portion) implies their land or inheritance. The land owes its existence to Yahweh (Lev 25:23), and he creates its inhabitants, continually supervising or monitoring their behavior. He allocates land to people (Gen 2:8; Deut 2:5, 9, 19; Josh 12–22). Conversely, he removes people from the land and gives it to their enemies when they do not behave in worthy manner (Gen 3:23–24; Lev 26:33; Deut 28:49–68).[26] Yahweh's sentence in 2:4 is that those who violate his requirements will forfeit their fields. In this regard, "we are thoroughly miserable" (שדוד נשדנו) communicates an ironic, poetic justice as it calls to mind the themes in 2:2. Those who coveted and seized the fields of others now lament the loss of their own; those who schemed to exploit, defraud and steal the inheritance of others now weep as they lose their rights to shares of ancestral inheritance from Yahweh.[27] This forfeiture of ancestral inheritance is reinforced in the following verse.

Yahweh's just sentences reach their climax with the transitional particle לכן (therefore) in 2:5. Micah 2:5 announces the consequences of land-magnates being deprived of their fields and allocated to their enemies. The verse assimilates

---

[25] Nogalski, *Book of the Twelve*, 537.
[26] McKeown, "Land," 487; Waltke, *Commentary on Micah*, 108.
[27] O'Brien, *Micah*, 19; Nogalski, *Book of the Twelve*, 538.

vocabulary from traditions of the first land allocation (Josh 14–15 and 18–20) and actualizes them for the entire community as well as reversing the conquest.[28] The idea of "stretching a measuring line for you by lot" finds expression in the original allocation of the land (Josh 18–22), which was carried out through the casting of lots by the priest (Num 26:55–56; Josh 14:2; 18:11; 19:51). The implication of this sentence is reflected in Wolff's remarks, "Whoever has been dispossessed of his land can no longer expect his lost property to be returned in a future social distribution of the land."[29] As a defender of the oppressed against the dishonest social elites, "Micah speaks of the achieving of social and religious ideal from which the covetous and their descendants will be excluded. The future 'assembly of Yahweh' will consist of the oppressed."[30]

The analysis of the unit (2:1–5) highlights the multi-layered picture of a cold-hearted indulgence that violated Yahweh's blueprint for healthy covenant community living. This violation evoked the cause-and-effect theology. The alternation in his wordplays between רע and רעה (1, 3), חשבי and חשב (1, 3), ונחלתו and חלק (2, 4), תמישו and ימיש (3, 4), נשדנו and שדינו (4), highlights the conflict that exists between prejudice and justice, while stressing that human transgression will be dealt with by Yahweh's justice. Carol J. Dempsey writes,

> By means of vignettes occurring throughout the book of Micah, all readers of the book are prompted to visualize a causal relationship between negative social behavior, namely, sin and divine punishment. The present vignette (vv. 1–5) suggests a direct relationship between the harshness of the actions of those who deserve punishment and the harshness of their own coming punishment.[31]

At the foundation, the elites in Judah had misguidedly mistaken covenantal responsibility for covenantal advantage and freedom. This development gave way to a high sense of security that eventually led to self-gratification.[32] Their reprehensible acts were an affront on Yahweh's character and attack on the basic ethical structure of his people in covenant community.[33] The development of Micah's rhetoric indicates that Yahweh does not put up with attitudes that are

---

[28] Nogalski, *Book of the Twelve*, 538.

[29] Wolff, *Micah*, 80.

[30] Delbert R. Hillers, *Micah: A Commentary on the Book of the Prophet Micah*, Hermeneia (Philadelphia: Fortress, 1984), 33.

[31] Carol J. Dempsey, "Micah 2–3: Literary Artistry, Ethical Message, and Some Considerations about the Image of Yahweh and Micah," *JSOT* 85 (1999): 120–21.

[32] Mignon R. Jacobs, 'Micah,' in *Theological Interpretation of the Old Testament: A Book-by-Book Survey*, ed. Kevin J. Vanhoozer (Grand Rapids: Baker Academic, 2008), 278; R. Walter L. Moberly, "In God We Trust? The Challenge of the Prophets," *ExAud* 24 (2008): 24.

[33] Carroll, "Passion for Justice and the Conflicted Self, 171; Hillers, *Micah*, 33.

unethical. Consequently, the connection between the literary form and ethical thrust makes the unit very stimulating.

3.2. Distorted Theological Rationalization and Condemnation of Injustice (2:6–11)

Micah 2:6–11 is a disputation oracle that focuses on Micah and his prophetic colleagues. The text is quite irregular and the links between thoughts are difficult to comprehend. The unit presents its readers with the challenge of coping with the density of changes in speaker or speakers, grammatical inconsistencies, and the presence of some uncommon forms.[34] The content of the speeches indicates that it is clearly a disputation or dialogue that sketched out the perspective of Micah's opponents—or distorted their theological justification of crimes (2:6–7), and the prophet's perspective and counter argument—of condemnation of injustice (2:8–11).[35] The fluidity in the characterization of the misdeeds of those who neglect or oppose the godly voice, using the language of oppression and imagery of dispossession, is shared by the accusation in 2:1–2.[36] The increased degree of charges of shameful crimes against the weak and marginalized is strongly suggested by the transition from the image of economic piracy and dispossessing male owners (2:1–5) to that of continuity of similar actions against women and children (2:9). Radically, within this unit, there is the heightening of the negative characterization of the powerful enemies of the people, which does not end with their description as thieves without any integrity, as they undermine Yahweh's honor as the patron of women and children of his people (2:9), but with the mockery of their theological wisdom (cf. 2:7, 11).[37]

The historical setting of the (re)reading for which the unit of 2:6–11 is written, as well as the setting of the speaker, is similar to the setting of the previous unit (2:1–5),[38] but it is probably not the same occasion. It is an attempt by Micah to respond to those who had a cheerful and optimistic message and thus urged him to curtail his message of divine judgement. Those to whom he addressed the announcement of Yahweh's judgement found his message not only personally provocative and offensive, but theologically unimaginable.[39] The claims and counter claims of rival prophets to be the official guides of the nation, legitimate spokesmen of Yahweh, were one of the most fascinating features of Israel religion throughout the classical period. The Hebrew Bible presents ample instances

---

[34] Ben Zvi, *Micah*, 56.
[35] Dempster, *Micah*, 80; Sweeney, *Twelve Prophets*, 357.
[36] Dempster, *Micah*, 80.
[37] Ben Zvi, *Micah*, 59–60.
[38] Ben Zvi, *Micah*, 62–63.
[39] Mays, *Micah*, 67.

in Israel where prophet confronted prophet in religious controversy.⁴⁰ They announced contradictory oracles and hurled contradictory messages at one another. In fact, "the charge 'venal' was countered by the charge 'insane.'"⁴¹

In this unit, the text links the attitude of the evildoers with their distorted understanding of Yahweh's relationship with them as covenant community members. Their distorted theological perspective is presented not on the basis of understanding "a communally accepted, trusted description of YHWH's attributes and doings, but of their rejection of the message of prophetic voices that interpret those accepted descriptions from a viewpoint informed by the particular circumstances of their time."⁴² The unit concludes with shocking perspective that the community accepts only highly exaggerated and ridiculed prophets or preachers, or both, and snubs godly ones.⁴³

The structure of the unit indicates the speaker's citation of the speech of the evildoers (2:6), a presentation of the theological thought of the evildoers, that is, the theological foundation of the justification of evildoing (2:7) and the lack of applicability of the aforementioned theological thought, that is, the ethical foundation of the condemnation of injustice (2:8–11). An exegetical analysis of the unit is presented below.

3.2.1. Identity of the Speaker (2:6)

> "Do not prophesy," they prophesy.
> They shall not prophesy concerning these things.
> Disgrace shall not overtake us.

The first task in this unit is the identification of the speaker or speakers. Micah's opponents are variously understood to include the false prophets, the land-grabbers, the powerful men denounced in the previous unit, or "the house of Jacob" (cf. 2:7), or a combination of the above.⁴⁴ Hiller believes that אל־תטפו (Do not prophesy) is directed at more than Micah alone. He notes, "Though especially the rich are in mind, the speakers represent the people.... Perhaps it is a situation where oppressor and oppressed alike regard prophecy as irreligious."⁴⁵ Similarly, Jenson observes that Micah's emphasis on land rights indicates that

---

⁴⁰ In 1 Kgs 22, one finds the stories of Micaiah ben Imlah versus Zedekiah ben Chenaanah; Jeremiah versus Hananiah in Jeremiah 28; Isaiah (28) and Hosea (4:5; 9:7–8) were opposed by other prophets, Amos (7:10–17) by a priest and Micah by prophet and priest (3:11) in collusion.
⁴¹ Andersen and Freedman, *Micah*, 296–97.
⁴² Ben Zvi, *Micah*, 64.
⁴³ Ben Zvi, *Micah*, 64.
⁴⁴ See, Ben Zvi, *Micah*, 57.
⁴⁵ Hillers, *Micah*, 36.

3. Socioeconomic Transgressions and Power Relations

he is not addressing economic pirates and murderers but rulers and merchants who oversee and control the economic base of the nation and are familiar with the legal system.[46]

Although the MT is believed to be corrupted and thus cannot be understood without emendations and reconstructions,[47] the main thrust of the oracle is clear. In verse 6, the verb (*hiphil*) נטף (to drip) appears three times in the opening line of the unit and twice in the conclusion in verse 11. It is usually associated with the dropping of liquid, as in raindrops (Judg 5:4; Ps 68:8), honey (Prov 5:3; Song 4:11; Joel 4:18), or ointment (Song 5:5),[48] and it is used metaphorically for preaching or prophesying (Ezek 21:2; Amos 7:16). The most reasonable inference that one can make of the text is that the previous oracle of judgement illustrates the kind of preaching or prophecy which the religiously secure oppose (cf. Amos 7:12–13; 9:10; Hos 9:7) at the beginning of this unit. The unit documents Micah's confrontation with rival prophets, his publicity of their collaboration and conspiracy in crimes against society, and the unpleasant conclusion that only a highly exaggerated and ridiculed prophet who would collude with their sordid desires could please them.[49] Thus the imperative אל־תטפו (Do not prophesy) pictures Micah and his prophetic opponents in discussion (cf. Amos 2:12). In this regard, יטיפון (they prophesy) signals the quotation of what the opponents say. It is probably an ironic comment that sums up the attitude of the audience who, judging from their behavior, have little or no understanding of the moral and religious foundation of genuine prophecy. According to Jenson, "Truth and justice, not rhetoric and forcefulness, are the ultimate judge of speech."[50]

The expression לא־יטפו לאלה (They shall not prophesy concerning these things), presupposes a situation in which the prophet has been verbally assaulted and reproached and it consequently represents Micah's counterattack. The literary context of "these things" points back to the unsolicited and annoying preaching of condemnation (2:1–2) and the announcement of judgement (2:3–5). The remark in the second segment of the verse, לא יסג כלמות (disgrace shall not overtake us) becomes a fitting summary of the words of Micah's opponents in this context. The *niphal* verb יסג from the root נשוג (translated as overtake) usually means "turn back" or "turn away," and the feminine plural noun כלמות (disgrace) is the subject of the verb יסג. Here the speaker implies that the subject of the verb יסג will not be humiliated "by reproaches."[51] In absolute confidence

---

[46] Jenson, *Obadiah, Jonah, Micah*, 123.
[47] See Mays, *Micah*, 68; Andersen and Freedman, *Micah*, 297–301.
[48] Dempster, *Micah*, 88.
[49] Hillers, *Micah*, 34.
[50] Jenson, *Obadiah, Jonah, Micah*, 124.
[51] Andersen and Freedman, *Micah*, 306.

in their sense of security, knowledge about Yahweh and the uprightness of their life, these opponents reject the prophecies about judgement and hold that the disgrace of humiliating disaster, of any misfortune that would leave them exposed to reproaches, would never come near them.[52]

So Waltke notes, "Thus Micah is saying, 'since these prophets will not preach about judgement, Yahweh will not remove disgrace.' He may have in mind the Assyrian crisis that is happening as he speaks."[53] This implies a prophecy of punishment, since shame will not depart.[54] Regarding the relationship between shame and disgrace Jenson notes, "'disgrace' is often parallel to 'shame' (Jer 20:11; Ezek 16:63), and by metonymy it can also refer to the disaster that is the cause of shame and that allows others to mock and insult its victims.... Lack of shame for their sinful deeds was one of Jeremiah's criticisms of the false prophets opposing him (Jer 6:15; 8:11–12)."[55]

3.2.2. Theological Justification of Evildoing (2:7)

> Should this be said, O house of Jacob?
>   Is the Spirit of the LORD impatient?
>   Are these His doings?'
> Do not my words do good
>   to the one who walks uprightly?

Micah 2:7 contains four argumentative rhetorical questions. The questions arose out of a conviction about the wrongdoers' identity and character. The first question asks the house of Jacob if it is certain that something should have been said. A slight emendation results in reading הֶאָמוּר (said) as הֶאָרוּר (cursed) and thus the question: "Is the house of Jacob accursed"?[56] This reading fits well as a comment of Micah's opponents. However, the following three rhetorical questions expand the defensive denials of these opponents. The first question, as it stands, without any emendation focuses on the divine election of the house of Jacob and thus not only refers to the preaching of judgement but also to the follow up questions. "Should this be said?" (הֶאָמוּר) hints at their complacent conviction and dependence on traditional covenant theology (Ps 114:1–2). In their mindset and conviction, it is inconceivable that the house (descendants) of Jacob who obtained the promise and blessing of Yahweh could be thrust irrevocably beyond the sphere of salvation to suffer the misfortunes which express

---

[52] Mays, *Micah*, 69.
[53] Dempster, *Micah*, 89.
[54] Waltke, "Micah," 2:642.
[55] Jenson, *Obadiah, Jonah, Micah*, 124.
[56] Mays, *Micah*, 66; Dempster, *Micah*, 89.

Yahweh's anger and rejection.[57] Such an unreflective dependence on a religious heritage that makes them stand secure and unthreatened characterizes the two following questions. They are rhetorical questions intended to cast doubt and are tantamount to denial.[58]

By appealing to the very character of Yahweh himself, they ask, הקצר רוח יהוה (Is the Spirit of the LORD impatient? lit. "Has the Spirit of the LORD become shortened?") It is an expression that indicates exhaustion of patience in the classic characteristic description of God (Exod 34:6; cf. Prov 14:29). From the very description of the character of God in the Israelite credo (Exod 34:6–7), Micah's opponents find his message in apparent and irreconcilable contradiction to a long-held creed, basic to Israel's confession of faith. With this theological disagreement over the reading of Israelite history, the next question מעלליו אם־אלה (Are these His doings?) indicates that the threatened events are not what Yahweh intends.[59] These two questions continue the polemic of Mic 2:6 and serve as an indignant rejection of Micah's declaration. The demonstrative אלה (these) in verse 7 links back to אלה (these) in verse 6 and in both occurrences has the same referent, specifically 2:1–5. The announcement of impending judgement in 2:3 indicates that Yahweh's patience is exhausted and the announcement of permanent exclusion from the congregation of Yahweh (2:5) implies deed of Yahweh which is inconsistent with his character.[60]

In contrast, the last question in verse 7 sounds like a refutation of these charges. Here Micah adds an essential condition that his opponents have overlooked and taken for granted, namely, the issue of walking uprightly. The question indicates the ethical condition of the covenant. Contrary to being rebellious to faith and harmful to national well-being, Micah insists that his words or deeds (דברי), which could as well mean Yahweh's "words or deeds" referring back to "these things" whose antecedent is the announcement of doom in 2:3–5, benefit those who walk uprightly.[61] Those who were asking these questions ignore the moral and religious dimensions of their covenant responsibility before God. Obviously, Israel's traditions and confessional narratives positioned salvation and blessing firmly in the context of obedience, generosity, and stewardship of the economic asset of land.[62] However, Micah's opponents take their prosper-

---

[57] Mays, *Micah*, 70.
[58] Andersen and Freedman, *Micah*, 307.
[59] Deeds (מעלל) in the prophets are usually wicked acts of men (cf. Mic 3:4); of Yahweh's saving acts only in Pss 77:12; 78:7, and are not expected of God, whom they believe. Mays, *Micah*, 70.
[60] Andersen and Freedman, *Micah*, 307–8.
[61] It is a consistently repeated lesion taught by wise, that Yahweh rewards the upright (ישר; cf. Ps 1; Prov 2:7, 21; 11:3, 6, 11; 14:9, 11). Mays, *Micah*, 70.
[62] Jenson, *Obadiah, Jonah, Micah*, 125.

ity as a sign of Yahweh's favor and as a confirmation of their uprightness. Consequently, success and complacency became their unshakable foundation for a theology against the prophetic announcement of doom. Micah goes on the attack. Concisely, if the "house of Jacob" is ruthless in plundering the homes of its own people, it does not walk uprightly and cannot be a recipient of Yahweh's blessing. In fact, Yahweh's Spirit will lose patience, and the announced words of judgement are positive proof that God will act in this manner.[63]

In the following verses (8–11), Micah accuses his opponents by stating the reality of their lives in terms of social ethics as evidence of the inappropriateness and inapplicability of the aforementioned theological thoughts.

3.2.3. Ethical Condemnation of Evildoing (2:8–11)

> But recently my people
>   have arisen as an enemy.
> You strip the robe off the garment,
>   from unsuspecting passers-by,
>   from those returning from war.
> The women of my people you evict,
>   each one from her pleasant houses.
> From their children
>   you take away my splendor forever.
> Arise and go;
>   for this is no place of rest.
> Because of the uncleanness that brings destruction,
>   and a grievous destruction.
> If a man walking after wind
>   and falsehood had told lies,
> 'I will preach to you concerning wine and strong drink',
> Such a person would be prophet for this people.

Micah 2:8–11, especially verses 8–9, is a concise narrative belonging to an argumentation between rival factions of prophets. Mignon R. Jacobs notes that in view of the emendation of the MT of verse 8, "In light of the characteristic of the text and the presence of the elements typical of the disputation speech, it is more plausible that the speaker in this verse is the prophet."[64] The conjunction "and" or "but" marks a transition from questions to statements.[65] By using the adverbial particle אתמול (recently, lately, yesterday) in verse 8, Micah does not

---

[63] Dempster, *Micah*, 89.
[64] Mignon R. Jacobs, *The Conceptual Coherence of the Book of Micah*, JSOTSup 322 (Sheffield: Sheffield Academic, 2001), 293.
[65] Andersen and Freedman, *Micah*, 313.

need to research too far into the past to illustrate evidence of inappropriate lifestyle and covenant violations on the part of his opponents. Judging from the grammatical structure of verse 8, these opponents are not morally upright, "they are 'the enemy of my people', and have accumulated a record of successful oppression that would justify the wrath of God many times over."[66]

Micah describes the victims of exploitation and oppression as "my people" (עמי) while his opponents play the role of enemy (אויב). Here, Micah attempts to create a distinction in the general population of Judah, disconnecting the weak from their oppressors, and leaving out the latter from the group of which he is a part. Thus, expanding the image of the powerful oppressors as the enemy, with their passionate drive for materialism, Micah describes how they claim the cloak of those who make efforts to live in peace, working for their bread and endeavoring to keep together the bonds of their community. The expression, "You strip the robe off the garment" (ממול שלמה אדר תפשטון) may literally translate "You strip off from the outside, a wrapper (cloak, garment, mantle), and so magnificence (glorious, splendor)." It implies the practice of reducing someone to destitution and leaving them naked by means of robbery, especially of a cruel kind. The feminine noun שלמה (wrapper) implies clothing, and refers to "an outer garment, of whatever design, some kind of cloak, easily removed (Gen 39:12)."[67] In many cultures, clothing is an insignia of glory, honor, and identity. In ancient Israel, a שלמה was a necessity of life, as essential as bread (Deut 10:18; Isa 3:7; 4:1). Andersen and Freedman note that,

> References to the שַׂלְמָה or its equivalent in legal texts, in mourning customs, in folklore, indicate that this part of a person's dress has an enormous social significance as a mark of status and identity. To take away a person's 'cloak' especially when it was their last possession, was a devastating indignity and an ultimate crime (Job 22:6).... If taken in pledge, the garment had to be returned to its owner by nightfall so he would have something to sleep in (Exod 22:25–26).[68]

The למהש (garment) and a person's dignity are inseparable. In fact, Yahweh himself is alerted on the violation of this obvious and remarkable testament of Israelites' sensitivity to a simple but basic human value (Exod 22:26–27). Obviously, the picture of robbery that Micah presents regarding his opponents' victims is that of the removal of whatever dignity, honor, and identity that the

---

[66] Mays, *Micah*, 71.
[67] Andersen and Freedman, *Micah*, 317. The שלמה (garment) is the basic article of clothing that people were prohibited from taking as a pledge (Deut 24:13) and אדר (robe) can also mean "splendor," "glorious," "majesty" or implying a more elegant and expensive covering (Jonah 3:6). Jenson, *Obadiah, Jonah, Micah*, 126.
[68] Andersen and Freedman, *Micah*, 318.

people have left. This is reprehensible and deserves condemnation. In the last phrase in verse 8, if taken word for word, the MT מעברים בטח שובי מלחמה reads, "from those who pass by (in) security, returned from war."[69] It indicates a specific injustice, and most probably refers to travelers in general. However, the translation of the phrase implies that these people are refugees escaping the threat of war, perhaps from the northern kingdom, or survivors of the 701 BCE Assyrian invasions. Jenson imagined that "They expected safety in Jerusalem and help from their fellows, but instead found themselves being robbed of the clothes off their back."[70] Under treaty, safe passage of travelers could be guaranteed and thus a journey could not be made without advance assurances (Num 21:21–24). Thus, when a traveler is making a journey based on this understanding and is robbed (cf. Hos 6:9), the crime is complicated by treachery. Obviously, it would have been a disgraceful crime, if such refugees, consisting predominantly of women and children, had been robbed along the way as they were passing by with the assumption of security. Micah's rhetoric and specific, concrete outrages suggest something very familiar in meaning and memory to his hearers and thus require no explanation.[71]

In verse 9, Micah continues the negative portrayal of his opponents. They are not only greedy and ruthless marauders who despoil their helpless victims and captives (2:8), but also those who undermine Yahweh's honor as patron of the women and children of his people.[72] The crimes of verse 9 cut to the heart of Israel's social ethics. The law made exhortations to public charity and protection against oppression on behalf of four conventional and symbolic groups of disadvantaged, defenseless, weak, and vulnerable individuals, namely, poor, homeless aliens, widows and orphans (cf. Exod 22:21–22; Deut 24:17–18). The protection of their land also constitutes a prominent aspect of ancient Israelite law (Deut 19:14) and wisdom teaching (Prov 15:25; 22:28; 23:10–11; Job 24:2–4). These issues are all given special attention in the prophetic critique of the major administrators of Israel and Judah (Hos 5:10).[73] The litmus test of good leadership was how it cared for these socially disadvantage people (Ps 72:2–4, 12–14; Jer 22:15–16). The crimes that are listed in these verses (8–9) are not the immediate

---

[69] Hillers, *Micah*, 35.

[70] Jenson, *Obadiah, Jonah, Micah*, 126. Dempster remarks that the phrase "refers to the peaceful return of soldiers from battle who have already fought—the war is over—and the last thing they expect is to be ambushed at home" (Dempster, *Micah*, 91).

[71] Andersen and Freedman, *Micah*, 320.

[72] Ben Zvi, *Micah*, 59–60.

[73] Zechariah expresses deep concern for the widow, orphan, foreigner, and the poor (Zech 7:10). Jeremiah's temple message includes a similar concern (Jer 7:6). Reinhard Achenbach, "The Protection of *Personae Miserae* in Ancient Israelite Law and Wisdom and in the Ostracon from Khirbet Qeiyafa," *Semitica* 54 (2012): 122–23.

actions of a foreign attacker, but obviously violations of covenant within the community of Judah. The specific details indicate some occasion, very recent according to verse 8, provisionally identified with the devastating strife in Israel in the reign of Ahaz.[74]

If נשי עמי (women of my people) is a reference "to the wives of the debt-ridden husbands, it shows a poignant divine concern for the women who are robbed of the place where they flourished."[75] In the construct phrase מבית תענגיה (house of her delight, or pleasures), the word תַעֲנֻגֶיה does not necessarily connote luxurious or comfortable homes, but the value of the house for the occupant.[76] If the husbands of these women had died, no doubt their houses would be essentially symbols and sources of joy, delight, comfort and security. The parallelism with עלליה (their young children) suggests that the women here are not necessarily widows, even though they would be vulnerable and protected by covenant law. According to Andersen and Freedman, תענגיה (pleasant) is an attribute of children in 1:16 and the repetition of this rare word in 1:16 and 2:9 (and elsewhere in Prov 19:10; Eccl 2:8; Song 7:7) indicates a connection of theme in Mic 1 and 2. In 1:16, the bereaved mother is addressed in the singular and could be taken as metaphorical for each listed city, but especially for Jerusalem, as the mother of lovely children. However, the plural נשי עמי (women of my people) in 2:9 tilts the balance in favor of human mothers.[77]

Micah underscores that children deprived of parents are victims. In 1:16, only one atrocity is involved—the expulsion of children (not women or mothers), but in 2:9, the atrocity involves separation of mothers and children.[78] Separating children from their homes is tantamount to removing them from their potential to be Yahweh's image bearer, flourishing in the land that Yahweh has graciously given to his people as a glorious inheritance. This again is an egregious violation, namely, stripping God of his הדרי (splendor) by taking away the weak and helpless children, the future of the nation, and robbing them of their destiny.[79] הדרי (my splendor, glory) refers to exclusively divine privileges which these children are expected to enjoy as Yahweh's people and his peculiar care. By means of injustice, violence, and oppression these enemies ruined the posterity of the children by driving them out of their houses and separating them from their parents. The enemies either carried out these contemptible acts continually or they intend to stand by what they have done forever (לעולם).

---

[74] Andersen and Freedman, *Micah*, 321.
[75] Dempster, *Micah*, 91.
[76] Andersen and Freedman, *Micah*, 321.
[77] Andersen and Freedman, *Micah*, 321–22.
[78] Andersen and Freedman, *Micah*, 322.
[79] Dempster, *Micah*, 92.

In view of the reference to a garment in verse 8, there is a progressive intensification as those less privileged are taken advantage of. The language is extravagant, and the hyperbole communicates God's outrage at such callous behavior. A sequential and composite reading of these crimes will indicate a portrait of the typical family where fathers are robbed and disconnected from their families (possibly by slavery or forced labor), followed by the eviction of their wives and finally their children are disinherited.[80] Micah's rebuttal of their claim to uprightness is thus aptly sketched out in violation of social ethics, shameful robbery, and oppression of the powerless. He has been provoked enough by the behavior of his opponents and now burst out with rage in 2:10. While there are difficulties in understanding the altercation between Micah and his opponents, the imperatives of Mic 2:10 reflect the message that one action is intrinsically interconnected with the other, namely: wrongful deprivation of others leads to Yahweh's dispossession of the dispossessor.[81] The command in 2:10 could be the quotations of the land dispossessors, possibly the expulsion order to the women and children in 2:9. However, it seems more likely that Micah is the speaker as he moves from vehement indictment to a declaration of judgement.

The first poetic line summons the people under judgement to leave because their habitation is no longer a place of rest and security. The land has been stolen by the greedy land grabbers to enlarge and enrich their estates, the inheritance that Yahweh has given graciously to his people (Deut 12:9) and is no more the מנוחה ("rest") promised by God. מנוחה ("resting place") is a theologically significant Deuteronomic term for undisturbed enjoyment of Yahweh's gift of the land for inheritance (נחלה) (Deut 12:9; 1 Kgs 8:56).[82] As the greedy land grabbers ordered the poor and helpless to get off the property being expropriated, so too will they find no home as a place of rest and security (cf. Ruth 1:9).

In the second line of 2:10, the text uses words that show the land can no longer be a place of rest and security for Yahweh's people because of impurity. The word טמאה ("uncleanness") is a highly religious term, used to describe pollution and the result of certain kinds of unethical behavior in priestly texts (Lev 18:24–28; Num 35:33; Deut 21:23). This term fits more appropriately the present prophetic context in which the entire land has become polluted by the moral contamination of the rich.[83] As one can deduce, these materialistic and avaricious creditors have seized garments taken in pledge, which was traditionally a symbolic sign of debt, and not real property (Exod 22:25–26; Deut 24:12–13; cf.

---

[80] Jenson, *Obadiah, Jonah, Micah*, 126.
[81] Ben Zvi, *Micah*, 61.
[82] Jenson, *Obadiah, Jonah, Micah*, 127.
[83] In other prophetic texts טמאה is a cultic metaphor for sin or a term for idolatry (Jer 19:13; Ezek 22:5, 15; 24:13; 36:25, 29; 39:24). Dempster, *Micah*, 92; Jenson, *Obadiah, Jonah, Micah*, 127.

3. Socioeconomic Transgressions and Power Relations 65

Amos 2:6), robbed widow's houses and destroyed the livelihood of those evicted. In the process, they have gained power in the land, but at the same time defiled it, and thus made it unclean.[84] The following verb תְּחַבֵּל (*piel* of חבל), has several meanings including "pledge" or "corrupt," but "destroy" is most probable. Destruction (חבל) reinforces the announcement of threat and the *niphal* verb נמרץ (grievous) is from the root מרץ (to be sick). It is used in Micah in the sense of terrible, and thus וחבל נמרץ (terrible or grievous destruction). Because the land has been defiled (טמאה) by their manifold atrocities, therefore utter destruction (תחבל), even a sore and grievous destruction (וחב נמרץ), should come upon them.

Micah 2:11 brings the unit to a close with a well calculated, scornful and contemptuous restatement of the relationship of Micah's opponents to prophecy. The verse picks up the language and theme of verse 6, by using similar expressions to describe prophesying. Micah's version of the interchange reflects a negotiation in which there is a conspiracy of reciprocal self-deception. He caricatures at his audience a specific job requirement of the preacher they desire; an enthusiastic and charismatic preacher in the old style of prophets who are under the influence of the Spirit (1 Sam 10:6; 1 Kgs 18:12; 22:21; 2 Kgs 2:9, 16), one who lies and whose preaching would intoxicate his audience in a drunkenness that would make their blind folly worse.[85] The use of רוח (spirit, wind) and שקר (deception, falsehood) together in the first line of the verse indicates that the two words function as hendiadys (empty falsehood) and thus describe the inspiration of false prophets (1 Kgs 22:22).[86] If רוח is taken as an adverbial accusative of הלך (walking), which makes for the best poetic arrangement, then the translation would be "a man walking in the spirit." Walking (הלך) is a religioethical metaphor, "to bring out the person's character, shown particularly in deceitful speech. Micah 2:11bA catches a similar aspect, the charlatan's self-advertisement, at least in the sarcastic words of his critic."[87]

Consequently, the message which Micah puts in the mouth of the "approved" preacher is probably a sarcastic metaphor; he caricatures the prophet as having a monotonous and anticipated message. In the expression לך ליין ולשכר אטף (I will preach to you concerning wine and strong drink), "wine and strong drink" (יין ולשכר) indicate "the content of the message rather than payment for

---

[84] Hillers, *Micah*, 37.
[85] Hillers, *Micah*, 37.
[86] The messages of false prophets were seen to be windy (Isa 41:29; Jer 5:13) and deceptive (Jer 14:14). In Isa 9:15 (MT 9:14), Isaiah speaks of a prophet who teaches falsehood and Jer 14:14 talks about prophets who prophesied falsehood in Yahweh's name. They announce false vision, divination, futility, and the deception of their own minds. Jenson, *Obadiah, Jonah, Micah*, 128.
[87] Andersen and Freedman, *Micah*, 328.

services rendered. The words mean prosperity and pleasure ... as opposed to the words of Micah, who preached about 'these things'—God's judgement (2:6)."[88] The sarcastic and discourteous conclusion of 2:11 is clear; the one qualified to be the "trickler" (i.e., prophet or preacher) of this people is "a man of the spirit" who convincingly utters more and more deceptive lies, and with such utterances, "I will preach to you concerning wine and strong drink." The people are only too excited to be deluded and tricked.

3.3. Corrupt Economic, Political, and Religious System (3:1–12)

Micah 3 is a judgement oracle that has been interpreted to be a reaction to Mic 2:6–11.[89] The unit (2:12–13) preceding this section concludes with a graphic presentation of a righteous leader, a divine king as leader of Yahweh's people (משברא), delivering them in the future as they go together through (לפניהם פרצו הפרץ) the shut gate (שַׁעַר) of their exilic bondage. It provides a bridge between the idea of the anticipated status of Israel/Judah in view of their relationship to Yahweh, their king, leader, patron, and the fate of monarchic Israel/Judah on the one hand, and the status of the post-monarchic community of readers of the book.[90] However, in chapter 3 the situation changes to the current leaders of Jerusalem, who are heads and leaders of their people, spreading out the flesh (שאר) of their people in a cooking pot (כאשר ופרשו בסיר) and then grinding their bones to produce food (פצחו).[91]

This section takes up this unit as Yahweh's primary requirement and demand on Israel's leaders, their failure to embody justice and its attendant consequences. The three subunits: 3:1–4, 3:5–7, and 3:9–12 (with the exclusion of v.8), are connected by their shared addressees (Israel's ruling classes), their shared form (judgement oracles), as well as their shared theme (manipulation of justice for personal interest). The indictment and judicial sentence are connected with appropriate participles: אז (then, in v. 4) and לכן (therefore, in vv. 6 and 12).[92]

3.3.1. Economic Cannibalism of Judean Leadership (3:1–4)

> Then I said,
>   Hear now, heads of Jacob
>   and leaders of the house of Israel.
>   Is it not for you to know justice?

---

[88] Dempster, *Micah*, 93.
[89] Jacobs, *Conceptual Coherence of the Book of Micah*, 84–85.
[90] Ben Zvi, *Micah*, 69.
[91] Dempster, *Micah*, 109.
[92] Waltke, "Micah," 656.

> You who hate good
>> and love evil,
>> Who tear off their skins from them
>> and their flesh from their bones;
> And who eat the flesh of my people (like meat),
>> and strip off their skin from them,
>> and break their bones to pieces
>> and spread them in the pot
>> and as meat in a cooking cauldron.
> Then they will cry out to the LORD,
>> but He will not answer them;
> and he will hide His face from them at that time,
>> because they have practiced evil deeds.

This subunit of doom oracle has three sections: an address (3:1a), accusations (3:1b–3), and sentence (3:4). Micah begins and ends his indictment by accusing Israel's leaders of רע (evil; 3:2, 4).[93] Coming again to his accusations, Micah describes in horrific language the depredations of the ruling class throughout the whole country (Judah/Israel). The opening clause, ואמר (then I said) in verse 1, is often read to link what follows with what has gone before. Here Micah's call to attention, to "listen" (שמעו־נא) signals a particularly strong turn in his rhetoric. The text calls the hearers (and readers) to hear with understanding so as to heed. Micah's accusing question indicates that the "heads of Jacob"[94] (יעקב ראשי) and "leaders/rulers of the house of Israel" (וקציני בית ישראל) are expected to know justice by experience (as part of the responsibilities of their positions) and it thus takes as a premise that these leaders do know their responsibilities.[95] The verb ידע (to know) is used not just for intellectual discernment but to indicate a preferred option.[96] It means to be skilled in association with normative

---

[93] Waltke, "Micah," 656.

[94] The word ראש (head) in the text has a clear association with the court of ancient Israel. The title was applied to judges of the tribe, city, and nation. These judges were involved in judicial arbitration. Some of them were military deliverers. The king also instituted professional judges over the nation just as Moses appointed competent laity to administer justice (Exod 18:13–26; Deut 1:15–18). See Wright, *Old Testament Ethics for the People of God*, 270; De Vaux Roland, *Ancient Israel: Its Life and Institutions*, trans. John McHugh (New York: McGraw-Hill 1961), 152–53.

[95] The two nouns ראש (heads) and קצין (rulers) are parallel terms that refer to those who held administrative position in Jerusalem. Although the king is not mentioned in the accusation, probably because the actual deeds take place among the lower officials in hierarchy, the king can be included in the accusation, since he has the ultimate responsibility to maintain justice, the strongest test for the corruption of power. Jenson, *Obadiah, Jonah, Micah*, 132.

[96] Dempster, *Micah*, 110.

legal traditions of justice and sound judgement. Those who know justice will make informed judgement.[97]

Micah's question requires an answer in the affirmative. Instead of intimately knowing justice, these heads and leaders are woefully ignorant and are pictured as habitual haters of good (שנאי טוב) and lovers of evil (ואהבי רעה) (3:2a). Both pairs of opposites (good/evil—cf. Prov 11:27; 12:2; Ps 34:14 and love/hate—cf. Prov 1:22; 8:36; Ps 45:7), suggest that justice embodies fundamental and universal values as well as emphasize that the judges' attitudes in law and society reflect the deepest personal passions. According to Jenson, "These people have not only overturned the required legal standards, they have also rejected the fundamental moral basis for their society, which in turn is a rejection of the God who stands behind Israel's law and who ensures that it is obeyed."[98] This is a clear reversal of the norm which is also familiar to Micah's contemporaries, "Woe to those who call evil good and good evil; who substitute darkness for light and light for darkness; who substitute bitter for sweet, and sweet for bitter!" (Is. 5:20) and is implied in Amos's statement in 5:15 "Hate evil and love good, and establish justice in the gate."[99] As people in covenant relationship with Yahweh, they must hate evil by doing good (Ps 97:10). Good in this context is a shortened description for the requirements of the covenant (cf. Mic 6:8). Micah's charge that they are "haters of good and lovers of evil" is uniquely pointed, "What these judges 'hate' and love is טוב and רָע, that is 'good' and 'bad' as these general terms relate to the courts, hence 'right' and 'wrong' or 'justice' and 'injustice.'"[100] These judicial leaders are driven by greed and they thus define what is good as the objects of their covetousness and what is evil as the hindrance that prevents their satisfaction and fulfillment.[101] The passion of these greedy judges to satisfy their lusts brought threatening effect on the weak and helpless.

With no passion to protect and preserve the familial covenant community, the vile leaders perversely destroyed it. Instead of being the good shepherds taking care of the flock of Yahweh, they transformed themselves into cannibals "who tear off their skins from them and their flesh from their bones" (3:2b). Micah does not withdraw from his gruesome imagery to describe the brutality

---

[97] Mays, *Micah*, 78.
[98] Jenson, *Obadiah, Jonah, Micah*, 132.
[99] Smith-Christopher, *Micah*, 109. The failure of justice in the courts in Jerusalem is a recurrent theme in Isaiah and Micah (Isa 1:17, 21–23, 26; 5:7, 23). Micah imagines these leaders in light of traditions like those recorded in Exod 18:13–27 and in Deuteronomy 1:9–18 that define the responsibility to be faithful judges, free from partiality and corruption. Mays, *Micah*, 78.
[100] Hillers, *Micah*, 43.
[101] Dempster, *Micah*, 111.

and corruption of these heartless leaders. Changing his style from relative participles to verbal clauses, he depicts the horrifying scenes not only in chronological order but in ever greater detail, hoping to stir the soured consciences of his audience, by his shocking depictions: "they eat the flesh of my people," "strip off their skin from them," and "break their bones to pieces" (3:3a). As if these are not horrible enough, by simile in verse 3b Micah expounds further the incomplete metaphors of verse 3a: "spread them in the pot" and "as meat in a cooking cauldron." The combination of שאר (inward flesh) and בשר (outward flesh) underscores the complete feasting on Yahweh's people.[102]

Micah's sentence on these leaders is just. Since they refused to change their minds before the cries of their victims, so now Yahweh will not change his judgement. The verb זעק (to call, cry out) which also occurs as an aspect of a legal appeal (2 Kgs 6:26; 8:5) is used to describe the painful and desperate plea of those who are going through an acute distress to someone who can save, answer, or deliver them. God answered the cry of his people when they called upon him in their distress (Exod 5:8, 15) and has promised to answer those who cry out to him in repentance (Isa 58:9). But because they have abandoned their obligations and responsibilities as people in covenant relationship with Yahweh, so they have no claim when they cry to him (cf. Jer 11:11). Truly, those who imposed misery on others without relief will in turn know and suffer the terror of unrelieved distress and helplessness.[103] They will repeatedly cry to him when the hour of punishment comes, but he in turn will not respond and will hide his face from them (3:4).[104] The turning away of his face is a sign of no mercy (cf. Isa 1:15; 8:17; Deut 31:17–18); it is a very concrete act of his anger and wrath. Because of the evil they have done, justice must take its course and the worst form of judgement for Israel is Yahweh's absence, not affliction itself.

3.3.2. Corrupt Prophetic Advisers (3:5–7)

> Thus says the LORD concerning the prophets
>   who lead my people astray;
> When they have something to bite with their teeth,
>   They cry, "Peace,"
> But against him who puts nothing in their mouths,
>   they declare holy war.
> Therefore, it will be night for you without vision,
>   and darkness for you, without divination.

---

[102] Waltke, "Micah," 658.
[103] Jenson, *Obadiah, Jonah, Micah*, 134.
[104] This is a clear opposite of what is envisioned in the priestly blessing, when Yahweh is asked to make his face shine upon his people with protection, gracious blessing, and peace (cf. Num 6:24–26).

And the sun will go down on the prophets,
    and the day will become dark over them.
The seers will be humiliated
    and the diviners will be embarrassed.
and they will all cover themselves up to their moustache,
    because there is no answer (from) God.

As in chapter 2, where Micah reproached the prophets (2:6–11) after a sharp sentence on the greedy land magnates (2:1–5), so also in chapter 3 a judgement oracle against the greedy prophets (3:5–8),[105] follows one against greedy leaders (3:1–4). The structure of this subunit is clear: the messenger formula with inserted addressees (3:5a), the accusation (3:5b) and the judicial sentence (3:6–7).[106] In this section, Micah turns his attention to those prophets who have misled the people into thinking that they will soon find peace, if the people are willing to pay them. The oracle denounces these prophets, whose pessimistic attitude allows them to take advantage of the trust of the people who come to them to request a prophecy about the future.[107]

The first paragraph of this unit begins with the prophetic messenger formulae כה אמר יהוה (Thus says the LORD) with the inclusive addressees על־הנביאם המתעים את־עמי (concerning the prophets who lead my people astray). The addressees are described and characterized by verbal participles as in 3:2, 9–10. The common noun with the construct suffix first person עמי (my people) indicates the whole nation and suggests that Yahweh is speaking but through his messenger. While the immediate context (3:1–4) and the concluding section (3:9,12) reveal that the larger issue is that of the administration of justice and establishment of equity in society generally, Micah's indictment here is on Judah's charismatic leadership and twisted prophetic oracles (3:5–8).

The participles describing these prophets show that they cause the people to wander off, go astray, feed on them and announce peace when Yahweh has not allowed such announcement. The verb תעה (to err, wander) is used in the *hiphil* participle. It conveys the idea of misguiding people to wander morally or mentally (cf. Deut 13:6; 27:18). "The implied norm is the moral and religious path that the prophets should have been helping the people to follow (Jer 23:13, 32)."[108] Although the verb נשך (to bite) usually describes the action of serpent biting or wounding (Gen 49:17; Num 21:8, 9; Amos 5:19; 9:3) rather than eating, the antithetical clause הנשכם בשניהם (biting with their teeth) introduces a metaphor of food and may imply that these prophets may not be ignorant of the

---

[105] Andersen and Freedman, *Micah*, 359.
[106] Waltke, *Commentary on Micah*, 168.
[107] Nogalski, *Book of the Twelve*, 547.
[108] Jenson, *Obadiah, Jonah, Micah*, 134.

3. Socioeconomic Transgressions and Power Relations

mischief of the leaders but active beneficiaries of the systemic order, echoing the vicious image (3:2–3).

The motivation or driving force of these prophets for ministry is that which goes into their mouth; namely the service fees paid to them by those who trusted them as Yahweh's vehicle for the transmission of his will and thus requested direction concerning the future at their mouth. The well-fed or well-paid prophets will declare oracles of peace (שלום)—welfare, prosperity and general well-being,[109] "but against the one who could not put anything in their mouths" (ואשר לא־יתן על־פיה) they announce a holy war (וקדשו עליו מלחמה).[110] Though the Hebrew expression וקדשו עליו מלחמה (they sanctify a war or consecrate a war) may have some allusion to religious rites (cf. Jer 6:4; Joel 3:9), for Micah in all probability it implies that when the customary service fees are not given or withheld, these prophets announce an inevitable calamity; and they do so in the name of Yahweh (cf. Jer 23:16).[111] These prophets are far more malicious. They announce war on those who will not pay them. In addition to slandering reputations, humiliating people, and spiritually abusing the poor, this also meant cursing them. It is noted by James L. Mays that, "Probably the prophets produced oracles of misfortune against those who did not support them."[112]

There is nothing wrong with a prophet receiving a "prophet offering or clergy fee." Undoubtedly, it was traditional for prophets in ancient Israel and Judah to be given gifts or fees in return for services (cf. 1 Sam 9:7–8; 1 Kgs 14:3; 2 Kgs 4:42; 8:7–9). However, the transgression of Micah's contemporaries is that "What comes out of the mouth of these prophets depends on what has been put into it."[113] Their appetites and audiences determine their messages; those who can pay them hear the "gospel of prosperity," "something good is going to happen to you!" In Micah's rhetoric, he highlights the ostentatious claims of racketeering prophets to declare the vengeance of God against those who could not afford or would not give them money. That these prophets exchange their oracles for fees is pointedly repeated in 3:11: ונביאיה בכסף יקסמו (her prophets divine for money). Thus, the clear ideological reasoning is that

---

[109] The Hebrew term שלום (peace) is regarded as the Old Testament's richest word to denote the blessings of salvation (Deut 28:1–14). It "included bodily health, social harmony, economic plenty, and political security. The prophets promised such peace, but without its essential ethical and religious foundations (Jer 6:14; Ezek 13:10)." Jenson, *Obadiah, Jonah, Micah*, 135.

[110] Wolff, *Micah*, 102.

[111] This is very similar to the experience of Jeremiah when he contradicted the words of Hananiah, who publicly humiliated him (Jer 28).

[112] James Luther Mays, *Micah: A Commentary* (Philadelphia: Westminster, 1976), 83.

[113] Wolff, *Micah*, 102.

these prophets and their oracles are unreliable since their visions are motivated by greed and not from Yahweh.[114]

Micah pronounces an ironic judgement on these racketeering prophets (3:6–7): "'night', 'darkness', 'the sun going down', 'the day growing dark' are a series of images for the experience of distress and dereliction."[115] Their sight will be removed, and they will be unable to speak. These prophets, who ought to have been the moral guardians of the nation, will lose their gifted insight. They will no longer be able to see through the wall of darkness to the bright mysteries of divine revelations. The image of loss of sight is explored first in 3:6, symbolizing the absence of Yahweh for the prophet. Since the prophets cannot see in darkness, this image conveys the loss of power for these prophets and specifies how the visionaries will be discredited.[116] Micah 3:7a conveys the removal of speech from those who make their livelihood by speaking. A prophet without vision and speech is worthless. One of the essential media of revelation for the prophets was חזון (vision), a legitimate Israelite way of discovering God's will (Prov 16:10). It has similarity to an inspired dream (Isa 27:9; cf. Num 12:6–8) and it is a positive equivalent to קסם (to practice divination) (Jer 27:9; Ezek 21:21) which was sternly condemned (Deut 18:10, 14; 1 Sam 15:23; 2 Kgs 17:17).[117] Since prophets see visions from Yahweh and speak on his behalf, the removal of sight and speech goes to the heart of their identity. This sentence of judgement removes their ability to function as prophets because they falsified the right to act as Yahweh's spokesmen.[118]

The implication of this dark silence from God will be the disgrace of the prophets (3:7). The two terms בוש (shame) and חפר (disgrace) are often rendered as embarrassment and humiliation (Job 6:20; 19:3; Pss 6:10; 22:5; 44:7; Prov 14:35).[119] These prophets will be ashamed at their loss of position and influence, they will be exposed as unclean, and God will not answer them when they cry for the restoration of their gift.[120] As a result of this embarrassment and humilia-

---

[114] Nogalski, *Book of the Twelve*, 547.
[115] Mays, *Micah*, 84.
[116] Nogalski, *Book of the Twelve*, 548; Andersen and Freedman, *Micah*, 376.
[117] חזון is a technical term used to describe the contents of a prophetic book especially in its superscription. As a way of describing the contents of a prophetic book Dempster notes, "Both noun and verb are used in Isa 1:1; the verb is used in Amos 1:1; Mic 1:1; and Hab 1:1; the noun is used in Obad 1 and Nah 1:1. The rest of the prophetic inscriptions use the term 'word of Yahweh' (Jer 1:2; Ezek 1:3; Hos 1:1; Joel 1:1; Jonah 1:1; Zeph 1:1; Hag 1:1; Zech 1:1; Mal 1:1). The term 'burden' also seems significant (cf. Hab 1:1; Mal 1:1)." Dempster, *Micah*, 112.
[118] Nogalski, *Book of the Twelve*, 548.
[119] Smith-Christopher, *Micah*, 117.
[120] Waltke, "Micah," 664–65.

tion, they will "cover themselves up to their moustache." This is an expression of wonder and amazement at the action of God; they will have nothing to say. They will cover their faces with sorrow to hide their shame when their separation from Yahweh becomes a public knowledge (cf. Lev 13:45; Ezek 24:17, 22).[121]

Like the ruling elders who gruesomely flayed Yahweh's people in Micah's depiction (3:1–4) and who will experience Yahweh's absence, these well-fed prophets are apprehended in a darkness of their own creation. They will lose their ability to prophecy and the consequence of their prophetic bankruptcy will be disappointment and dishonor (בוש) and humiliation, scorn or mockery (חפר). Since their oracles are considered to be delusive, they will lose the respect of the people and become a laughingstock. For them, it shall be a time when their prophecies of שלום (peace) are seen to be empty deceptions and they are embroiled in a disaster for which they have no convincing oracles.

3.3.3. Judgement on Gross Sin and Crime (3:9–12)

> Now hear this, heads of the house of Jacob
>   and rulers of the house of Israel,
> You abhor justice
>   and twist everything that is straight.
> You build Zion with bloodshed
>   and Jerusalem with injustice
> Her leaders pronounce judgment for a bribe,
>   and her priests instruct for a price,
>   and her prophets divine for money.
> Yet they lean on the LORD saying
>   "Is not the LORD in our midst?
>   No calamity will come upon us."
> Therefore, because of you,
>   Zion will be plowed as a field;
>   and Jerusalem will become a heap of ruins,
>   and the mountain of the house
>   will become high places of a forest.

This subunit of judgement oracle has an elegant form: an invitation to listen, accusation with development and judicial sentence. It is addressed directly to the transgressors, with the exception that the indictments are developed in the third person (3:11).[122] Using the traditional call to attention, Judah's rulers are called first to pay attention and then castigated for failing to seek justice and equity.

---

[121] Alfaro, *Micah*, 37–37.
[122] Waltke, *Commentary on Micah*, 184.

The parallel terms "heads" and "rulers" expand the charges against the political leaders of Judah and Israel. The accusations against the religious leaders mark the climax of Micah's prophetic judgement. He goes straight to the foundation of the evil, their internal disposition: "abhor justice and twist everything that is straight" (3:9). He outlines their crimes: they pervert justice and build Zion with blood; greediness rules their lives, and they think God is unconditionally on their side.[123]

Like the pairs in 3:1, on the one hand these heads and leaders' primary responsibility is to know in every situation in the social life of the people what the right decision is and to implement it. But on the other hand, they twist the law and so weakens the norms and limits that are essential for a just society; they detest justice (המתעבים משפט). They not only take twisted and dishonest paths themselves, but by bribery, influence, and deceptions "they pervert the right" (כל־הישרה יעקשו), literally, "twist everything that is straight" (3:9). The expression is used by the wisdom teachers to characterize the wicked (Prov 10:9; 2:18; Job 33:27).[124] As evidence of this general indictment of the abomination of justice, Micah cites the way they build Zion by bloodshed (בנה ציון בדמים) and Jerusalem by violence (וירושלם בעולה). The city of peace has been built as a result of social oppression and murder. In fact, Micah is not the kind of character that approves and appreciates tourism. To "build a city with blood" (cf. 3:10; Hab 2:12)[125] according to Smith-Christopher, "involves carefully planned injustices and perversion of God's intention."[126] Only poetic style can separate "bloodshed" from "wrongdoing." This kind of Hendiadys refers to oppression of the weak by the powerful, which Micah attacks frequently and which he considers as amounting to the taking of life for profit.[127] The blood of the poor in Micah's shattering imagery is converted into money and buildings. Where others see beautiful palaces, comfortable homes, and monumental structures, Micah sees the human price tag of such apparent prosperity. The riches of the few are based on the poverty of many. The whole city is but a glittering monument to Mammon.[128]

Like the judges and prophets in the previous subunits, so in this unit, judges, prophets, and priests are openly and cruelly corrupt (3:11). An administration of avarice grips the city. Zion's leaders who preside as judges sell the justice they dispense. While prophets divine for money and complete the triad of greed

---

[123] Alfaro, *Micah*, 38.
[124] Mays, *Micah*, 88.
[125] Micah's vision of the bloody city finds parallel in Jeremiah's denunciation against Jehoahaz (cf. Jer 22:13–17).
[126] Smith-Christopher, *Micah*, 123.
[127] Hillers, *Micah*, 48.
[128] Alfaro, *Micah*, 38.

3. Socioeconomic Transgressions and Power Relations

(3:11a), this relegation of office to avarice has spread like an infection to the priests as they too request their fees. Priests were charged with the responsibility of supervising and guarding the cultic life of the people, arbitrating between families and social groups, and teaching and expounding the law. They were expected to gratuitously enforce compliance with ethical standards as criteria for admission into the sanctuary and instruct the people in the ethical traditions of their covenant with Yahweh (cf. Lev 10:11; Deut 17:8–13; 33:30).[129] But these priests, like their religious counterparts—the prophets—perverted this privilege by commercializing their religious teachings for selfish interest.

Those who were to uphold religious traditions and order were participating in a tyranny of transgression.[130] Though the support for the priests was through the divinely apportioned tenth in Israel (Num 18:20–21), whether provided for or not, these priests traded the grace of God upon receipts of covetous fees. Their perspectives toward what they do are regulated by their own sense of entitlement. They mistakenly believe their positions of power and privilege will protect them. Thus, they traded their responsibility to rule, teach, and speak for Yahweh for symbols of power and wealth. According to Mays, it is probable that it was not the service fees or profits from the work that Micah sees as repugnant, "but the fact that gain had become the overriding basis of the practices of leader, priest and prophet alike ... the obligation to God and neighbor had little chance."[131]

The most incriminatory aspect of the attitude of each of these groups was that they claimed to be relying on Yahweh, while they were violating his laws and defrauding the people. Micah attributes the lack of social conscience to a theological error, a distorted, laughable, and one-sided doctrine of election that takes no account of attitude and Israel's covenant traditions. They live with assurance and in confidence of their relation to Yahweh. The verb שען (rely on, lean on) is a frequent synonym of "trust" in the Old Testament vocabulary of faith. To "rely on Yahweh" is used for dependence on divine help in a military setting (Isa 10:20; 2 Chr 13:18; 14:20; 16:7–8). However, these people had forgotten that moral integrity is an essential prerequisite of this trust. When this is lacking, the consequence will be judgment not salvation (Isa 30:12; 31:1).[132]

The expression "Is not the LORD in our midst!" sets out the premise in the argument, reflecting a strong presumption of Yahweh's encouraging disposition and presence. The motif of Yahweh's continued presence with Israel finds expression in both Sinai and wilderness narratives (Exod 33:3, 5; 34:9; Num

---

[129] Gerhard von Rad, *Old Testament Theology*, vol. 1 (London: Oliver & Boyd 1962), 244.
[130] Leslie C. Allen, "Micah's Social Concern," *VE* 8 (1973): 28.
[131] Mays, *Micah*, 89–90.
[132] Mays, *Micah*, 90; Jenson, *Obadiah, Jonah, Micah*, 139–40.

11:20; 14:4; cf. Deut 6:15). The motif relates to the ark and its importance as an objectification of Yahweh's presence with Israel in war (1 Sam 4:3; Deut 7:21; Josh 3:10), in a time of severe famine and return of fertility and plenty after drought (Jer 14:9; Joel 2:27), and in hymnic documents praising Yahweh for deliverance from enemies (Zeph 3:15, 17; cf. Isa 12:6). In Micah, the concrete reference of this confident assurance and confession must be "the mountain of the house (of the LORD)" mentioned in 3:12.[133]

With Yahweh in the midst of Jerusalem, the city was guaranteed safety and deliverance (Pss 46:5; 48; 84; 87) and a positive summary of the consequence is their one-sided interpretation of the tradition, "No calamity will come upon us." The claim to be relieved from calamity (רעה) is a reaction to the announcement of punishment in 2:3 and it is equivalent to the peace (שלום) of 3:5. This theological theme of confidence has, however, not always guaranteed security in Israel's past, especially when they lived in disobedience (cf. Exod 32:9; 33:3, 5; Num 14:14). The theological validity of this theme of trust depends on how they behave, particularly in realizing that Yahweh does not compromise justice and thus ensures that the weak and the powerless find justice (Exod 22:22; 23:6; 2 Sam 12). But for leaders who have clearly compromised justice and have turned the city of peace into a center of bloodshed and violence, to appeal to Yahweh is to invite nothing but disaster.

Micah 3:12 thus ties the fate of Zion to the shortcomings of its judicial, religious, and political leaders. The impending destruction of Jerusalem is related to the greed and cynicism of its leaders. The metaphors in 3:12 invoke images of destruction. A ploughed field and a heap of rubble could be seen as part of the planting process, where the soil is tilled and the debris piled up; however, when applied to a city, the image of a leveled field implies devastation.[134] Thus the oracle unit ends on the climactic note that Zion, the most historically holy city in Judah on account of Yahweh's presence, will become the most unclean place.[135]

---

[133] Mays, *Micah*, 90–91.
[134] Nogalski, *Book of the Twelve*, 549.
[135] יער (forest) is a metonymy for unclean animals and death. Delbert R. Hillers notes that in figurative fashion prophets frequently threatened that wild animals would inhabit the deserted city (Isa 13:21–22; 34:11–17; Jer 50:39; Zeph 2:13–15), and that the city becomes a ruin-heap and then is overwhelmed with wild animals. Hillers, *Micah*, 48.

4

RELIGIOUS UNFAITHFULNESS AND COMMUNITY MORAL DEPRAVITY IN MICAH'S ORACLES

> Prayer is often a temptation to bank on a miracle of God instead of on a moral issue, i.e., it is much easier to ask God to do my work than it is to do it myself. Until we are disciplined properly, we will always be inclined to bank on God's miracles and refuse to do the moral things ourselves. It is our job, and it will never be done unless we do it.
> —Oswald Chambers

The book of Micah condemned socioeconomic transgressions and abuse of power, and the oracles also present deficiency of moral value at both religious and national levels. The prophet's metaphors used to describe the miserable moral morass of society form a kind of compendium with a progression of thoughts and coherence of moral depravity. This chapter continues with exegetical analysis of oracles dealing with aspects of religious dishonesty and corruption.

4.1. Israel's Religious Sins (6:1–8)

Micah 6:1–8 falls within the third movement (6–7) that stresses a call to repentance and renewal. The distinction between these sections is noticeably clear with the opening signature imperative שמע (hear) in striking head-to-head connection (1:2; 3:1; 6:1). The first section (1:2) addresses the nations (i.e., calls the entire world to attention), the second (3:1) addresses the leaders of the nation, and in the third, the spotlight falls on the people (6:3, 5). This third section opens with Yahweh's rebuke of an ignorant, haughty, and immoral people and ends with a people who express faith, hope, and praise.

Accordingly, it includes disputation elements (6:1–8), a lament (7:1–7) and a conclusion with hymnic elements (7:8–20).[1]

In its literary context, this didactic dialogue unit (6:1–8) is not specifically anchored in the world of the text to any particular settings, place, time, and location.[2] Thus like the rest of other units in the book of Micah, the reading falls within an eighth century setting that assumes knowledge of Judah's story on several levels as well as suggesting anticipations of the looming Assyrian invasion.[3] The oracle was probably first delivered at the temple where a large number of worshippers were gathered, as it is an indictment of them and not of specific leaders. Illuminating the probability that the prophet presented this oracle in the sanctuary at Jerusalem are references to torah teachings with its sacred history, pronouncements of priests, the fragrance of sacrifices and the call to an ethical life. One can imagine the Assyrian crisis of 701 BCE when the people were attempting to make atonement for their transgressions.[4] Concerning the didactic thrust of the unit, Wolff remarks, "A didactic sermon-in-outline, the passage leads the reader from the present reality of Yahweh's great deeds of salvation, through a discussion of inappropriate cultic responses, and then on to clear statements of 'what is good' for human beings."[5]

A hypothetical priestly or liturgical setting could be envisaged as antecedent of 6:1–8. Thus the close relationship of this unit with the cult indicates that the oracle "derives from temple ceremonial '*in einer kultischen Gerichtszene.*'"[6] In his form critical interpretation of Mic 6:1–8, Paul L. Watson submits that the *Sitz im Leben* of the unit is probably where priests assemble to judge cases that deal with questions of the covenant and the cult and where, as judges in a trial, they are expected to pronounce the judgement in a manner that is traditional to the priestly office.[7] The setting-in-life assumed by the style indicates a situation in which a sinner, conscious of his predicament because of sin which endangers his relationship with God and familiar with the fact that a sacrifice of atonement is a basic requirement, seeks to receive direction as to what is adequate.[8] Although the sphere of competence and influence to which the question is directed is the responsibility of the priest, "the language in these verses cannot be characterized as priestly ... there are no reference to entering the temple, nor to anyone

---

[1] Jenson, *Obadiah, Jonah, Micah*, 166.
[2] Ben Zvi, *Micah*, 151.
[3] Daniel J. Simundson, *Hosea, Joel, Amos, Obadiah, Jonah, Micah*, AOTC (Nashville: Abington, 2005), 338.
[4] Dempster, *Micah*, 162.
[5] Wolff, *Micah*, 183.
[6] Andersen and Freedman, *Micah*, 509.
[7] Paul L. Watson, "Form Criticism and an Exegesis of Micah 6:1–8," *RQ* 7.1 (1963): 64.
[8] Mays, *Micah*, 137.

wishing to enter a temple; ... the basic structure of the entrance liturgies consists of question, response, and promise (cf. Pss 15:1–5; 24:3–4; Isa 33:14b–16); there is no such promise in Mic 6:6–8."[9] However, it is challenging to keep the intensely personal and dynamic relationship between Yahweh and Israel within a legal and covenantal framework of giving the consideration of formal justice. There is a conflict between the legal background that provides some of the ideas and vocabularies for the dispute and the more literary expression of the emotional and interpersonal aspects of the covenant in the drama of the unit.[10]

The unit illuminates the world of knowledge of the audience and readers. Accordingly, the audience of the book is imagined as being familiar with some foundational traditions of Israel; the exodus from Egypt, the Balak-Balaam story, and the crossing of the Jordan. They were also aware of the literary as well as theological and didactic routine of the supremacy of morality over rituals. This is not to say that supremacy as understood was that rituals had no significance; rather, ritual performances in the midst of covenant faithlessness have no value.[11] The subunit (6:6–8) raises and addresses fundamental questions which are vital not only to those on trial, but to adherents of biblical faith throughout history. In it, the voice of the prophet confronts the nation and people at every level with accusations that their own inattentiveness to Yahweh's demands of משפט (justice), חסד (mercy, kindness), and humility before God (6:8), has endangered the land to a degree that Yahweh can no longer ignore.[12] Thus it stresses a call to repentance and renewal.

A majority of scholarly opinions hold that the unit (6:1–8) is constructed in order to evoke the images and associations of a covenant lawsuit, a manifest example of the so-called *rîb* form (appearing three times in 6: 1–2).[13] Consequently, J. Carl Laney remarks that Mic 6:1–8 is an illustration of juridical procedures for dealing with covenant violation "brought by a messenger (a prophet) against the vassals (the people of Israel) for their violation of their treaty (the Mosaic covenant) with the Great Suzerain (Yahweh)."[14] Although this

---

[9] Ben Zvi, *Micah*, 151.
[10] Andersen and Freedman, *Micah*, 507.
[11] Ben Zvi, *Micah*, 152.
[12] Nogalski, *Book of the Twelve*, 580.
[13] A covenant dispute is conducted as a lawsuit in which indictments are brought on the people of Israel by Yahweh over breaches of various covenant requirements (cf. Deut 32:1–43; Ps 50; Isa 1:2–3, Jer 2:2–37; Judg 10:11–14). Herbert B. Huffmon, "Covenant Lawsuit in the Prophets," *JBL* 78 (1959): 285, 295; Ronald T. Hyman, "Questions and Response in Micah 6:6–8," *JBQ* 33.3 (2005): 158; J. Carl Laney, "The Role of the Prophets in God's Case against Israel," *BSac* 138 (1981): 321; Timothy M. Pierce, "Micah as a Case Study for Preaching and Teaching the Prophets," *SWJT* 46.1 (2003): 83.
[14] Laney, "Role of the Prophets in God's Case against Israel," 323.

literary form has been mostly accepted as it allows readers to interpret the text with limited difficulties, it is observed that Micah does not use one specific literary genre for each separate oracle unit. In fact, he scarcely uses a piece in line with the literary and social conventions that govern the normal function of its literary genre.[15] Commenting on the inconsistency of Micah's use of genre, Ronald T. Hyman observes, "Complexity and some confusion arise because Micah does not follow the lawsuit analogy to its fullest and does not identify the speakers explicitly while he himself speaks all the roles within the dramatic analogy."[16]

Surprisingly, one can observe that Yahweh's role in this lawsuit analogy is subverted in the unit. Usually, Yahweh is expected to be either the prosecuting attorney or judge. As an alternative, Yahweh plays the role of the aggrieved petitioner appearing before an anonymous prosecuting attorney or judge.[17] Micah 6:1–8 shares with Isa 5:1–7 the rhetorical use of interrogation. Both recite the benevolent actions of Yahweh. In line with Isaiah who begins his poem by giving it a title that stimulates the expectation that it will be a love song and then faces other directions, so Micah opens the unit with a covenant lawsuit (*rîb*) and then betrays the usual procedure for such an adventure.[18] As it stands, the literary background of Mic 6:1–8 is diverse; as an artistic composition, the unit seems to be a mix of literary features. At its opening, the unit does evoke the mental image of legal procedures (6:1–3). Micah utilizes wordplay in the invocation to the mountains and hills to be the inanimate witness to the proceedings.[19] The rhetoric of verses 4–5 demonstrates creedal recitation of Yahweh's mighty deeds. In fact, Yahweh's covenant faithfulness led to Israel's liberation rather than bondage, but on the contrary Israel turned its faith back into bondage.[20] The legal procedure is continued with further interrogations about requirements of true worship. These questions of truly ethical religion have given rise to the proposal that 6:6–8 reflects the genre that belongs to the cult; a temple entrance ritual or a priestly torah liturgy (cf. Pss 15:1–5; 24:3–6; Isa 33:14b–16).[21]

---

[15] Andersen and Freedman, *Micah*, 508.
[16] Hyman, "Questions and Response in Micah 6:6–8," 158.
[17] Ben Zvi, *Micah*, 148–49; Watson, "Form Criticism and an Exegesis of Micah 6:1–8," 70.
[18] Andersen and Freedman, *Micah*, 508.
[19] Waltke, *Commentary on* Micah, 375.
[20] Dempster, *Micah*, 154.
[21] Andersen and Freedman, *Micah*, 510; Ben Zvi, *Micah*, 150; Wolff, *Micah*, 167.

4. Religious Unfaithfulness and Community Moral Depravity

Although one can observe a sharp difference between the legal character of 6:1–5 and the cultic/priestly nature of 6:6–8,[22] the kerygmatic equilibrium between 6:1–5 and 6:6–8 binds the two subunits together.[23] The MT presents these verses (1–8) as a unit in its traditional division. The speakers and/or participants in the dramatic dialogue can only be identified by means of vocative and pronouns: unidentified you (masc. pl. 6:1); unidentified you (masc. sg. 6:1); hills (3rd fem. pl. jussive, 6:1); mountains (6:2); my people, that is, Israel (named in 6:2, 3–5); no identification of intended audience—presumably Yahweh is indirectly addressed (6:6–7); and Adam—man, that is, mankind (6:8).[24] The constituent literary structure of the unit (6:1–8) is presented below.[25]

A. Call for attention (6:1a)
B. Commissioning of the prophet (1b)
C. Invocation of inanimate witnesses of Israel's actions (1b–2a)
D. Yahweh's questions: Israel's indebtedness to Yahweh (3–5)
 a. Initial question (3)
 b. Yahweh's liberation of Israel and Israel's benefits from Yahweh's actions (4)
 c. Address that stresses a need for repentance (5)
E. Israel's response with questions pertaining to true worship (6–7)
 a. First rhetorical question: Implicit admission of guilt (6a)
 b. Escalating question exemplifying Judah's distorted theology of worship (6b–7)
  1. Second rhetorical question: Quality (6b)
  2. Third rhetorical question: Quantity (7a)
  3. Fourth rhetorical question: Desperation (7b)
F. Yahweh's verdict and remedy (8)
 a. The verdict: You have been told already (8a)
 b. The remedy: Three compact answers in intensifying significance (8b)
  1. First answer highlights the necessary action: To act justly
  2. Second answer accentuates inner attitude of solidarity: To love kindness
  3. Third answer stresses the wellspring of both actions: To walk humbly (live cautiously) with your God

---

[22] May observes that the two appear to be quite distinct literary types with no clear example elsewhere in the Old Testament of this kind of mixture in a disputational, didactic rhetorical unit. Mays, *Micah*, 138.
[23] William McKane, *Micah: Introduction and Commentary* (Edinburgh: T&T Clark, 1998), 177–79.
[24] Andersen and Freedman, *Micah*, 505.
[25] I have followed Laney, "Role of the Prophets in God's Case against Israel," 322; and Dempster, *Micah*, 155, here with modifications.

The following subsections present a literary analysis expressing both the emotional and dynamic interpersonal aspects of the covenant relationship between Yahweh and Israel.

4.1.1. The Controversy between Yahweh and His People (6:1–5)

> Hear now what Yahweh is saying,
> Arise, contend with the mountains
>   And let the hills hear your voice.
> Hear, you mountains, Yahweh's controversy,
>   And you everlasting foundations of the earth,
> Because Yahweh has a case with His people;
>   Even with Israel He will dispute.
> My people, what have I done to you?
>   And how have I wearied you?
> Answer me.
> Because I brought you up from the land of Egypt,
>   And I redeemed you from the house of slavery;
> And I sent before you
>   Moses, Aaron, and Miriam.
> My people, remember now
>   What Balak king of Moab counseled,
>   And what Balaam son of Beor answered him?
>   From Shittim to Gilgal,
> In order that you might know the righteous acts of Yahweh.

The two opening verses (6:1–2) summon the people and witnesses while the remaining three verses (6:3–5) present Yahweh's implicit accusation of the people's covenant unfaithfulness. The identification of who is speaking and to whom in the opening verses is difficult to determine. Interpreters of the Hebrew text are not unanimous on the addressee in the two commands in 6:1. For example, Waltke believes that Yahweh is addressing the prophet, Micah, and commanding him to arise and plead Yahweh's case against Israel.[26] On the other hand, Mays and Wolff imagine that Yahweh is addressing Israel.[27] There is a close connection between Yahweh's voice and the prophetic voice. Consequently, the imperative introductory formula is naturally taken as the speech of the prophet who in this manner conveys what follows as Yahweh's word.[28] The formula emphasizes the characteristic dialogical character of the relationship between God and his people as mediated through the prophet.

---

[26] Waltke, *Commentary on Micah*, 344–45.

[27] Mays, *Micah*, 128–31; Wolff, *Micah*, 172.

[28] Mays, *Micah*, 131.

4. Religious Unfaithfulness and Community Moral Depravity

In the summons, the people are called first to hear (שמעו) what Yahweh is saying. This clearly indicates that an oracular speech is about to be delivered. According to Ben Zvi, "The first summons creates the expectation that the following text will be directly associated with YHWH. Given that there are no clear markers to the contrary in 6:1b, it seems that the following text was constructed to suggest to the readers that they should understand it as YHWH's direct speech."[29] They are summoned to arise and defend their case before the mountains (קום ריב את־ההרים) and hills (הגבעות). Here, the mountains and hills and the everlasting foundations of the earth (והאתנים מסדי ארץ) are addressed as universal and enduring witnesses in the legal case that Yahweh has against his people. These witnesses describe the scope of the audience (as universal) and the history of the audience (as timeless).[30] The invocation of the mountains and primeval streams as witness in the controversy between Yahweh and Israel has connection to ancient treaty and covenant practice in which Huffman argues that heaven and earth are invoked not as judges or members of the divine council but as witness to the covenant.[31] According to Waltke, "the mountains served as sober and salient witnesses to the truthfulness of *I AM*'s accusation. They 'saw' both his saving acts that demanded as the only reasonable response Israel's heartfelt commitment to *I AM* and also Israel's unfulfilled obligations."[32]

In this manner, the language of "contesting a legal case" in verse 1 indicates what is expected of Israel in a covenant lawsuit that she would bring against Yahweh, and in verse 2, the language indicates the passing down of a sentence in court and describes what Yahweh would do in his role as judge regarding the covenant lawsuit with Israel. As permanent and all-seeing entities, the mountains would be witnesses to Israel's offences against the covenant, and to Israel's past and present failures. Although, strictly speaking, Yahweh does not need these entities, they strengthen the validity of the charges. The setting indicates that Yahweh is always open to reason and argument, but he will certainly ensure that the dispute is resolved, and justice is established.

Following the announcement of the prophet that Yahweh has a case—dispute, controversy (ריב)—with his people Israel, Yahweh begins to speak. Verses 3–5 present Yahweh's ריב with or against Israel in two segments, each beginning with the vocative עמי "my people" (6:3–4, 5). The speech of verse 3 ironically begins by entertaining the notion that Yahweh may have given the people reason for complaint (cf. Isa 5:4). The tone is not accusatory but conciliatory; the purpose is to awaken Israel's awareness of their lack of any cause for complaint. The implication is that the people are acting as if Yahweh has

---

[29] Ben Zvi, *Micah*, 142–43.
[30] Dempster, *Micah*, 156.
[31] Huffmon, "Covenant Lawsuit in the Prophets," 292.
[32] Waltke, *Commentary on* Micah, 375.

wronged them, and this attitude must be investigated, but it must begin with Yahweh's vindication of his ways to them.³³

The expression מה־עשיתי לך "what have I done to you" (6:3) is the aggrieved complaint of a wounded and innocent party (cf. Num 22:28; 1 Sam 26:18). While there might still be little space before Israel is required to answer the accusation (cf. Gen 4:10; 1 Sam 13:11), they only have an excuse for their attitude if Yahweh had "wearied" (הלאתיך) them beyond what they can stand. The reversal of the accusation indicates a remarkable testimony to the patience and long-suffering of Yahweh who, though wearied, is yet to burst out in judgment. Yahweh thus demands an answer (ענה בי) to be set as evidence to the contrary before the parties. This is obviously ironic, since it is Yahweh who is blameless and the people who are guilty.³⁴

To refute Israel's imagined complaint, Yahweh's saving acts which constituted the people as a community are swiftly recited with four emphases: redemption from Egypt (6:4a), inspired leadership of Israel: Moses, Aaron, and Miriam (6:4b),³⁵ salvation from the schemes of Balak and Balaam in the wilderness journey (6:5a) and entry into the Promised Land (6:5b).³⁶ According to Robert B. Chisholm, the similarity in sound between the Hebrew verbs הלאתיך (I wearied you, 6:3) and העלתיך (I brought you up, 6:4) emphasizes the radical difference in content and attitude; that is, the contrast between false accusation and reality.³⁷

In the second segment of the vocative עמי (my people, 6:5), Yahweh's appeal that Israel should remember implies not just the issue about Balak and Balaam; but the purpose of the entire recitation. The *qal* imperative זכר (remember) is mostly used in contexts that imply a memorialization of the past by means of the intellectual reflection of recalling Yahweh's saving deeds in history and acting upon that understanding, by connecting the will in conformity and obedience to present realities (cf. Deut 32:7; Pss 119:52; 143:5).³⁸ Thus in view of Israel's forgetfulness, an appeal to Yahweh's saving acts becomes a necessary and common vehicle for motivation in the attempt to change attitudes (cf. Deut 7:18; Judg 8:34; Ps 106:7).

---

[33] Hillers, *Micah*, 77.

[34] Jenson, *Obadiah, Jonah, Micah*, 169.

[35] The mention of Moses indicates the great leader through whom the torah was mediated. Aaron is cited with Moses and evokes associations of priesthood, perhaps as an indirect preparation for the priestly language of 6:6–8, and it is likely that Miriam is thought of here especially as the prophetess (Exod 15:20). Hillers, *Micah*, 77–78.

[36] Hillers, *Micah*, 77.

[37] Robert B. Chisholm Jr., *Handbook on the Prophets* (Grand Rapids: Baker Academic, 2002), 425.

[38] Mays, *Micah*, 135.

4. Religious Unfaithfulness and Community Moral Depravity

The reference to King Balak of Moab and Balaam son of Beor falls within the context of favorable divine acts and assumes knowledge of Numbers 22–24, where Balak hires Balaam to curse Israel, but through Yahweh's intervention he could only bless Israel, by predicting her future delightful greatness (cf. Deut 23:5–6). The expression "from Shittim to Gilgal" serves as an addition to what happened in the past and it is governed by זכר (remember) at the beginning of the verse. Shittim represents the place in Moab, where Israel was encamped when the Balak and Balaam incident occurred. Here, the Israelites broke the covenant and succumbed to the enticement of Moabite idolatry (Num 25:1), but Yahweh's faithfulness brought his people across the Jordan (Josh 3:1) to their first foothold in the promised land, Gilgal (Josh 4:19). In this regard, "the summary of sacred history leads from Exodus to conquest, from promise to fulfillment."[39]

The final phrase clarifies the purpose of the review of Yahweh's saving acts (צדקות). In the purpose clause (in order that you may know), the verb ידע (to know) "can describe a very fundamental religious attitude. In some occurrences, and it may be plausible here, it is covenant language."[40] It indicates a personal, ethical knowing that is authoritative for living. Yahweh's saving acts, in this context, is shorthand for all the deeds mentioned previously: liberation from Egypt, leadership in the wilderness, deliverance from Balak, and crossing the Jordan into the Promised Land. The recounting of Yahweh's righteous acts delegitimizes the Israelites' unstated accusations, and by implication their unreciprocated faithfulness presents them as guilty. The brief dialogue that ensues in the next verses (6:6–8) brings reconciliation to the situation, reconciliation expressed in a recognition of personal duty and responsibility rather than murmuring, loss of trust and extravagant rituals.

4.1.2. Extravagant Rituals as means of Reconciliation (6:6–7)

> With what shall I come to the LORD
> (With what) shall I bow before the God on high?
> Shall I come to Him with burnt offerings,
>   With yearling calves?
> Does the LORD take delight in thousands of rams,
>   In ten thousand rivers of oil?
> Shall I present my first-born for my rebellious acts,
>   the fruit of my body for the sin of my soul?

---

[39] Hillers, *Micah*, 78.
[40] Hillers, *Micah*, 78.

The central issue hanging in the balance between Yahweh and Israel is that of *relationship* that requires immediate attention. The word מה (what) used repeatedly in 6:3, 5, 6, 8 underscores the dialogical character of the questions and issues requiring attention by both Yahweh and the people.[41] In the opening legal section (6:1–5), Micah provides a vision of who Yahweh truly is to Israel. Yahweh compellingly declares his case and protests his guiltlessness regarding any form of wrongful behavior in his relationship with Israel. This is aptly captured in his redemptive deeds on behalf of Israel (6:3–5). Most interestingly, Yahweh's redemptive acts demonstrate his right behavior and commitment towards Israel and the essence of his being. According to Rick R. Marrs, "The recitation is vivid and compressed. Four emphases appear: redemption from Egypt, inspired leadership (Moses, Aaron, Miriam), deliverance from the schemes of Balak and Balaam, entrance into the land."[42]

While Yahweh's questions to Israel function as declarations of guiltlessness, the switch from the recitation of Yahweh's saving deeds (6:3–5) to the response of the people (6:6–7) is obviously abrupt. The opening interrogative, במה (with what) in verse 6 introduces a lame defense that is highly illogical.[43] The rhetorical question indicates the procedure which the interrogator believes he must follow (cf. Gen 15:8; Exod 23:15; 1 Sam 6:2; 2 Sam 21:3). It is based on a specific assumption and orientation that focuses on the possibilities which that assumption allows. In dealing with Yahweh, the response of the speaker implies that Yahweh is the problem. The response grows out of textual orientation such as "none shall appear before me empty-handed" (Exod 23:15; 34:20), which has a growing significance of cultic sacrifice in Israel's religious development.[44] With the interrogative (במה), the questioner is wondering aloud and trying to determine what is required and adequate to enter into Yahweh's presence; namely "to meet Yahweh with" and "bow before the God on high." Access to Yahweh's presence by an individual or group usually requires various form of speech, and Israel's three great annual festivals (Exod 23:10–19; 34:18–

---

[41] Philip P. Jenson, *Obadiah, Jonah, Micah: A Theological Commentary*, LHBOTS 496 (New York: T&T Clark, 2008), 167.

[42] Rick R. Marrs, "Micah and a Theological Critique of Worship," in *Worship and the Hebrew Bible: Essays in Honour of John T. Willis*, ed. M. Patrick Graham, Richard R. Marrs, and Steven L. McKenzie, JSOTSup 284 (Sheffield: Sheffield Academic, 1999), 201.

[43] Marrs states that "the startling 'with what shall I come before the Lord … ' (במה) counters Yahweh's earlier questions ('What have I done to you? In what have I wearied you? [מה … מה])." Marrs, "Micah and a Theological Critique of Worship," 201.

[44] Mays, *Micah*, 139.

26; Deut 16:1–17; Lev 23:4–44; Num 28–29) show that the major features of Israel's worship are great offerings of sacrifices.[45]

Since coming before Yahweh imagines the shrine where he is present and where sacrifices can be accepted, the verbs in verse 6 characterize the approach not in the usual manner but in a highly particular way. The first two phrases "to meet Yahweh with" and "bow before the God on high" demonstrate both parallelism and progression. The verb (קדם) with the preposition (ב) in verse 6 evoke the picture of an approach to someone else with gifts meant to achieve a complementary reception and approval (cf. the story of Jacob's preparation to meet Esau in Gen 32:13–21; in a cultic context, Ps 95:2).[46] The image of prostration and adoration is also very striking. The *niphal* verb אכף (bow down) in other contexts indicates bowing down in distress, oppression, and humiliation (Pss 57:7; 145:14; 146:8). The uniqueness of the form in this verse suggests a reflexive meaning "bow myself down."[47] The self-abasement is a way of acknowledging and confessing the absolute sovereignty of Yahweh; who in the imagination of the inquirer is unreachable (לאלהי מרום—God on high). Here, מרום stands for the high home of Yahweh from where he supports the needy and distressed (Pss 7:8; 18:17; 68:19; 144:7; Isa 58:4; Lam 4:13).[48]

Verses 6b–7 unfold a litany of possible "adequate" offerings. The list does not suggest ethical or social justice rhetoric, but it ranges across a spectrum of sacrificial offerings, and it is comprehensive in its descriptive character. The sequence of the response indicates an ascending intensity from quality, quantity, to the unimaginable offerings (child sacrifice). The list obviously exhausts the available possibilities in the realm and practice of sacrifice and leaves no stone unturned in the search for what is adequate enough to achieve reconciliation with Yahweh. The first sacrifice is that of quality: "Shall I come to Him with burnt offerings with yearling calves?" The burnt offering (עלה) is specifically mentioned while other items are most probably objects to be offered as or with the עלה. The עלה was a sacrifice totally dedicated to God, with no share for the worshipper. It is proposed as a gift and its primary purpose is to deal with sin.

---

[45] For a mode of access into Yahweh's presence see, Patrick D. Miller, *They Cried to the Lord: The Form and Theology of Biblical Prayer* (Minneapolis: Augsburg, 1994), 46–49; Danijel Berković, "Aspects and Modalities of God's Presence in the Old Testament," KAIROS—*EJT* 3.1 (2009): 51–72; John Kessler, *Old Testament Theology: Divine Call and Human Response* (Waco, TX: Baylor University Press, 2013), 382, 398.

[46] Mays, *Micah*, 139.

[47] Dempster, *Micah*, 159.

[48] Jenson, *Obadiah, Jonah, Micah*, 171; Mays, *Micah*, 139; Andersen and Freedman, *Micah*, 524.

While a calf was adequate for sacrificial purpose after eight days old; a yearling calf would be more expensive than most individual offerings (Lev 9:3; 22:27).[49]

The verb רצה (to be pleased) in verse 7 is a technical term in priestly text for the acceptance of a sacrifice by Yahweh (Lev 1:4). It is used elsewhere to indicate that sacrifice is inseparable from the life it represents (Lev 1:4; 22:23; 2 Sam 24:23; Jer 14:10–14). רצה illustrates a hint of Yahweh's delight in and approval of an honest sacrifice (cf. Ps 51:18; Mal 1:10). However, the speaker's critical tone in the intensification of the proposal with a second consideration of quantity "reverses the intended assurance of acceptance, suggesting instead an impossible level of demand."[50] Rams and oil appear in other sacrificial acts (Lev 2:1), but the multiple, countable rams and innumerable rivers of oil to be poured upon the sacrificial altar and raise the value of the sacrifice (Exod 29:2) are deliberately fanciful.[51]

The list of alternatives and possibilities reaches its pinnacle of human delusion, as the speaker proposes to offer his first-born child (בכורי). The proposal "to present or give my firstborn" to Yahweh is astonishing. Yahweh's claim of the first born is well articulated in Israel's normative tradition and redemption is to be made by a substitute offering (Exod 13:2; 22:28; 34:20). Although reported cases of human sacrifice in Israel are rare and are told as exceptional cases (cf. Lev 20:2–5; Judg 11:30–40; 2 Kgs 3:27; 16:3; 17:17; 21:6; 23:10; Jer 7:31; 19:5), the practice is strictly prohibited in Israel (Deut 12:31; 18:10; Lev 18:21; 20:2–5).[52] The proposal does not draw from any recognized spectrum of possibilities in the cultic tradition of Israel. Thus far from being extravagant evidence of piety, it defiled the primary, most essential moral and religious norms of Israel.

The second phrase פרי בטני (the fruit of my body) refers to the same act, but escalates through the use of an animal metaphor (cf. Deut 30:9).[53] The necessity of offerings lies in guilt before Yahweh. In the later part of verse 7, the questioner speaks of "my transgression" and "the sin of my soul." Here, "transgression" (פשע) and "sin" (חטאת) are a synonymous pair used as a general category for acts that violate Yahweh's norms for the sacral and social spheres

---

[49] Hillers, *Micah*, 78; Mays, *Micah*, 140; Andersen and Freedman, *Micah*, 525.
[50] Jenson, *Obadiah, Jonah, Micah*, 171.
[51] Hillers, *Micah*, 78; Tremper Longman III and David Garland, *The Expositor's Bible Commentary* (Nashville, TN: Zondervan, 2008), 539. However, this proposal is not without precedent. Solomon who is reported to have sacrificed a thousand offerings (1 Kgs 3:4; 8:63) is perhaps the model of extravagant piety in view here. Mays, *Micah*, 140.
[52] Although the practice of human sacrifice has been outlawed (Lev 18:21; Deut 18:10), it is particularly noted that such practice did take place in the time of King Ahaz, a notorious and certainly influential king during Micah's life and prophesy (Mic 1:1; cf. 2 Kgs 16:2–4). Dempster, *Micah*, 159.
[53] Jenson, *Obadiah, Jonah, Micah*, 172.

4. Religious Unfaithfulness and Community Moral Depravity 89

(cf. Mic 1:5; 3:8; 7:18; Ps 54:4). All who fall into this category as sinners need reconciliation with Yahweh.[54] However, despite the apparent sincerity and willingness or lack thereof of the people to offer the best so as to repair their standing with Yahweh, Yahweh's reply simply rejects the substance, the desperation and the attitude it reflects with what seems a studied disdain. The proposals and assumptions are all false; Yahweh requires something much better than burnt offering, countable rams, innumerable rivers of oil, and first-born child.

4.1.3. Social Obligations as markers of Ethical Religion (6:8)

> He has told you, O man,
>   what is good?
> And what does the LORD require of you?
>   But to do justice,
>   to love kindness,
> And to walk humbly with your God

The indignant confrontation and misguided "what" (מה) of the people (6:6) is granted a calm, authoritative and composed response in the "what" (מה) of the prophet in the crowning verse (6:8), which has been rightly celebrated as the supreme definition of ethical religion and one of the great moral breakthroughs in history.[55] The petitioner's questions deal with "what" but the prophet's answers deal with how someone should approach Yahweh.[56] The concentration on the thing to be offered moved to a focus on the quality of life that is lived with the person with whom one is joined by a social bond such as covenant. In the answer, reproachful in its restraint, the petitioner is addressed with the surprisingly indefinite and inclusive vocative "man" (אדם)—which is a generic Hebrew term for humanity, and as Mays suggests it refers to "the generalizing and paradigmatic intention of the saying as a whole; its teaching is meant for any *man* in Israel."[57] The "offering" that Yahweh truly desires is neither new nor previously unheard, "He has told you." Micah's answer to what constitute an ethical religion is conveyed by the very fundamental understanding of Israel's faith.[58] The declaration belongs to Israel's tradition and as such the petitioner needs only a reminder. It is however difficult to ascertain what setting the appeal to the past refers to. According to Mays, "Probably the answer rest on a memory of what

---

[54] Mays, *Micah*, 141.
[55] Andersen and Freedman, *Micah*, 504.
[56] Hyman, "Questions and Response in Micah 6:6–8," 161.
[57] Mays, *Micah*, 141.
[58] Longman III and Garland, *Expositor's Bible Commentary*, 540.

earlier prophets had said. The prophets spoke of YHWH's requirements under the theme of 'good' (Isa 1:17; 5:20; Amos 5:14–15; Mic 3:1)."[59]

The meaning of the expression "what is good" is determined within the context and narrowly defined as what God requires of humanity. The "good" is what Yahweh requires; the right and true way to live, and this must have a positive effect on people in community. In the torah, what Yahweh desires is remarkably expressed and is similar to the requirement in Micah:

> And now, Israel, what does the LORD your God require from you, but to fear the LORD your God, to walk in all His ways and love Him, and to serve the LORD your God with all your heart and with all your soul, *and* to keep the LORD's commandments and His statutes which I am commanding you today for your good? (Deut 10:12–13, NASB)

There is a correspondence between what Yahweh is telling Israel and what he is doing; he distinguishes himself as someone who does justice and is interested in the plight of the week and oppressed (Deut 10:17–18). Thus the offering Yahweh "seeks"; "what is good" and "what the LORD requires" has been fractured by transgressions,[60] but they are found in three infinitival compact expressions that are related and mutually self-defining: "to do justice," "to love mercy" and "to walk humbly" (live cautiously) with your God.

The first two requirements are fundamental to Israel's faith. To do justice is "to uphold what is right according to the tradition of YHWH's will both in legal proceedings and in the conduct of life."[61] Proverbs 21:15 states, "The execution of justice is joy for the righteous, but is terror to the workers of iniquity" (NASB). The fundamental requirement to seek justice, though universally applicable, is given special emphasis by the covenantal character of Israel, who knew what it was to maintain the rights of the weak and oppressed (Deut 10:17–19; Ps 146:7).[62] The combination of verb and noun, "love" and "kindness" (אהבת חסד), is unique in the Old Testament "since one usually does kindness."[63] The Hebrew word חסד is variously translated: "mercy" (NIV), "loyalty" (REB, NJB), "goodness" (NJPS). It usually implies help provided by a stronger person to a weaker member in a covenant relationship, the covenant relationship not always being necessary.[64]

---

[59] Mays, *Micah*, 141.
[60] Walter Brueggemann, "Walk Humbly with Your God: Micah 6:8," *JP* 33 (2010): 14.
[61] Mays, *Micah*, 141–42.
[62] Jenson, *Obadiah, Jonah, Micah*, 173.
[63] Dempster, *Micah*, 161.
[64] Dempster, *Micah*, 161.

4. Religious Unfaithfulness and Community Moral Depravity 91

Like justice, אהבת חסד (love and kindness) is pre-eminently a quality of Yahweh (Ps 89:14); which must also characterize Israel's internal communal life (Hos 4:1; Mic 7:2). The practice of justice must rest on kindness and mutuality which recognizes the rights of the weak and oppressed and respond in brotherly identification. The combination of the requirement of justice and kindness does not imagine any form of divorce between the actions and the intentions; the inward and the outward expressions must correlate. The "love of kindness" is interpreted by Brueggemann as "to practice a life of reliable solidarity."[65] Remarkably, the requirements of doing justice and loving kindness are quite clear in the Hebrew Bible/Old Testament but the inclusive summary of the series, traditionally translated as "to walk humbly" (הצנע לכת) with your God is unique to Micah.[66] While walking describes a quality of behavior in relation to the fundamental metaphor of life as a journey, the verb הצנע is used to describe a way of life that is humble, not so much by modesty, as by considered attention to others. According to Hillers, "if correctly translated and explained here, the modifier would refer to employment of discretion, prudence, and wisdom in the religious life."[67] The humility implied here lies not in following one's own presumptuous way, but in attending to the will and way of Yahweh.[68] A similar understanding is expressed by Stephen B. Dawes: "The worshipper is to be humble towards God (recognizing his dependence upon him and being willing to subject himself to him?), towards his fellows (being ready to put others first and give himself away in service to them?), and towards himself (shunning undue ambition, and cultivating a realistic sense of his own place and value?)."[69]

The final phrase, "with your God," resonates in the traditional covenant description associating Yahweh with "my people" (6:3, 5) and such ideas as: "you shall be my people, and I will be your God" (Jer 30:22; cf. Exod 6:7; Hos 1:9).[70] This idea of walking with God is a fundamental metaphor for Israel, and it contrasts later with walking in the statutes of the house of Omri (6:16). The good that Yahweh requires are the practice of justice, which is a way of loving kindness, and which consequently manifests in walking humbly with God. These are the essential pillars upon which Israel's covenant rests, but which in all of its aspects Israel has miserably been unsuccessful. While the answer does call for sacrifice, it is rather a different sacrifice from that proposed by the question. (The ethical and application chapters 5 and 6 below provide insight on this development).

---

[65] Brueggemann, "Walk Humbly with Your God," 14.
[66] Hyman, "Questions and Response in Micah 6:6–8," 164.
[67] Hillers, *Micah*, 79.
[68] Mays, *Micah*, 142.
[69] Stephen B. Dawes, "Walking Humbly: Micah 6:8 Revisited," *SJT* 41.3 (1988): 338.
[70] Jenson, *Obadiah, Jonah, Micah*, 174.

4.2. Cheating and Violence (6:9–16)

This unit (6:9–16)[71] is a bill of crimes connected with threats of punishment. It establishes a connection between extravagance in ritual disallowed in 6:7–8 and the accumulation of unmerited wealth (6:9–11) which serves as its theme. The oracle unit is composed in first person style. Verse 9 contains an introduction formula that identifies the addressee as "the city" and summons it to hear Yahweh's message. Verses 10–12 articulate the motivation for the indictment (emphases on commercial crimes) of the city's population. On account of their gross misconducts (verse 13), Yahweh has already begun punishment (verses 14–15) which will be a curse of frustration on the natural sequence of life. A similar scheme of indictment and announcement of punishment is found in verse 16 but it speaks of sin that echoes the practices of the leaders of the northern kingdom of Samaria (16a; compare the opening reference to Samaria in 1:5–7), the consequence that the city shall be devastated (16b). Yahweh requires justice, kindness, and humble walking (cautious living) in his way (Mic 6:8); but there is wickedness, violence, and a demonstration of a lifestyle that is reminiscent of the precepts of Omri and the practices of the house of Ahab (6:10–12, 16). Thus, Judah is on the verge of suffering the same fate as Samaria for replicating its sins (6:13, 16).

Although one of the characteristic features of the unit is its obscurity, in language and style, the unit bears a resemblance to similar material in chapters 1–3 that are accepted as authentic Micah materials.[72] The oracle addressees "tribe" and "assembly" but the indefiniteness of the text makes it difficult to identify the city as Jerusalem, or Samaria, pointedly.[73] While various assumptions exist regarding the setting of the unit,[74] "the setting within the world of the book is left open as possible, within the restrictions associated with 1:1."[75] As it stands, the unit makes a quick and smooth transition from the cult to the culture,

---

[71] Ben Zvi treats it as a "prophetic reading explaining the reasons for divine judgement against the monarchic 'city'" (Ben Zvi, *Micah*, 155–65); Hillers regards it as a literary unit that invokes Yahweh's curse on the cheating city (Hillers, *Micah*, 80–82); and May considers it as a divine announcement of guilt and punishment (Mays, *Micah*, 143–49).

[72] "One of the hallmarks is obscurity; obscurity to us, that is." This may be due to textual deterioration as a result of transmission process or it may inhere in the very nature of prophecy. Andersen and Freedman, *Micah*, 541.

[73] Hillers, *Micah*, 81.

[74] Mays holds that the oracle is addressed to Jerusalem during the late Babylonian crisis, in a period when a citizens' assembly was in charge of its affairs, and disasters which are interpreted as punishment have already commenced (v. 13). Mays, *Micah*, 145.

[75] Ben Zvi, *Micah*, 163.

4. Religious Unfaithfulness and Community Moral Depravity 93

from the temple to the market and workplace, and the disconnection between Yahweh's desired requirements and the people's aspiration is fixed and clear.

4.2.1. Addressee and Summons (6:9)

> The voice of Yahweh
>   calling out to the city.
> And it is an efficient wisdom to fear your name.
> Hear O tribe
>   and who has appointed it.

Micah 6:9 contains three sentences. The first sentence introduces, though in an inconsistent manner, the direct words of Yahweh to the city. The expression קול יהוה (voice of Yahweh) replaces the traditional prophetic messenger formula כה אמר יהוה (2:3; 3:5). While this expression lacks parallels in prophetic literature,[76] קול יהוה is presented as an articulated voice and as a metonymy for Yahweh.[77] Yahweh's voice is employed during the disclosure of the torah at Sinai (Deut 5:25), and reference to the thunderous voice of Yahweh is seen in Ps 29, where it indicates his authority and power possibly on account of Israel's disobedience to that torah. Since the voice of Yahweh is mentioned in 6:1b, the opening of 6:9 can be taken as a reactivation of that theme. In 6:1, Yahweh addressed the mountains and in 6:9 the city. Here, קול (voice) may be taken to mean "hear," an equivalent of שמע (listen).[78] The voice cries out to the city, which represents monarchic Jerusalem and its people (Mic 1:1; 3:12).[79] Given the continuation of Mic 3 in chapter 6, the king would be Ahaz, who was culpable for following Ahab's practices.[80] In the context of the text, it is clear that this voice addresses an Israelite audience with a driving force to hear and respond.

The second sentence is directed at Yahweh, expressing reverence for what is announced in his name: "And it is an efficient wisdom to fear your name." The noun תושיה (sound or efficient wisdom) which appears here and mainly in wisdom literature (cf. Prov 2:7; 3:21; 8:14; 18:1; Job 26:3) is a term from the vocabulary of wisdom (cf. Prov 1:7; 9:10; 15:33), associated with prudence and knowledge in the positive sense. Like its parallel terms חכמה (wisdom, Prov

---

[76] Mays, *Micah*, 146.
[77] Ben Zvi, *Micah*, 157.
[78] Andersen and Freedman, *Micah*, 547.
[79] Mays, *Micah*, 146. The city is represented by the pronoun "her" in follow up verses (12, 16) but it is not a city that is addressed in verses 13–16 where the masculine plural "you" is used.
[80] It is also possible to imagine a northern origin of the text since verse 16 refers to Omri and Ahab. Thus, the city could be Samaria and the unspecified addressee could be a king on that hypothesis. Andersen and Freedman, *Micah*, 546.

11:6) and עצה (advice, counsel, Prov 8:14), תושיה is a divine gift and a human acquisition necessary for success (Prov 3:21).[81] The expression יראה שמך (to see your name) is usually read as "to fear your name" since the familiar expression יראה יהוה "fear of Yahweh" (which is the beginning of wisdom)[82] has related idioms such as "fear God," "fear his word," "fear (his) name" (Deut 28:58; Isa 59:19; Mal 3:20; Pss 61:6; 86:11; Neh 1:11).[83] Since true religion is associated with the "fear of Yahweh," the sentence indicates that it is wisdom to pay attention to words uttered with the signature of Yahweh's name. The announcement to the city from the voice and signature of Yahweh's name conveys his wisdom and it is expected to impart תושיה (sound wisdom) into the addressees, in addition (or aspect of) the fear of his name. These ideas, according to Andersen and Freedman, are similar to those already described in 6:8 as requirements from humans. The three compact infinitival expressions "to do justice," "to love mercy," and "to walk humbly" in verse 8 (in response to the question "What is good?") are here in verse 6:9 amplified by two more requirements: "sound or efficient wisdom" and the "fear of Yahweh's name."[84]

The third sentence is the summons to hear, conveyed by a masculine plural imperative and addressed to the collective noun מטה (staff or tribe)[85] of the city. Thus, a number of probable explanations have been given to the expression, שמעו מטה ומי יעדה (hear, O staff and who appointed her). Considering the plural form of the verb שמעו (hear) Ben Zvi notes that "the city or better, the people of the city are asked to listen to the staff (i.e., the [sound of] the rod of punishment; cf. Isa 30:32; Job 3:18; see also Isa 10:5, 24; Lam 3:1) and above all to YHWH, the one who appointed the staff and who is about to present a speech to this audience (cf. Jer 47:7)."[86] Here, the staff is understood to be a symbol of a ruler, and "her" refers to Jerusalem, although a different word (שבט) is usually used for royal scepter (Isa 14:5).[87] Following the translation of מטה as "tribe," the expression that follows—ומי יעדה "and who appoints her"—is phonetically close

---

[81] Jenson, *Obadiah, Jonah, Micah*, 175.
[82] The biblical concept of יִרְאַה יהוה is generally understood and acknowledged as both the credo and epistemological and theological foundation of the book of Proverbs. Bruce K. Waltke, *The Book of Proverbs, Chapters 1–15*, NICOT (Grand Rapids: Eerdmans, 2004), 180; Allen P. Ross, "Proverbs," in *The Expositor's Bible Commentary*, ed. Frank E. Gaebelein, 12 vols. (Grand Rapids: Zondervan, 1991), 5:907.
[83] Andersen and Freedman, *Micah*, 546.
[84] Andersen and Freedman, *Micah*, 546.
[85] מטה (rod) could also be an instrument of chastisement (Exod 4:20; Isa 10:5) or oppression (Isa 30:32).
[86] Ben Zvi, *Micah*, 158.
[87] Jenson, *Obadiah, Jonah, Micah*, 175.

4. Religious Unfaithfulness and Community Moral Depravity

to and suggestive of מועדה "her [the city's] assembly" (cf. Isa 14:13; Ps 74:4).[88] Mays notes that in the NRSV the summons ("Hear, O tribe and assembly of the city!") with the plural imperative שמעו (hear) is addressed to the collective nouns "tribe and assembly of the city." In this case, "the indictment speaks of the sins of the city's inhabitants; the announcement of punishment is addressed to the corporate group and the assembly responsible for its life."[89] Here, Yahweh speaks directly to the city—understood to be Jerusalem, whose leaders and people have been in view throughout the book.

4.2.2. Dishonest Business Practices (6:10–12)

> Are there yet in the house of the wicked
>   treasures of wickedness
> and the scant ephah-measure that is cursed?
> Shall I justify as pure the scales of wickedness,
>   and the bag of deceptive weights?
> For the rich men of the city are full of violence,
>   and her inhabitants speak falsehood,
>   and their tongues are deceitful in their mouth.

This subunit contains two rhetorical questions about features that characterize the entire city (vv. 10–11) and a further characterization of the city in general terms (verse 12). They describe Yahweh's abhorrence at crimes of injustice in commercial centers and violence in society, both in action and word. The first two verses emphasize the magnitude of lawlessness and injustice that characterize the city. In more specific descriptions, the indictments are focused on those who enrich themselves by dishonest commercial transactions. Micah accuses them of falsifying measures and weights; such wickedness cannot be tolerated. Two specific examples of dishonest business practices are mentioned. First, verse 10 indicates that in measuring, a merchant or trader could use an ephah smaller than required. The word איפה (measure) is literally an ephah, a dry measure estimated to be "anywhere from 3/8 to 2/3 of a bushel, used to measure flour, barley or other grains."[90] The איפה has been doctored by the merchant to make "scant" (רזון) and less grain were being measured out to potential custom-

---

[88] Accordingly, Ben Zvi notes that the text conveys a secondary meaning similar to: "The voice of YHWH calls to the city ...: 'Hear, O tribe, and her [the city's] assembly'" (cf. Isa 1:1; Jer 11:2; Joel 4:6 [NRSV 3:6]; Mal 3:4; etc.). Ben Zvi, *Micah*, 159.
[89] Mays, *Micah*, 146.
[90] According to Dempster, the German equivalent of "a hungry purse" has been suggested. See Dempster, *Micah*, 168. Such despicable practice is decried in Israelite law (Lev 19:35–36; Deut 25:13–15; cf. Ezek 45:10; Amos 8:5), and thus recognize as a transgression in any society of a certain intricacy in business transactions. Hillers, *Micah*, 82.

ers, who felt that they were purchasing the required measurement. Micah describes such a scant measure, designed to defraud buyers as זעומה (cursed), a term usually associated with the cursing or denouncement of people (Num 23:7; Prov 22:14). Those defrauded have no option than to curse (זעם) the merchants, and invariably such a curse would be enacted by Yahweh (cf. 6:13–15).[91]

Second, when weighing for purchase or transaction a merchant could use inequitable scales or stone weights of unbalanced sizes, one for buying and another for selling. Thus, false weights are placed alongside accurate weights so as to reduce the איפה (ephah of the grain being sold) and increase the shekel (the amount of money being received) from the transaction. This is the direct opposite of justice and equity.[92] The main verb זכה (to pronounce just or righteous, to be morally pure or blameless) in verse 11 serves as the subject of the two clauses: במאזני רשע (scales of wickedness) ובכיס אבני מרמה (and the bag of deceptive weights). The verb brings to mind a pronouncement in trial or court in which the actions of the lawless person are tried. Since scales can be manipulated or falsified,[93] the use of scales may not necessarily vindicate a person who is violating the law. The noun כיס (measuring bag) relates to a bag that holds weights in Deut 25:13. However, in this passage it refers to a bag to carry and measure grain (cf. Gen 42:27, 28; 43:12–18, 21; 44:1, 11). A כיס (measuring bag) may appear to be sanctioned or official, but it may not give a right measure of grain. The common noun מרמה (deceit, fraud) which modifies אבני (weights) functions as an attributive genitive and forcefully describes the inherent character of the weights (אבני); they are "deceitful weights" (אבני מרמה). These ways of defrauding people in business transactions are repeatedly prohibited in the Mosaic law and wisdom literature (Deut 25:13–16; Lev 19:35–36; Prov 11:1; 16:11; 20:10, 23; cf. Amos 8:5; Hos 12:8).[94]

In verse 12, Micah characterizes these acts of dishonesty in commercial dealings in the city by the rich and its inhabitants as "violence and injurious deception against those who are defrauded."[95] The noun חמס (violence) is the direct opposite of חסד (mercy, kindness), which leads to משפט (justice). חמס suggest destructive, violent, physical attacks on people, including murder, which resulted in wealth and property taken by naked force.[96] The clause העיר מלאה חמס (the city is filled with violence) is synonymous with הארץ מלאה משפט דמים

---

[91] B. Wiklander, "זָעַם," *TDOT* 4:106–111 (110), cited in Jenson, *Obadiah, Jonah, Micah*, 176.
[92] Dempster, *Micah*, 168.
[93] According to Waltke, ancient scales "could be falsified by inaccurate pans, a bent crossbow, or mishandling." Waltke, *Commentary on Micah*, 410.
[94] Dempster, *Micah*, 168–69.
[95] Mays, *Micah*, 147.
[96] Wolff, *Micah*, 194.

4. Religious Unfaithfulness and Community Moral Depravity

(the land is filled with murder or bloody crimes) in Ezek 7:23.[97] The speech of the wealthy may be open-minded and pious, but it is contradicted by their behavior, which is characterized as חמס (violence, outrage).[98]

The venue for this characterization of the dishonest city may be the law court, where the inhabitants speak lies and exercise their deceitful tongues on behalf of their benefactors. Most probably, the wealthy have been indicted of dishonesty and cheating by the poor (farmers) but because of their wealth, they could buy false witnesses and so manipulate the law. Thus, a reversal existed at the law court, where, rather than being a viable center for establishing justice, it becomes a vehicle for violence (Exod 20:16; cf. 1 Kgs 21).[99] The use of such language to characterize the ingenuity of the wealthy and their agents places such practices in their broadest social context and illuminates the bitterness of the complaint against the city in Micah. Accordingly, "the injury is more than economic; it damages the lives and status of persons in the fabric of society and destroys that fabric."[100] Significantly, ethical violations are the focal emphasis of these verses and the charges of violence and dishonesty on a societal level are comprehensive generalizations that portray the city's population whose behavior bears little resemblance to the standard expected of Yahweh's people in covenant community.[101] The next section of the unit moves into the announcement of punishment.

4.2.3. Announcement of Punishment (6:13–16)

> And I also will make you sick, striking you down,
> > desolating you because of your sins.
> You will eat,
> > but you will not be satisfied,
> And there will be gnawing hunger in your midst.
> > You will try to bring to safety but will not be successful,
> > and what you do preserve I will give to the sword.
> You will sow but you will not reap.
> You will tread the olive
> > but will not anoint yourself with oil;
> > > and the grapes,
> > but you will not drink wine.

---

[97] In Ezek 28:16, trade and violence are linked in the paradigmatic case of Tyre and here in Micah, Jerusalem joins this notorious city.
[98] Hillers, *Micah*, 82.
[99] Jenson, *Obadiah, Jonah, Micah*, 176.
[100] Mays, *Micah*, 147.
[101] Nogalski, *Book of the Twelve*, 575.

> And he observed the statutes of Omri
>> and all the works of the house of Ahab.
> And you have walked in their devices.
> So I will give you up for destruction
>> and her inhabitants for derision,
> and you will bear the reproach of my people.

This subunit, especially verses 13–15, describes the consequences of the transgressions of the city's inhabitants that were referred to in verses 10–12. Micah 6:13 presents a summary of Yahweh's punitive actions, and specific details regarding this punishment are described in 6:14–15; what Yahweh intends to do is primarily the focus of 6:13, while the effects of his actions constitute the focus of 6:14–15. Rather than using the transitional particle לכן (therefore, 2:3; 3:6) in 6:13, the particle גם (also) is used to emphasize the relationship between the crimes of the wicked and their own punishment.[102] The phrase על־חטאתך (because of your sins) at the end of the verse recapitulates the moral and religious transgressions of the city, previously described. Thus, the violence and treachery of the wealthy against their victims justifies the corresponding measures of Yahweh's punitive actions (verses 13–15).

The verb נכה (be hit, smitten, struck down) in the first clause החליתי הכותך (strike you down with sickness) is used to describe Yahweh's punishment of his people and military attacks. With the reference to sword in 6:14 and an outcome of international disgrace and public embarrassment, the historical circumstances point to those created by military invasion and siege.[103] In the second clause, the verb השמם (*hiphil* infinitive absolute of שמם; to devastate, ravage) appears again in 6:15 where it implies abolition of precepts. However, שמם is usually rendered as destruction or desolation (Lev 26:34; Isa 54:3; Jer 12:11). While the message conveyed by the verse is strong and might indicate the subjective and collective mood of the inhabitants of the city, it does not refer to the final and complete destruction of the people, since there is a reference to a remnant in 7:18–20 and a future compassion and forgiveness that they will experience (cf. 5:2–9). The imagined devastation of 6:13 is described quite clearly in 6:14–15.[104]

Verses 14–15 continue with the elaboration of Yahweh's verdict with the pronouncement that the people will experience hunger and military devastation. Moving from the first person pronoun אני (I) which served as the subject and referring to Yahweh in verse 13, the second person singular pronoun אתה (you) is the subject that dominates 6:14–15. The oracle subunit views the city as a

---

[102] Jenson, *Obadiah, Jonah, Micah*, 176.

[103] Mays, *Micah*, 147.

[104] Waltke, *Commentary on Micah*, 412.

4. Religious Unfaithfulness and Community Moral Depravity 99

corporate entity that is responsible for commercial crimes and cultic apostasy that provoke Yahweh's judgement.[105] These verses contain five threats of misfortunes, two in verse 14 and three in verse 15, against those who try to gain a living from the land (cf. Hag 1:6). These misfortunes are similar to those elsewhere (Lev 26:26; Deut 28:18, 30–31, 38–40; cf. Hos 4:10; 5:6; 8:7; 9:12, 16; Amos 5:11) and they are presented in the form of "futility curses," on account of the fact that whatever course of action the guilty undertake they will "inevitably be frustrated in it."[106] The curses are not an attempt to outline a precise picture of external events but simply a reversal of the natural sequence of blessing and fertility and a basic exposition of Yahweh's reaction to breach of covenant requirements.

In verse 14, the description of hunger depicts the curse of eating and not being satisfied based on Leviticus 26:26 that is set in the context of a military siege (Lev 26:25). What is in their midst, namely, ישחך, is not quite clear. The word ישח is a *hapax legomenon* that has inspired several suggestions. The LXX renders it as "darkness," the Vulgate "humiliation," and the Syriac "dysentery." The NRSV offers "gnawing hunger," while REB and NEB imply "indigestion" hence with the euphemistic expression "your food will lie heavy in your stomach." These versions all indicate a chaotic situation, and the meaning of this futility curse is graphically colored.[107]

The expression ותסג ולא תפליט (You will try to bring to safety but will not be successful) probably refers to an attempt by the people to put aside supplies for another day, but that day will not come, possibly because of a military attack where there is no one to save or deliver (cf. Isa 5:29). Even if someone makes a successful attempt to preserve anything it will only be short-term, because Yahweh will "give them over to the sword."[108] Since the wicked are city merchants who trade in commodities, verse 15 continues with three more maledictions— grain, oil, wine—all aimed at an agrarian community. The people would sow their various seeds, press their olives, and tread their grapes, but all the efforts and hard work in preparing these basic essentials would be in vain. Their expectations will be cut short; "there would be no opportunity for them to anoint themselves with oil (Deut 28:40), nor would there be time for the juice of the fresh grapes in the winepress to be fermented into wine (Deut 28:39; Amos

---

[105] Mays, *Micah*, 147.
[106] Hillers, *Micah*, 82. See also Waltke, *Commentary on Micah*, 412.
[107] Andersen and Freedman, *Micah*, 549.
[108] "The REB reflects a quite different interpretative tradition, since the word translated 'save' … can also occasionally mean 'deliver [a child]' (Job 21:10), hence 'you will come to labour, but not bring forth.' A curse on the womb (miscarriage, barrenness) is common (Deut 28:18; Hos 9:11), as is the loss of children to captivity or death (Deut 28:41; Hos 9:12–13)." Jenson, *Obadiah, Jonah, Micah*, 177.

5:11)."[109] Consequently, they will not find satisfaction, fulfillment of joy or prosperity. Noticeably, the anticipated season of peace and fertility of the land in 4:3-4 will not happen until after Yahweh's punishment. This situation brings to the fore an opposite expectation, namely, infertility of the land (resulting in a lack of food) and war. Consequently, Nogalski remarks:

> The threat of Micah 6:14-15 does double duty. In the short term, it evokes memories of Sennacherib's siege in 701 BCE when Jerusalem nearly fell to the Assyrians. In the long run, however, attentive readers cannot escape the nagging sense of doom hanging over Jerusalem in the Book of the Twelve on its march to the destruction of 587 at the hands of the Babylonians.[110]

The last verse of the unit (v. 16) contains a disorderliness of styles. The verb forms shift awkwardly between singular and plural, second and third person, and thus a range of emendations have been proposed to ease better reading. In its translation, the text reads:

> And he (3rd masc. sing.—an impersonal passive?) observed the statutes of Omri and all the works of the house of Ahab; and you (2nd masc. pl.) have walked in their devices. So I will give you (2nd masc. sing.) up for destruction and her inhabitants for derision, and you (2nd masc. pl.) will bear the reproach of my people.

Notwithstanding, the overall sense of the unit is clear: it concludes with a second indictment and punishment sequence, that involves the motivation of the accusation for punishment (6:16a) and a judgement (6:16b). Rather than enumerating specific transgressions, the speaker depicts actions by situating them in the categories identified by the names Omri and Ahab.[111] Although the precise sense of the phrases חקות עמרי (precepts of Omri) וכל מעשה עמרי בית־אחאב (and all the practices of the house of Ahab) escapes one, the manner of speaking indicates a tradition in which the policies and practices of Omri and Ahab are so malicious that the mention of their names can serve as a final motivation for indictment.[112]

---

[109] Jenson, *Obadiah, Jonah, Micah*, 178.
[110] Nogalski, *Book of the Twelve*, 576.
[111] Omri was the founder of Samaria (1 Kgs 16:24), the capital of the northern kingdom (Mic 1:5), but he was even more famous for being a renowned sinner (1 Kgs 16:25). However, Ahab is known for being more wicked than all the kings before him in the northern kingdom (1 Kgs 16:25-33); one whose deeds were the standard against which future kings were assessed (2 Kgs 8:18, 27). The seizure of Naboth's vineyard and judicial murder of Naboth has been clearly noted (cf. 1 Kgs 21). See Hillers, *Micah*, 82; Waltke, *Commentary on Micah*, 414.
[112] Mays, *Micah*, 148.

4. Religious Unfaithfulness and Community Moral Depravity 101

The verb שמר (observed, kept) in 6:16 has the basic sense of "adherence to and act in conformity with." Its object is חקות (statutes, precepts). The expression "statutes of Omri" is an ironic perversion of the "statutes of Yahweh."[113] The "statutes of Omri" might refer to "'rules' that Omri devised for the cult of Baal that the people of Israel were obligated to follow or economic practices of the northern kings, 'a law-code of the individualistic commercialism which was now displacing the ancient community economy of Israel's past.'"[114] Although חקות (statutes) might also refer to the idolatrous activities of Ahab, who encouraged the worship of Baal (1 Kgs 18; 2 Kgs 10:18), the present context indicates a moral nuance; חקות (statutes) and מעשה (practices) "describe behaviour that undermined traditional Israelite standards of justice and morality."[115]

The expression בית־אחאב (house of Ahab) includes family members who are regarded as notorious for their evil, including his wife Jezebel, who led him astray in the matters of Baal worship (1 Kgs 16:31), the murder of Naboth, and the theft of his vineyard (1 Kgs 21), his sons Ahaziah (1 Kgs 22:51–53) and Joram (2 Kgs 3:1–3). Judgment and destruction came upon the entire dynasty (2 Kgs 9:7–9; 10:11), which was certainly the eventual consequent fate of the entire northern kingdom (Mic 1:5–7).[116] Further elaboration of the indictment is seen in the clause ותלכו במעצותם (and you have walked in their devices). The verb הלך (walked, followed) has the basic sense of "following with a view to conformity." Its object is מועצה (counsel, plan, devices, policy). Since "house of Ahab" is parallel to Samaria in 2 Kgs 21:13, it is fascinating to note that the Micah text directs its message to people of Jerusalem and Judah for following after the standards and actions of the worst and infamous kings of the northern kingdom. This moral nuance does not only convey a severe insult to Judah's fidelity to Yahweh but also return to the theme that opened the book of Micah: Judah has followed the rules and deeds of Israel and her vilest kings imaginable rather than learning from them (cf. 1:5).[117]

The last phrases of verse 16 announce devastation and humiliation to Judah and Jerusalem as a consequence of their decision to follow the examples of Israel's worst kings which were diametrically opposed to the statutes of Yahweh by which they were expected to walk (cf. Mic 6:8). The conjunctive particle למען (therefore, so that, for the sake of, because of) in the verdict, is an illustration of the "'resultive' use of the conjunction, used here 'to indicate a result which was

---

[113] Cf. Deut 4:6, 8 where statutes (חקות) is a common term for Yahweh's commandments in the torah.
[114] Dempster, *Micah*, 169.
[115] Jenson, *Obadiah, Jonah, Micah*, 178.
[116] Jenson, *Obadiah, Jonah, Micah*, 178.
[117] Nogalski, *Book of the Twelve*, 576.

not necessarily intended by the subject marked by the verb in the main clause, but was bound to ensue.'"[118]

Since Micah has directed his oracles mainly against the nation's leadership, the resultive implication of the sins of the leaders of Judah and Jerusalem is here given a threefold exposition. First, Yahweh will give them over to "desolation," a situation that causes astonishment or horror (cf. 2 Kgs 22:19; Ps 46:8; Isa 24:12; Jer 25:18). Second "its inhabitants" will become "an object of derision." "Object of derision" is found mostly in Jeremiah in reference to the ruined and disgraced state of Jerusalem (Jer 19:8; 25:9, 18; 29:18; 51:37, in all these texts with "horror"). The dual nouns לשמה (desolation) and שרקה (object of derision) indicate that the city will become so devastated that the sight of it will stimulate horror and the surviving population will be a laughingstock to its enemies.[119]

The third resultive implication of the sins of the leaders is that "you will bear the reproach of my people." Because reproach, scorn or disgrace is usually heaped on others, this final verdict may imply, "you will endure the insults aimed at my people."[120] Yahweh's people are not exempted from the punishment of the leaders (you) who are mainly blamed and punished. Though the people are not as guilty as the wealthy residents in the city and despite the fact that they are mostly the victims of exploitation and oppression (Mic 2–3), they suffer as a result of the verdict aimed at the oppressors.[121] The empirical factor here is that the "reproaches of my people" is a reference to the reproach they will receive when they are defeated and taken into captivity by privileged classes of foreign invaders, who are common agents of Yahweh's punitive anger against his people; the wicked city will ultimately experience the reproach of the oppressed.[122]

4.3. Total Corruption of the People (7:1–6)

This unit is a lament bemoaning the moral condition of the nation in which the prophet lives.[123] The mournful dirge begins and ends with the first-person allusion. The literary context indicates that the prophet is speaking on behalf of the city of Jerusalem, as the opening cry of sorrow shows. Although the description of his circumstances is not adequately specified to enable one to establish a his-

---

[118] W. Edward Glenny, *Micah: A Commentary Based on Micah in Codex Vaticanus* (Leiden: Brill, 2015), 186.
[119] Mays, *Micah*, 148–49.
[120] Jenson, *Obadiah, Jonah, Micah*, 178.
[121] Andersen and Freedman, *Micah*, 550.
[122] See, Glenny, *Micah*, 186; Hillers, *Micah*, 82; Andersen and Freedman, *Micah*, 550.
[123] The identity of potential speaker(s) has been read to include Yahweh, Daughter Zion (or Jerusalem), and the prophetic speaker identified as Micah. Ben Zvi, *Micah*, 168.

torical setting with certainty, the general structure of the unit is similar to the preceding one (6:9–15). The unit begins with a unique metaphor of interjection that evokes a vulnerable despondency that he feels about the state of society (7:1) and then continues to state more pointedly his basic theme in graphic portrayal with assertions about the absence of "the righteous and the faithful" (7:2a) and presence of "the incorrigible and the corrupt" (7:2b) that creates hostility. His description of the social disintegration is presented in two levels, focusing on the one hand on the public domain and its officials (7:3–4) and on the private family domain (7:5–6) on the other hand. The unit can thus be understood as a response to the judgment portrayed in 6:13–16; the curses of 6:14–15 have been effected and the corruption in society (6:10–13) has escalated and reached the climax point, manifested in the breakdown of integrity at the highest level of leadership (3:11) and down to the lowest sphere of intimate relations of life, with friends and family (7:2–6).[124]

4.3.1. Loss of Genuine Spiritual Identity (7:1–2)

> Woe is me!
> For I am like the fruit pickers
> > and like the grape gatherers.
> There is not a cluster of grapes to eat,
> > or a first-ripe fig which I crave.
> The godly person has perished from the land,
> > and there is no upright person among men.
> All of them lie in wait for bloodshed;
> > each man hunts his brother with a net.

The opening verse of this subunit is a cry of lamentation in the first person: אללי לי (Woe is me!), illustrating through an agricultural metaphor (7:1 cf. 6:15) and its interpretation (7:2–4) the moral degeneracy of the entire city population, both of the people and its leadership. Micah utilizes an extended agricultural metaphor to compare the plight of the pious to one facing starvation after the harvest has failed. Like the gleaner after the harvest (7:1a cf. Lev. 19:9–10; 23:22; Deut 24:19–21),[125] the prophet is searching in vain for some last remaining virtuous person in the land (7:1b). The harvesting has been so ruthless that the fig trees and vines are completely stripped. Micah's metaphor evokes a feeling of depression and anguish; the world of his daily life has become effectively frustrating, one of a death sentence for a hungry person preparing for an unproductive win-

---

[124] Andersen and Freedman, *Micah*, 562.
[125] In these texts, harvesters were urged to leave some of the produce for the poor and strangers to glean after the gathering of grapes or figs. It was an important traditional means of securing the poorest of the land from starvation. Hillers, *Micah*, 85.

ter.¹²⁶ Embedded in the picture of a frustrated, hungry gleaner, is an accusation of injustice, corruption, and lack of kindness. The subsequent description of the human environment of Micah provides the literal counterpart to this initial metaphor.¹²⁷

In verse 2, the metaphor is explained and expanded with significant social detail that explicitly hints at Judah as evidently the vineyard (cf. Isa 5:1–7). In the first part of verse 2, the term used to depict the assertions about the absence of "the faithful" is חסיד. It is an adjective which describes those who live out their pieties toward fellow human beings and Yahweh with a sincere purpose in covenant community; they practice the expected חסד (mercy, loving-kindness of 6:8) as a lifestyle, and enact loyalty to Yahweh by their unconditional commitment to the practice of משפט (justice) with all whom they deal. The חסיד furnishes the values and norms assumed by the ישר (upright person). In this context, ישר is a reference to one who lives in obedience to Yahweh's ethical standards. The search for a חסיד (the faithful or godly person) whose indispensable qualities are basic for the flourishing of human life and society, which was conducted from among the masses or general population, as indicated by the references to באדם (among men) and מן־הארץ (from the land, i.e., a reference to Judah) was fruitless; all such persons have disappeared (אין) or perished (אבד).

This state of affairs, that is, the disappearance of the faithful and upright and consequently the barrenness of the land in terms of good people, is explained in the second line of verse 2 that supplies the antithesis to חסיד. The expression, "all of them" (כלם) does not refer back to the nouns in verse 2a but anticipates an approaching list. The pursuits of men are nothing more than a surprise attack and hunt in which their fellow human beings are the prime target. According to Jenson,

> Robbers usually 'lie in wait' for the unsuspecting and the helpless (Ps 10:9; Prov 1:11; 24:15), but if the righteous have disappeared, then the only alternative is to 'hunt each other with nets.' This is no longer a matter of relative gain but of 'blood,' of violence and murder (a stage beyond 6:10–12). Doing away with someone is simply equivalent to catching a fish (Ezek 26:5; Hab 1:15–17). 'Each other' (literally 'his brother,' NIV, NJB) refers not only to a blood brother but also a 'kinsman' (REB) or even 'fellow-countryman' (GNB). The law set out the responsibilities owed to the 'brother' (Lev 19:17; Deut 22:1–4), but now the closest family ties mean nothing.¹²⁸

---

¹²⁶ Jenson, *Obadiah, Jonah, Micah*, 179.
¹²⁷ Hillers, *Micah*, 85.
¹²⁸ Jenson, *Obadiah, Jonah, Micah*, 180.

Rather than creating a community where there is a viable structure for practicing traditional virtues of faithfulness, human relations simply became an occasion for violence and injustice toward fellowman.

4.3.2. Corruption of the Officials and Judges (7:3–4)

> Their hands are skilled at doing evil.
> The prince asks
>   And the judge for profit
> The great one speaks the desire of his soul;
> And they weave it together.
> The best of them is like a briar,
>   The most upright like a thorn hedge.
> The day of your keeping watch
>   of punishment has come
> Now their confusion will occur.

This subunit contains an elaborate self-examination. The first line of verse 3 continues the account of the people's sins from 7:2. It is expressed in dramatic irony: על־הרע כפים להיטיב (Their hands are skilled at doing evil). The verb היטיב (skilled) is derived from יטב (to do good) with the noun form as טוב (good). It often means diligently, thoroughly, but here, it is an ironic reversal of the moral norms implied by the good. Their efforts indicate a wholehearted commitment at making use of both hands. Dempster remarks that although there is evidence of ambidextrous soldiers in the Nubian army from Micah's time, it normally takes practice to learn how to become right-handed or left-handed. It is rare for people to be ambidextrous, however here in Judah the people have learned to do evil diligently with both hands.[129] Thus their evils were calculated and planned.

The inner structure of verse 3 involves three explicit substantives: שר (prince, officer), שפט (judge) and גדול (great one). These nouns are the subjects of two parallel participles שאל (asking) and דבר (speaking), with one appendage, בשלום (for profit) common to both participles.[130] The verse denounces Judah's political officials and judges as conspirators in perverting justice. The desires of official are what the judge delivers for a price. Both act from materialism and greed, and these are the leaders of the nation.[131] What is clear from the context of 7:1–3 is that these leaders in verse 3 manipulate the situation to their advantage; they are in collaboration with each other in defrauding the people (cf. 3:2–3). Apparently, besides the preparation of their hands for evil (7:3a), they

---

[129] Dempster, *Micah*, 175 citing Nadav Na'aman, *Ancient Israel and Its Neighbors: Interaction and Counteraction* (Winona Lake: Eisenbrauns, 2005), 104–5.
[130] Andersen and Freedman, *Micah*, 569.
[131] Nogalski, *Book of the Twelve*, 578.

also prepare a strategy by which the rulers can demand things from the people, and the judges will not reprove them but instead speak words in their favor. Consequently, the sins of the leaders are rooted in their minds and hearts with their selfish intentions. Rather than wholeheartedly loving and practicing חסד (cf. 6:8), they delight in materialism, wealth and treasures (6:12), and they strategize and conspire to acquire them unjustly by the abuse of their position, power, and privilege.

The full-blown corruption of the nation is emphasized in verse 4a where Micah uses a botanical metaphor to describe the leaders of society: "the best of them" (טובם) is like a useless plant, כחדק (brier) that serves no purpose other than to perpetuate their own existence at the expense of others.[132] Since the ישר (upright persons) has disappeared, the ones who are sarcastically called the upright (ישר) of the nation (who are in fact wicked) are comparable to a thorn hedge (ממסוכה). Perhaps this intertwining of thorns continues the rhetoric of the preceding verse, "and they weave it together." Marvin A. Sweeney aptly describes this intertwining of thorns, "Goodness and righteousness are so interwoven or tangled up with evil that they become like thorn bushes that are impossible to untangle."[133]

Verse 4b thus speaks of the punishment and confusion of these treacherous leaders on account of their intrigue and avarice. The judgement is described in the form of an enemy attack designed to punish Judah. The time when this devastation will take place is syntactically stressed as "the day of your watchmen." Usually, watchmen on the walls of fortified cities would blow an alarm when an enemy approaches. Biblical prophets regard themselves as Yahweh's watchmen who sounded spiritual alarms to caution the people of impending danger (Jer 6:17; Ezek 3:17; 33:2, 6, 7; Hos 9:8). According to verse 4b, that day of portended punishment that the prophets warned about (cf. Isa 10:3; 37:3) has arrived.[134] One obvious outcome of this divine visitation, of an appointed day of judgement, is the moment of their confusion; it shall be a time of confusion against the wicked.

4.3.3. Fragmented Appetite and Self-interest (7:5–6)

> Do not trust in a neighbor;
>> do not have confidence in a companion.
> From the woman who lies in your bosom;
>> guard the doors of your mouth.

---

[132] Nogalski, *Book of the Twelve*, 578.
[133] Sweeney, *Twelve Prophets*, 408.
[134] Dempster, *Micah*, 176; Jenson, *Obadiah, Jonah, Micah*, 181.

4. Religious Unfaithfulness and Community Moral Depravity

> For the son treats his father contemptuously,
>   a daughter rebels against her mother,
>   a daughter-in-law against her mother-in-law.
> A man's enemies are the people of his own household.

In view of the arrival of the day of portended punishment emanating from the conditions they have created for themselves, the appropriate attitude under the inevitable result is social disintegration and universal suspicion, for no one can be trusted.[135] The subunit begins with a new chain of imperatives that presuppose the crisis of judgement. The imperatives describe the state of society in terms that point to the breakdown of social solidarity and interpersonal relationship and responsibility. Obviously, there is confusion and social disorder in the city and society is characterized by anarchy.[136] The illustration of instances of failure moves through structures of intimacy that begin from proportionate relationships (7:5a) and increasingly into more and more disproportionate, traditionally oriented hierarchical relationships that culminate with that of the master to his family members.[137] The imperatives in verse 5 deal with the situation, beginning with two prohibitions (7:5a) and then with a positive charge (7:5b). Verse 6 serves as the explanation for the imperatives.

In verse 5, one finds three descriptions of intimate relations, in which trust cannot be guaranteed even to the closest. The רע (friend) is a neighbor (NJB, REB, NASB) or fellow member of the covenant community. The אלוף (companion) is an intimate friend (BDB 48; Prov 2:17; 16:28; 17:9; Jer 13:21), on account of whose betrayal the psalmist mourned bitterly (Ps 55:14). The closest of all is the relation between husband and wife; "from the woman who lies in your bosom." The noun חיק (bosom, embrace) is an aspect of the body that has sexual connotations (Gen 16:5, cf. 1 Kgs 1:2; Deut 13:17; 28:54, 56, cf. Prov 5:20; BDB 301), and the charge שמר פתחי־פיך (guard the doors of your mouth) is a metaphorical description of the lips as being the dual doors that allow speeches to proceed from the mouth. The metaphor portrays the individual "as a guarded house in a dangerous town, full of those who are looking for hostages to seize and use to the harm of the owner."[138] These warnings obviously reinforce the previous lament over a total collapse of society (7:2–4). No doubt, for a people whose very existence, identity, security, and happiness found expression above all in such intimate relationships within the community, this situation of polarization and suspicion is indeed a portrayal of agony and torment.

---

[135] Hillers, *Micah*, 85.
[136] Waltke, *Commentary on Micah*, 428.
[137] Ben Zvi, *Micah*, 169.
[138] Jenson, *Obadiah, Jonah, Micah*, 181.

Verse 6 continues with additional crescendo of intensification with pairs of asymmetrical, traditionally oriented hierarchical relationships to which the arrangement is one of hostile intimacy. According to Mays, "the stability and harmony of the basic family unit was of such crucial value to the Israelite (cf. Exod 20:12; 21:15, 17; Deut 21:18–19; Lev 20:9; Prov 20:20) that its disintegration by insolence and rebellion seemed the worst manifestation of times of woe."[139] The paradigmatic size of a family unit that realizes all the possible relationship has five significant members: a father-husband who is the head of the family, directly related to his wife (7:5) and his son (7:6); a wife-mother, wife of the head of the family and so related to her husband (7:5) and in charge of the women of the subsequent generation (daughter and daughter-in-law, 7:6); a son (7:6), a daughter (responsible to her mother 7:6), and a son's wife (7:6) who is related more directly to her mother-in-law.[140]

In this network of relationships, the closest lines of responsibility and authority are between the same members of the two sexes; males and females, who would spend most of their time together in exercising their respective tasks, most of which usually differed significantly for males and females. The unit reflects the authority structure as well as the living arrangements; the man is over his wife and son, and the wife is over daughter and daughter-in-law. According to the law, children are expected to honor and respect their parents (Exod 20:12; Lev 20:9) and an unruly son deserves death (Deut 21:18–21). The situation in Mic 7:6a is different, "for the son treats his father contemptuously." The verb נבל (to treat disdainfully, to be senseless, foolish, BDB 614) is used only five times, once to describe one who exalts himself as foolish. In the *piel* stem, it is used four times to express disgust or contempt (Deut 32:15), or to treats one's father contemptuously (Mic 7:6a). God makes vile the recalcitrant (Nah 3:6). The prophet prays to ward off God's wrath so that he will not disgrace the throne of his glory (Jer 14:21). If the nuance is correct, the son treats his father contemptuously as a fool, probably in public (cf. Gen 9:25; 2 Sam 15). Furthermore, Mic 7:6a reveals that the close relationship between mother and daughter in this network of family relationship and responsibility would make insubordination an even more appalling contrast: "a daughter rebels against her mother." While a daughter-in-law ought to respect and submit to her mother-in-law (cf. Ruth 1), here in 7:6a is a reversal: "a daughter-in-law against her mother-in-law."[141] These graphic illustrations of the breakdown in the fabric of society and family serve as particular examples of the principle in the last clause of 7:6b: איבי איש אנשי ביתו (a man's enemies are the people of his own household).

---

[139] Mays, *Micah*, 152.
[140] Andersen and Freedman, *Micah*, 569.
[141] Jenson, *Obadiah, Jonah, Micah*, 182.

4. Religious Unfaithfulness and Community Moral Depravity

What Micah presents in this unit (7:1-6) is a picture of anarchy, disorder, greed, distrust, and enmity, where the greatest loyalty a person has is to self and self-preservation. The prophet laments the moral condition of the nation in which he lives, at every level of society, from government to family. There is the obvious dearth of righteous people in the land (7:1-2), and the leaders are especially responsible for afflicting the weak and vulnerable in order to enhance their own fortunes (7:3). However, their punishment is sure (7:4) but their sins have shattered the moral and familial fabric of their society; the collapse of the basic family structure is both the result of a breakdown of society in general (7:2-4) and a cause of it. For Micah, in such an environmental situation the remnant cannot trust even the closest members of their households (7:5-6).

5

ETHICAL BURDENS IN MICAH'S ORACLES

> The nation's morals are like its teeth, the more decayed they are the more it hurts to touch them.
> —George Bernard Shaw

The basic task of this chapter is to identify and synthesize the ethical burdens of the analyzed oracle units in the book of Micah. Ethics is a reflective discipline concerning moral character and conduct. According to John Barton, ethics "may mean one of two closely related things. The moral code of a society, and thus be more or less synonymous with 'morality'.... But it may also be used to refer to reflection on morality from a philosophical perspective, and thus be equivalent to 'moral philosophy'; and in this sense it is clear that not all societies have 'ethics.'"[1] Varied scholarly discussions exist regarding the relevance and/or the applicability of the Bible in contemporary ethical formulation. Hector Avalos, for example, holds that the biblical ideas are "no longer viewed as valuable, applicable, and/or ethical."[2] Avalos's argument is based on the fact that the Bible is a relic of an ancient civilization, confined to the ancient times and no longer has relevance for contemporary societies. Thus, for him, the biblical customs, traditions, values, or ethical motivations are irrelevant for today.

While Avalos's criticism remains, there exist interesting discussions concerning the significance of the ethics of the Hebrew Bible/Old Testament for modern communities.[3] Although the significance of Hebrew Bible/Old Testa-

---

[1] Barton notes that while "German has a useful distinction between *Ethos* (an actual moral code or system) and *Ethik* (the study of moral philosophy or the theory of ethics)," it is not easy to draw such lexical distinction in English. John Barton, *Ethics in Ancient Israel* (Oxford: Oxford University Press, 2014), 1.
[2] Hector Avalos, *The End of Biblical Studies* (Amherst: Prometheus, 2007), 17.
[3] Emily Arndt, *Demanding our Attention: The Hebrew Bible as a Source for Christian Ethics* (Grand Rapids: Eerdmans, 2011), 5–7, 21; Andrew Sloane, *At Home in a Strange*

ment ethics for modern communities' reflection may not completely imply sufficiency alone, in this chapter the indispensability and the necessity of the descriptive paradigm will serve as a basis for an inherently prescriptive application of Micah's ethical concern for contemporary Christian ethical engagement in this chapter. A descriptive paradigm identifies various structures such as Christian Frevel's suggested outline of ethics *of, in, from/based on*, and *with* in the Hebrew Bible which he systematically pooled together and finally approached prescriptively based on the Hebrew Bible.[4] The texts of Hebrew Bible/Old Testament are of essential religious character. In this regard, the identification and discussion of ethical burdens will be described theologically. Indeed, theology and ethics are indivisible in the Hebrew Bible/Old Testament. Henry McKeating puts it thus, "Old Testament ethics is a theological construction, a set of rules, ideals and principles theologically motivated throughout and in large part religiously sanctioned."[5]

The Hebrew Bible/Old Testament does provide a basis for ethical reflection; but at the same time, it is considered not so much a document for ethical consideration since it usually makes recourse to invoking conformity to commands. Such ethical living usually implies obedience to prescriptions, coming from a deity, a prophet, or a parent, since the literature reflects a system of communal living rather than individual ethical life.[6] One's reflection on the instructions or commands given to Israel in the Hebrew Bible/Old Testament presumed and presented her as a potential ethical paradigm for developing a Christian ethos that would inspire fresh and practical expressions of an ethical, religious and community life today. Such an assumption and presentation of Israel as a paradigm for inspiring a moral community is rooted in her historical experience and relationship to God.[7] The theological and God-centered nature of

---

Land: Using the Old Testament in Christian Ethics (Peabody, MA: Hendrickson, 2008), 29–31.

[4] Christian Frevel, "Orientierung! Grundfragen einer Ethik des Alten Testaments," in *Mehr als Zehn Worte? Zur Bedeutung des Alten Testaments in ethischen Fragen*, ed. Christian Frevel, Quaestiones disputatae 273 (Freiburg: Herder, 2015), 9–57.

[5] Henry McKeating, "Sanctions against Adultery in Ancient Israelite Society, with Some Reflections on Methodology in the Study of Old Testament Ethics," *JSOT* 11 (1979): 70.

[6] Philip R. Davies, "Ethics and the Old Testament," in *The Bible in Ethics: The Second Sheffield Colloquium*, ed. John W. Rogerson, Margaret Davies and M. Daniel Carroll R., JSOTSup 207 (Sheffield: Sheffield Academic, 1995), 165.

[7] The term *Israel*, according to Birch, "relates to different socio-political or institutional forms, some historical, some shaped by the canonical traditions (wilderness wanderers, tribal federation, nation, socio-cultural group, religious community). But in all of the traditions these forms reflect, Israel is the community which serves as the shaper of moral identity, the bearer of moral tradition, the locus of moral deliberation and the agent of moral action." See Bruce C. Birch, "Divine Character and the Formation of Moral Com-

5. Ethical Burdens

ethics in the Hebrew Bible/Old Testament is considered as a response to Yahweh's grace, which patterns, stimulates and invests the action of Israel. Thus Israel is viewed as "a 'paradigm' of God's purpose for human community as a whole."[8] As a consequence, the best way for one to appreciate Hebrew Bible/Old Testament ethics is to identify with Israel's point of view and seek to understand how they grasped and embodied their relationship with Yahweh, and how that perspective modeled their ethical standard as a covenant community.[9] Essentially, the justification for ethical responsibility in the Hebrew Bible/Old Testament is compliance and commitment to Yahweh's will as declared. Such justification is furthermore embedded in the festive cultic community. Obviously, the several and different phases of Israel's existence would have necessitated a different context for ethics. However, the general point, as Barton notes, is "that lifestyle and social organization help to determine ethical outlook, remains entirely valid, and should rein in any tendency to complete skepticism about the development of ethical thinking."[10] Israel's morality can thus be viewed not as static but as something that developed in a logical and coherent manner.[11]

With respect to Israel's constitution of a standard of ethical conduct in the Hebrew Bible/Old Testament,[12] emphasis is placed on the Pentateuch which provides the foundation and basic information for its framework. Specific examples for insights are the legal system and ethical rules in the Decalogue (Exod 20:1–17; Deut 5:6–21), Covenant Code (Exod 20:22–23:33), Deuteronomic Law (Deut 12–26) and Holiness Code (Lev 17–26).[13] Eckart Otto sees most of Deuteronomy as importantly ethical, in many respects the center of Hebrew Bible/Old Testament ethics. In one of his essays, "Human Rights: The Influence of the Hebrew Bible," Otto notes how Deuteronomy presents a demand for a just ordering of society in a manner that Yahweh desired: "The Deuteronomic programme of social ethics did not provide for institutions of

---

munity in the Book of Exodus," in *The Bible in Ethics: The Second Sheffield Colloquium*, ed. John W. Rogerson, Margaret Davies, and M. Daniel Carroll R., JSOTSup 207 (Sheffield: Sheffield Academic, 1995), 119.

[8] Sloane, *At Home in a Strange Land*, 30.

[9] Christopher J. H. Wright, *Old Testament Ethics for the People of* God (Leicester: InterVarsity, 2006), 17.

[10] Barton, *Ethics in Ancient Israel*, 9.

[11] Barton, *Ethics in Ancient Israel*, 10.

[12] Barton discusses various sources of ethics in Hebrew Bible/Old Testament to include: wisdom literature, law, narrative, prophecy, psalms, and apocalyptic. Barton, *Ethics in Ancient Israel*, 17–39.

[13] See, Eckart Otto, "Of Aims and Methods in Hebrew Bible Ethics," *Semeia* 66 (1995): 162; Otto, "Myth and Hebrew Ethics in the Psalms," in *Psalms and Mythology*, ed. Dirk J. Human, LHBOTS 462 (London: T&T Clark, 2007), 26; Joseph Jensen, *Ethical Dimensions of the Prophets* (Collegeville: Liturgical, 2006), 20.

the state as being responsible for the political process. It denounced any coercion for the sake of social solidarity in society, but it trusted in the insight of the addressees, so that Deuteronomy did not speak in terms of legal prescription but rather as exhortation."[14]

The wisdom books are not negligible in the discussion of Hebrew Bible/Old Testament ethics. Except for the Ten Commandments, people outside the theological world think first, in connection with Israel's ethics, of the wisdom books (especially Proverbs and Ecclesiastes). The justification of this position is based on the fact that "these books are clearly designed to give advice on how to live and to observe the (alleged) moral order in the world; and they provide encouragement to practice virtue and incentives to avoid vice."[15] Although varied ethical instructions are found in the wisdom literature as well as the law codes, the literary nature of the wisdom literature was basically linked to the theological conversation that concerns the establishment of ethical instructions and the implications of moral behavior.[16]

As one approaches the prophetic literature, the theological traditions that strengthened prophetic ethics in the Hebrew Bible/Old Testament are primarily the wisdom.[17] Nevertheless, prophetic oracles that were preoccupied with moral issues cannot be restricted to certain traditions with a theological emphasis. Biblical prophecy does not approach ethics in a theoretical manner. The biblical prophets announced oracles within an ethical society that was characterized by diverse and manifold range of theological emphases. They were motivated in this direction, possibly having been influenced by such moral context declared prophetic oracles out of the pain and confusion of the Babylonian deportations and the destruction of Jerusalem.[18] Consequently, the prophetic books are a source of ethics in their own right. This is clearly demonstrated in the survey of M. Daniel Carroll R. where he notes that, "the prophetic literature is a rich resource for ethics, whether the goal is to describe the ethical thinking and moral behavior of ancient Israel (or of the authors of the books), or the purpose is to probe the Prophetic Books for contemporary ethical guidance."[19]

Since Israel is viewed as a paradigm of God's purpose, Yahweh speaks to them through the prophets. Though they arrived with a specific word for a spe-

---

[14] Eckart Otto, "Human Rights: The Influence of the Hebrew Bible," *JNSL* 25.1 (1999): 14.
[15] Barton, *Ethics in Ancient Israel*, 17–18.
[16] See Alphonso Groenewald, "Ethics of the Psalms: Psalm 16 within the Context of Psalms 15–24," *JSem* 18.2 (2009): 422; Barton, *Ethics in Ancient Israel*, 18.
[17] Barton, *Ethics in Ancient Israel*, 36.
[18] M. Daniel Carroll R., "Ethics," in *Dictionary of the Old Testament Prophets*, ed. Mark J. Boda and J. Gordan McConville (Downers Grove: InterVarsity, 2012), 186–87.
[19] Carroll, "Ethics," 191.

cific time, they nevertheless always reminded the people of Israel's story and their covenant relationship with Yahweh, which necessitated the people's faithful response. The prophets' moral teachings often take the form of condemnation rather than recommendation. Thus to reconstruct their moral code one has to look not only at "what they commended, but at what they condemned."[20] This is why prophetic texts are seen by many as being at the heart of what the Old Testament has to say about ethics.[21] Although contention still exists, especially in German speaking scholarship, regarding the prophetic tradition of "moral *denunciation* rather than moral *instruction*," Barton notes that "obviously anyone who denounces moral failings in others must have a set of moral convictions."[22]

The prophets, frequently driven by an absolute conviction of God's sovereignty and holiness, in resistance to unfaithfulness, articulate views of responsibility, self-determination, and social order that are still contested in contemporary ethical discourse. Essentially, the theological axioms of Yahweh's sovereignty and the responsibility of all people in covenant community to this sovereign God are the basis for the ethical framework and burdens in the book of Micah. The following subsections are a descriptive articulation of the basic ethical burdens in the book of Micah particularly within the scope of the analyzed oracle units.

5.1. Yahweh's Sovereignty and the Concern for Justice

Although Yahweh's sovereignty is one subject that creates differences of opinion among biblical scholars and Christian communities today, it could be defined as,

> God's power to do anything that is neither logically incoherent nor inconsistent with God's moral perfection. A singular exercise of his divine omnipotence is found in the divine creation of the universe *ex-nihilo*, out of nothing. Omnipotence also entails the ability to perform miracles, actions that lie beyond the natural potentialities of created being.[23]

---

[20] Barton, *Ethics in Ancient Israel*, 36.
[21] This is, however, not the case with Eckart Otto who completely omitted the ethical potential of narrative and prophetic texts, which are all together essential components of the Old Testament. Eckart Otto, *Theologische Ethik des Alten Testaments* (Stuttgart, Berlin, Cologne: Kohlhammer, 1994), cited in Barton, *Ethics in Ancient Israel*, 16.
[22] Barton, *Ethics in Ancient Israel*, 16.
[23] William Hasker, "The Problem of Evil in Process Theism and Classical Free Will Theism," *Process Studies* 29.2 (2000): 195.

Yahweh's universal sovereignty and uniqueness is well acknowledged. His absolute independence allows him to do whatever he pleases (Isa 46:9–18; Dan 4:34–35). This is why Israel's speech about Yahweh regularly affirms Yahweh's capacity to create and establish, govern and direct, in a fashion that confirms Yahweh's comprehensive sovereignty which at the same time assures a reliable and consistent direction of life and events in the world (cf. Job 42:2). According to Walter Brueggemann, Israel's all-encompassing and most generalized doxologies are found in the declaration of Yahweh's unequalled power; namely, Yahweh's potential to affirm sovereignty: "Indeed who is like Yahweh ... there is none like Yahweh."[24] This confessional declaration presents Yahweh as an actively functioning agent who is preeminently the subject of dynamic actions and thus acts in decisively convincing and transformative ways.[25] Of course, Yahweh's sovereignty underscores a concern for justice. Even though biblical data on justice are varied[26] and operate within wider religious and cultural worldviews,[27] the concern for justice is basic in every discussion regarding socioeconomic issues in every aspect of ancient Israel's manifold social space. As it is frequently used in biblical texts, justice is a call for action more than it is a principle of evaluation[28] (cf. Job 29:16; Isa 58:6; Jer 21:12). To be regarded as just, one must be seen as an active investor in community with a unique demonstration of concern and responsiveness to the needy and helpless.[29]

From the essential structures of Israel's covenant community, and at a basic level, justice is social (or distributive) or punitive (or criminal). Social justice deals with how opportunities, entitlements, and other privileges are allocated among individuals, and punitive justice focuses on how misconduct is discerned and punished. Much of what the Bible says about social (distributive) justice is directly related to punitive (retributive) justice. Commenting on biblical justice as an "essentially retributive conception of corrective justice," Chris Marshall notes:

> As a justification for inflicting punishment, retributive justice requires that the recipient must be *guilty* of wrongdoing ... and that the pain of the penalty must

---

[24] Walter Brueggemann, *Theology of the Old Testament* (Minneapolis: Fortress, 1997), 268.
[25] Walter Brueggemann, "Crisis-Evoked, Crisis-Resolving Speech," *BTB* 24.3 (1994): 95.
[26] It is found in the historical, legal, prophetic, and wisdom literature, and in the Psalms as well. Christopher J. H. Wright, *Old Testament Ethics for the People of God* (InterVarsity, Leicester, 2006), 253.
[27] Chris Marshall, "Divine Justice as Restorative Justice," *Center for Christian Ethics* (2012): 12. https://www.baylor.edu/content/services/document.php/163072.pdf.
[28] Stephen Charles Mott, *A Christian Perspective on Political Thought* (Oxford: Oxford University Press, 1993), 79.
[29] Walter Brueggemann, *Reverberations of Faith: A Theological Handbook of Old Testament Themes* (Louisville: Westminster John Knox, 2002), 177.

be *proportionate* to the seriousness of the crime (the principle of equivalence). In these circumstances the imposition of punishment is not only appropriate, it is morally *necessary* in order to satisfy the objective standards of justice (the principle of justice). Understood in this way, many justice theorists conceive of retributive justice as a moral alternative to revenge and as a check against arbitrary or excessive punishment.[30]

Although justice is essentially a question of world-order in the ancient Near East, Israel understands justice not as an abstract concept or a philosophical theory but as fundamentally theological. "It was rooted in the character of the LORD, their God; it flowed from his action in history; it was demanded by his covenant relationship with Israel; it would ultimately be established on earth only by his sovereign power."[31] The whole concept of justice is firmly entrenched in the covenantal framework of Israel's historical relationship with Yahweh. This covenantal and historical relationship made it possible for Israel to understand Yahweh's concern for justice and their comprehensive universalization of the affirmation (Mic. 6:8; cf. Ps 33:5). The urgency of justice was an urgency of aiding and emancipating the victims of oppression. The idea of justice and its interrelated concepts informed Israel's prophetic exhortation and encouragement communication as they act as intermediaries between God, kings, and covenant people.[32] It is used to evaluate social and economic relationships in covenant community (cf. Isa 1:11–17; Jer 22:3, 15–16; Amos 5:21–25).

One of the most persuasive ethical burdens of the book of Micah is Yahweh's sovereignty that revolves around two basic moral issues: judgement of Israel and Judah (1:2–3:12; 6:1–7:6) and restoration of God's people (4:1–5:15). The oracles open with the divine messenger's announcement of a theophany that invites the world to give attention as the king of the universe leaves his throne room (1:2–4), in his sovereign power to judge Samaria and Jerusalem (1:5).[33] While the theophany of 1:2–4 is specifically connected with the judgement of Samaria (1:5–7) and Jerusalem (1:8–16), the book's oracles end with Micah's penetrating rhetorical question, "who is like Yahweh?" (7:18). Such an ending depicts Yahweh's sovereignty in terms of mercy, forgiveness, cessation from anger, pardon, defeat of sin and eradication of evil.[34]

---

[30] Marshall, "Divine Justice as Restorative Justice," *13*.
[31] Wright, *Old Testament Ethics for the People of God*, 254.
[32] Hershey H. Friedman, "Messages from the Ancient Prophets: Lessons for Today," *IJHSS* 1.20 (2011): 297–305; M. Daniel Carroll R., "A Passion for Justice and the Conflicted Self: Lessons from the Book of Micah," *JPC* 25.2 (2006): 169–76; Carroll, "Ethics," 185–93.
[33] Leslie C. Allen, *The Books of Joel, Obadiah, Jonah and Micah*, NICOT (Grand Rapids: Eerdmans, 1976), 253–54.
[34] Dempster, *Micah*, 197.

Yahweh's supreme and unparalleled sovereignty which first finds expression in the meaning of Micah's name, "who is like Yahweh?" constitutes an essential ethical cornerstone in the book of Micah. Yahweh's sovereignty in Micah's oracles implies his supreme and ultimate power and wisdom in dealing with every form of evil that violates his moral order. The supreme and incomparable sovereign ruler of the world will judge all evil and nothing will escape his justice. As a God of justice, Yahweh does not allow evil to go unpunished. The frequency of punishment in Micah's oracles indicates Yahweh's commitment to justice which obviously corresponds to transgressions against societal order. The oracles hint at specifics of societal oppression and express anger at such infidelity of injustice in some of the most remarkable expressions of emotion in the literary prophetic book. They accentuate that such unfaithfulness of injustice was not just a moral matter; the one God of covenant demands justice, and the welfare of the poor, voiceless and powerless was the greatest index of covenant faithfulness. So, Micah denounced unjust rulers, greedy merchants and complacent rich, corrupt judges, prophets, and priests, and deplored social violence and the contamination of the social and familial order. The high point of his condemnation, however, was aimed at those who took solace in extravagant rituals and ceremonies but violated their social responsibility.

Although he predicted the destructive theophany that burst into flames a path of destruction in the northern and southern kingdoms (Mic 1), the concern for those who have become victims of injustice, namely the socially disadvantage and hapless poor, provokes Micah's deep and terrible swath of judgement in the second chapter. In Mic 2:1–5, the denunciation of the social evils of greed and violence highlights the multi-layered picture of a cold-hearted indulgence that violated Yahweh's blueprint for healthy covenant community living. The people have been disposed of their homes and estates on account of the covetous and greedy land-grabbling of the wealthy elite. Such violation of people's economic assets obviously evoked a cause-and-effect theology. These reprehensible acts were an affront on Yahweh's character and an attack on the basic ethical structure of his people in covenant community.[35]

The rhetorical development indicates that Yahweh does not put up with attitudes that are unethical. The connection between the literary form and ethical thrust makes the unit very stimulating. His soaring indictments and judgement sentences, provoked by the inner social ills of the people of Judah,[36] acknowledge the realization of Yahweh's sovereign rule in judgement by affirm-

---

[35] Carroll, "Passion for Justice and the Conflicted self, 171; Hillers, *Micah*, 33.
[36] Carr, *Introduction to the Old Testament*, 120.

ing the innocent and punishing the guilty.[37] Instructively, the understanding of justice as originating from the background of obvious violations of the traditional moral and social solidarities resulting from the covenant, which form the essential fabric of society, dominates the denunciations of Mic 3:1–12. The clear intention of the texts with all the embedded self-citations is to condemn the addressees who are described in positions of authority (positions associated in the world of the text with sinful leaders) and to declare Yahweh's judgement, occasioned by their actions, including the destruction of Zion/Jerusalem.[38] The judgement sentences highlight the essential value of justice and virtue as the primary standard by which one can judge the magnificence and permanence of a nation, and of the genuine foundations of societal structure. The absence of these basic criteria results in the immediate collapse of the social edifice with the entrance of social vice.[39]

5.2. Responsible Leadership and Accountability

The phenomenon of leadership in biblical texts is capable of different definitions that encompass forms, dimensions, and aspects. Katharina Pyschny and Sarah Schulz remark that the definition of leadership in "ancient *Traditionsliteratur*" (traditional literature) is complicated due to its interactions with ideas such as legitimacy, power, and authority, as well as various forms (such as monarchy, oligarchy, democracy, theocracy, hierocracy), dimensions (such as social, religious, political) and related aspects (e.g., guidance, management, delegation, participation, office, succession, institutionalization).[40] In the broadest sense of the term, leadership may be defined as "'the power or ability to lead other people,' but also more specifically as any way of public guidance, direction, management, stewardship, and governance including military-political decision making."[41]

---

[37] David J. Reimer, "The Prophet Micah and Political Society," in *Thus Speaks Ishtar of Arbela: Prophecy in Israel, Assyria, and Egypt in the Neo-Assyrian Period*, ed. Robert P. Gordon and Hans M. Barstad (Winona Lake, IN: Eisenbrauns, 2013), 216.
[38] Ben Zvi, *Micah*, 87.
[39] Alfaro, *Justice and Loyalty*, 38.
[40] For a discussion on various forms, dimensions, and aspects of leadership in the Hebrew Bible/Old Testament see, Katharina Pyschny and Sarah Schulz, "Debating Authority—Concepts of Leadership in the Pentateuch and the Former Prophets: An Introduction," in *Debating Authority: Concepts of Leadership in the Pentateuch and the Former Prophets*, ed. Katharina Pyschny and Sarah Schulz (Berlin: De Gruyter, 2018), 4.
[41] Christian Frevel, "Leadership and Conflict: Modelling the Charisma of Numbers," in Pyschny and Schulz, *Debating Authority*, 89.

From the foregoing, one could differentiate subjects (leaders), structures of leadership (institutions) and means of leadership (guidance). But in view of the complexity of the multiplicity of various and occasionally conflicting theories of leadership in the literary scope of the Hebrew Bible/Old Testament, the attempt here is to examine some precise relationships and contrasts in the typology of leadership functionaries mentioned in Micah's speeches. There is no denying the fact that leadership is an essential and central concern in the book of Micah. The typology of leadership offices and functionaries like judges (rulers and leaders), prophets, and priests is especially hinted at in Micah's oracles. The speeches, most especially 3:1–12; 6:1–16; 7:3–4, indicate genuine personal confrontation with leaders who appeared to be "power brokers" of the socioeconomic, political, and religious establishment of the time. The rhetoric of Micah indicates an intriguing and stimulating perspective on the chain of relationship found among these leaders, their followers/community, and the circumstances created by their leadership approaches.

From the synchronic perspective of the texts (3:1–12; 6:1–16; 7:3–4), these units and their subunits demonstrate remarkable interest in the comprehensive failure of the leaders in the administration of their duties and responsibilities. Micah's indictments highlight and connect several aspects of the contemptible catalogue of moral deficiency and decadence these leaders established and perpetuated in their society.

5.2.1. Perversion of Justice in the interest of Materialism

Micah's denunciations indicate a nation that had a dearth of virtuous and competent leadership. In the litany of comprehensive condemnation, the first subunit (3:1–4) of the indictment of the leadership in Jerusalem is directed at the judicial officials. The rhetorical flow of Mic 3:1–4 unfolds relatively clearly, as Micah uses gruesome and shocking metaphors to sensitize as well as invite them into reality. The unit speaks of the leaders of Jerusalem as heads of their people and "leaders/rulers of the house of Israel,"[42] who by following God's standards of right and wrong (cf. Deut 1:13–17) are to administer justice. In the Pentateuch and former Prophets, the hierarchy that existed between specific leadership functions is not easily determined. According to Frevel, the frequent references to elders in the book of Exodus (3:16, 18; 4:29; 12:21; 17:5–6; 18:12; 19:7; 24:1, 9, 13; cf. Lev 4:15; 9:1) indicate representative roles rather than functionary positions. However, the combination of the parallel stories of Exod 18 with Num 11, which share similar aspects and are both connected by redactional rewriting, brings together the group of seventy elders that were chosen by Moses

---

[42] See explanations on the parallel terms ראש (heads) and קצין (rulers) in the exegesis section.

on Yahweh's behalf. These elders are described as "office holders, officials, or administrative functionaries" (Num 11:16).[43]

The narrative of Exod 18:21 which is based on Jethro's counsel to Moses designates men of unquestionable integrity and influence, who fear God, are reliable and trustworthy, and hate dishonest and unjust practices. They are to judge the people at all times and are thus described as "officials, functionaries" (Exod 18:22). Although the elders do not have a share in institutionalized leadership in the book of Exodus, when Num 11 is read against the background of Exod 18, these elders become judges (Exod 18:22).[44] In the event of the nation's growth, the legal codes functioned as foundational principles and as collections of judgements that were examples of how Israel was to conduct itself as a society. These judgements, sometimes contextually embedded as implicit commentaries on the function of torah, constituted the legislative arm of Israel's judicial system. Accordingly, Israel's tribal representatives who are chosen as appointees from the community as judges[45] were to thoughtfully deliberate and execute justice by ensuring that Yahweh's ways find justifiable expression and application in society.[46] Generally, people will bring their cases to a judge, who is expected to make informed judgement (cf. Judg 4:5; 2 Sam 15:2). Consequently, the exhortation is normally and repeatedly given not to pervert justice by showing favoritism in judgement (Deut 1:17; cf. Prov 18:5; 24:23) or accepting a bribe (cf. Deut 16:18–19; Prov 17:23). Since the right and executive administration of justice is necessary for the flourishing of a covenant society, justice would not only be implemented in the courts but would be carried out within society in general. It was to be the essential responsibility of the powers within society.[47]

Micah's picture of his contemporaries indicates leadership functionaries whose duty was the administration of justice. He castigates the political and judicial officials in Israel who were supposed to render the appropriate verdicts and ensure their implementation. They were expected to be acquainted with what was right and equitable so as to ensure that the marginalized were not oppressed by the powerful. Contrarily, Micah's condemnation indicates that criminals have taken the reins of the courts and government and that vice has become virtue. Micah pictures these leaders as tyrants who have a strong pas-

---

[43] Frevel, "Leadership and Conflict," 91–92.
[44] Frevel, "Leadership and Conflict," 92.
[45] For the representative structure of leadership, see Frevel, "Leadership and Conflict," 94–95.
[46] The collection of judgements and commitment to the torah is regarded as the embodiment of Yahweh's way. Thus, texts mediating on torah and implementing it are viewed as providing direction for the righteous. Dempster, *Micah*, 208.
[47] Dempster, *Micah*, 208–9.

sion for evil rather than good (2:2–3). In his bizarre metaphors, the deep depravity of these officials is highlighted: rather than defending justice and protecting human rights, especially the underprivileged Judeans, they aided and abetted the powerful, greedy, land-grabbing wealthy criminals in the Judean society. The report card of the judicial leaders indicate that they were bereft of the ethical requirement of justice (3:1) and thus consistently gave unjust answers to plaintiffs (3:9), having sold their expertise and influence for "a bribe" (3:11). The total corruption of the entire justice system is summarized in 3:11. The rhetoric of 7:2–6 indicates once again an entire society that is in disarray due to lack of virtue and the obvious manifestation of injustice. The oracle rebukes Judah's officials and judges as collaborators in perverting justice. Clearly, the desires of the officials are what the judges deliver for a price. The nation's leaders are driven by avarice and greed.

As was the case with court functionaries, the dedication of office and function to avarice spread like an infection to the dual religious—charismatic (prophets) and cult (priests)—functionaries (3:5–7, 9–11). The basic and normative role of prophet in the Hebrew Bible/Old Testament, ancient Israel and Judah, was that of an intermediary: transmitting Yahweh's word to the people.[48] They undoubtedly and absolutely based their messages upon direct encounter and personal relationship with God and at God's own initiation. The authority of their message (the word of Yahweh) came to them practically as an unbiased, real and definite entity through Yahweh's Spirit (cf. 2 Sam 23:1–3; Ezek 11:5; Mic 3:8),[49] dreams and visions (cf. Num 12:6; Hos 12:10). Consequently, prophets were key personae empowered by God as channels for the transmission of his will to the human society of their time. Their actions and declarations gave their community momentary foretastes of the consequences of the attitude of their leaders.[50] Beyond their involvement in national affairs,[51] prophets coun-

---

[48] Pancratius C. Beentjes, "Constructs of Prophets and Prophecy in the Book of Chronicles," in *Constructs of Prophecy in the Former and Latter Prophets and Other Texts* 4, ed. Lester L. Grabbe and Martti Nissinen (Atlanta: Society of Biblical Literature, 2011), 37.

[49] Johannes Lindblom, *Prophecy in Ancient Israel* (Oxford: Blackwell, 1962), 174–79; Daniel I. Block, "Empowered By the Spirit of God: The Holy Spirit in the Historigraphic Writings of the Old Testament," *SBJT* 1.1 (1997): 43.

[50] Victor H. Matthews, *Social World of the Hebrew Prophets* (Peabody, MA: Hendrickson, 2001), 21–26.

[51] Moses, who is, described as the prophet *per excellence*, or "the prophet of prophets," was national leader. Karel Van der Toorn, *Scribal Culture and the Making of the Hebrew Bible* (London: Harvard University Press, 2007), 34. This description of Moses as a prophet *per excellence* is based on Deut 18:15; 34:10, although his burning bush experience (Exod 3) also suggests a prophetic function. Herbert B. Huffmon, "A Company of Prophets: Mari, Assyria, Israel," in *Prophecy in its Ancient Near Eastern Context: Meso-*

seled and advised kings to walk in the ways of God and most times confronted and challenged them. They were actively involved in significant national moments, like those of political-military catastrophes occasioned by the menace of enemies, internal power conflicts and wars.[52]

A shift of emphasis is however noticeable among the eighth-century prophets.[53] While they still had oracles from God to announce to kings and other leaders of their nations, their prophetic messages were directed more pointedly towards the people and society generally. This may be a result of deteriorating existential challenges confronting the nations. The failure of kings and leaders of the nations to maintain righteousness and justice necessitated prophetic oracles of impending judgment. In this regard, they were basically preachers who announced Yahweh's word with different dramatic and rhetorical means to invite the attention of their listeners and drive home their message.[54] These prophets, when reproaching the political establishment and religious institutions and their leaders, simultaneously indict other prophets and priests. This goes to show that prophets may also have had a formal position like the national leaders.[55] Conse-

---

potamian, Biblical, and Arabian Perspectives, ed. Martti Nissinen, SemeiaSt 13 (Atlanta, Society of Biblical Literature, 2000), 63; Reinhard Achenbach, "'A Prophet like Moses' (Deut 18:15)—'No Prophet like Moses' (Deut 34:10): Some Observations on the Relation between the Pentateuch and the Latter Prophets," in *The Pentateuch: International Perspectives on Current Research*, ed. Thomas B. Dozeman, Konrad Schmid and Baruch J. Schwartz (Tübingen: Mohr Siebeck, 2011), 441.

[52] Before embarking on a military operation, a king consulted with his prophets (1 Kgs 22:6–7; 2 Kgs 3:11). Elisha is said to have given military intelligence delivered to him by God to the king of Israel during his war with Syria (2 Kgs 6:8–12). De Jong, *Isaiah among the Ancient Near Eastern Prophets*, 342.

[53] The eighth-century prophets are otherwise known as classical prophets. Although there appear to be a slight shift in emphasis, it is however difficult to create a clear and significant distinction between them and earlier prophets. See comments by Horst D. Preuss, *Old Testament Theology* (Louisville: Westminster John Knox, 1996), 2:70–73; Rolf Rendtorff, *The Canonical Hebrew Bible: A Theology of the Old Testament*, trans. David E. Orton, Tools for Biblical Study 7 (Leiden: Deo, 2005), 157–62.

[54] The prophets sometimes presented their messages using allegorical forms, parables or "prophetic symbolism." For example, Isaiah went "naked and barefoot" (Isa 20:2–3) to dramatize the fate of the Egyptians and Cushites at the hands of the Assyrians. For other illustrations, see Jer 13:1–11; Ezek 4:1–6. Robin L. Routledge, *Old Testament Theology: A Thematic Approach* (Apollos: Inter-Varsity, 2008), 212–13.

[55] See, for example, Isa 28:7; Jer 2:26; Ezek 7:26; Mic 3:11; Neh 9:32; Zech 7:1–3. The expression "prophet of Israel" (Ezek 13:2) suggests an official position. Aside from Amos 7:14, where there is the reference to a בן־נביא (son of the prophets or member of a prophetic guild), such references are lacking in the classical period. This may imply that all such prophetic groups had become 'official.'

quently, this formal position may have compelled them to compromise with their employers thus lowering the standard of the divine demands.[56]

Within the Hebrew Bible/Old Testament, on the other hand, is the convergence of a broad spectrum of different priestly groups: Levitical, Zadokite, and Aaronic priestly traditions.[57] A pan-Levitical or Deuteronomistic priestly ideology holds that all Levites are priests who are commissioned with the offerings and sacrificial aspects of the cult. The biblical sources for the Levitical priestly traditions are those of Deuteronomy (18:1–8), Jeremiah (33:21), and Malachi (1:6–2:10).[58] Zadokite exclusivism appears in Ezekiel's extreme anti-Levitic polemic and narrowest definition of legitimate priesthood in the Hebrew Bible/Old Testament (Ezek 40:46; 43:19; 44:15–31; 48:11).[59] Aaronic priestly ideologies are developed in priestly sources (Exod 28:40–43; 29:1–9; Num 18:1–4), in Ezra-Nehemiah and Chronicles (Ezra 10:39; Neh 12:44–47; 2 Chr 26:18; 29:21; 31:19; 35:14). Typically, both the Jewish and Christian traditions associate Israel's priestly groups with the temple in Jerusalem. In this tradition, the descendants of Moses's brother, Aaron are regarded as exclusive and distinctive lineage who are dedicated to the worship of Israel's God, and commissioned with the teaching of the knowledge and will of Yahweh. In his examination of priesthood in ancient Israel Mark Leuchter notes:

> The social, textual, mythic and political concerns of Israel's priestly groups are evident throughout the biblical record, and reveal the depth of influence the priesthood exerted not only on the formation of the Bible but on the growth of Israelite religion into early Judaism.… Priests functioned as mediators between the realm of the divine and the realm of common activity and experience.[60]

In light of their communal responsibility and religious interest, the priests' sphere of influence is thus represented and expressed in the temple and every-

---

[56] De Jong, "Fallacy of 'True and False' in Prophecy," 4.

[57] For details of explanation regarding these priestly circles, see Dongshin Don Chang, *Phinehas, the Sons of Zadok, and Melchizedek: Priestly Covenant in Late Second Temple Texts*, LSTS 90 (New York: Bloomsbury T&T Clark, 2016), 55–65.

[58] Saul M. Olyan, "Ben Sira's Relationship to the Priesthood," *HTR* 80 (1987): 273.

[59] Zadokite priestly ideologies are also reflected in Chronicles with Hasmoneans development (1 Chr 24; 29). The non-inclusion of Abiather, one of the pillars of David's priestly establishment, in this record is perhaps due to the assistance of Adonijah rather than Solomon (1 Kgs 1:7; 2:26–27). Alison Schofield and James C. Vanderkam, "Were the Hasmoneans Zadokites?," *JBL* 124 (2005): 86.

[60] Mark A. Leuchter, "The Priesthood in Ancient Israel," *BTB* 40.2 (2010): 100. https://journals.sagepub.com/doi/10.1177/0146107910364344.

thing that is associated with it.⁶¹ Priests were mediators between Yahweh and the larger human population, providing opportunities for individuals, families, groups and communities to make offerings, offer prayer requests and carry out religious responsibilities as occasions demand. Besides their religious function of supervising and guarding the cultic life of the people, priests were also entrusted with judicial responsibility. Priests arbitrated between families and social groups. Their judicial functions, which are preserved in Deut 17:8–13, included issues such as land disputes, marital faithfulness and responsibilities, inheritance, and civil relations. By this function, they maintained the sacredness of daily life within society as much as they regulated and guarded the cultic life of the people.⁶²

One other integral aspect of priestly functions is the educational responsibility. Priestly instructional or pedagogical duty is hinted at in quite a number of biblical materials. Priestly commission to educate the people is found in the priestly material of Lev 10:10–11. Here the priests are charged with the responsibility of establishing a distinction between the holy and the profane, and between the unclean and the clean, and to teach all the children of Israel the statutes which Yahweh has spoken to them through his servant, Moses. Within the background of Moses' blessing in Deuteronomy, the family of Levi is singled out for praise on account of its faithfulness in discharging their instructional responsibility (Deut 33:10). Both prophetic literature (Isa 7:26; Ezek 44:23; Jer 18:18) and historical writings of Ezra-Nehemiah (Ezra 7:10; Neh 8:1–8, 11) and Chronicles (2 Chr 17:7–9) attest to the teaching aspect of the priestly function.⁶³

While prophets and priests functioned in different spheres of the communal and religious life of ancient Israel and Judah, it appears that individual prophets assumed prophetic status in the Jerusalem temple cult together with the priests. This relationship is seen in individual and corporate religious service of lamentation (see, for example, Obadiah, Habakkuk, and Zechariah). The resentful declaration of Jeremiah's opponents (Jer 18:18) indicates that a close relationship existed among the three religious authorities: priests, sages and prophets. The same relationship is emphasized in Ezek 7:26: "they will seek a vision [חזון] from a prophet, but the law [תורה] will be lost from the priest and counsel [עצה] from the elders." Both prophets and priests obviously spoke with authority and evidence of unethical practices is observed in their common element of prophecy and teaching; namely, the giving of תורה (Isa 1:10; 8:16, 20; 30:9; Zech 7:2–14). They announced a number of their communal oracles in the temple's court,

---

⁶¹ Bohdan Hrobon, *Ethical Dimension of the Cult in the Book of Isaiah*, BZAW 418 (Berlin: De Gruyter, 2010), 10.
⁶² Leuchter, "Priesthood in Ancient Israel, 101.
⁶³ Lena-Sofia Tiemeyer, *Priestly Rites and Prophetic Rage: Post-exilic Prophetic Critique of the Priesthood*, FAT 2/19 (Tubingen: Mohr Siebeck, 2006), 113–15.

whether or not they were officially involved in the cult (Jer 7:2; 26:2; 36:5–6; Hos 4:4–5; Amos 7:13; Hag 1:3–12).

The analyses of Micah's oracle units (3:5–7, 9–12) indicate that these religious functionaries (prophets and priests), rather than speaking with the priority and authority of their divine commission and through their common element of prophecy and teaching combined with the judicial leaders and thus traded their sacred commission for symbols of wealth and power. Micah indicts them for deceptively leading the people and perverting Yahweh's word for them. His indictment of deceptive leadership is amply strengthened with supportive evidence of selfishness driving their prophecies, divinations, and teachings. They commercialized their ministries and placed materialistic and economic consciousness far above Yahweh's interests and the concerns of the people they were commissioned to serve. According to Micah, they announce and teach favorable and complimentary messages only and continuously to those who have satisfied their greed with sufficient remunerations.

Contrary to the embodiment of desired characteristics and virtues of justice and righteousness (measuring standard and plumb line) by which both the leaders and the people in covenant community are to be evaluated (Mic 6:8; cf. Isa 28:17), the judicial (political) leaders were perverting justice and the religious leaders (prophets and priests) were perverting Yahweh's word. Micah lambasts these leaders for considering justice as an abominable virtue. Micah's apology (3:8) however, contrasted his self-understanding of ministry with those unjust and thoughtless profiteers. Distinct from these hucksters, he was filled with power and strength (i.e., courage), Yahweh's spirit and justice, which are essentially inseparable; and he was courageous enough to address his nation's wickedness and corruption manifested especially in the sphere of power and influence. He knew that the unfaithfulness of injustice as evidenced in society would be a terrible cancer that would remain untreated unless addressed and put under control. Rather than being influenced by his audience he expressed "God's concern for the oppressed and victims and right order in society, the very things loathed by the leaders of Israel.... It is clear that God ... determined his message."[64]

5.2.2. Abuse of Position, Religious Self-Deception and False Security

One of the thematic cornerstones of Micah's indictments is the abuse of position and privilege in the name of Yahweh. It is observed that personnel of the judicial, political, and religious institutions were men of great influence and power in ancient Israel and Judah's society. The rulers and leaders of Judah, especially

---

[64] Dempster, *Micah*, 116.

judges are to administer justice in society, the priests were to teach, give precise and adequate interpretation of the Law and answer questions relating to religion and rituals without charges (cf. Deut 17:8–11), and the prophets are to relevantly provide well-informed divine guidance. But contrary to expected norms and standards, Micah's indictment reveals how Judah's judicial, charismatic, and cultic leadership grossly abused their position and privilege. Micah decries them for degrading and perverting their sacred commission and function through their disgusting mercenary attitude in discharging their duties. Their failure in providing the required godly leadership led many to wander off in misery and destitution, and consequently their gross and immorality and hypocritical religious practices ultimately necessitated Yahweh's judgment upon them and their nation (3:4, 12).[65]

In addition to abuse of leadership position is a whole system that was sustained by a terrible theological foundation. Micah confronted the insidious strategy of a perverted religion which alienated creed from lifestyle and guarantee grace and peace to transgressors so as to enable them to continue with transgression. He confronted advocates of this theology of cheap grace (2:6) with his informed, intellectual, and rhetorical might. In their self-styled quasi-orthodoxy, they believed that grace would guarantee victory while keeping it away from their own lifestyle. This obviously distorted theology was at home with socioeconomic exploitation of the poor, with unfaithfulness of injustice in the judiciary and in the marketplaces, and with purchasing spiritual and religious approvals. It was easily accompanied by flamboyant demonstrations of religious enthusiasm, including extravagant rituals (6:6–7). Such religious ideology in Micah's perspective defines the leaders as agents of social injustice. The religious hucksters, by their choosy emphasis upon Zion and Yahwistic theology violated and frustrated the genuine intent of the covenant. This form of religious deception was the opium of an influential minority of oppressors that pacified their consciences to disregard their responsibility. It is impracticable, unrealistic, and disastrous and must be condemned in its entire ramification. Accordingly, "Micah's task was the difficult one of attacking not irreligious immorality but the subtle combination of social injustice and a religion which virtually gave it its blessing."[66]

The deficiency of moral integrity among these religious helmsmen of Micah's society is astonishing. Though they belong to a theocracy, they forgot its associated implications. The most incriminating aspect of their attitude is that they claimed to be relying on Yahweh (3:11), while they were obviously violating his laws and holding the people captive. According to Allen, "They saw no inconsistency between selfishly exploiting their wards and sanctimoniously expressing faith in the protective presence of their God. But such promises cannot

---

[65] Nogalski, *Book of the Twelve*, 551.
[66] Allen, "Micah's Social Concern," 26.

exist in a moral vacuum."[67] They presumptuously demonstrated high level religious conviction but such that divorced religion from ethical values of honesty, responsibility and accountability. Truly, their outward religious formalism was devoid of inner religious beauty and reality; the fruits of their lives could not match their sacred commission.

These religious leaders, having lost their sense of spiritual reality and responsibility (3:4, 7) and filled with the spirit of self-sufficiency and self-confidence deceived the people into thinking that their artificial and perverted religious ideology and false sense of security would deliver them from justice and retribution. Micah observes the religious system with shoddy and morally corrupt resources as that which only encouraged materialism and social injustice and would ultimately prove useless. According to Micah, such sheer hypocrisy that stimulates vainglory will incur terrible responsibility. He declares judgement in a climatic manner (3:12) described by Wolff as:

> It is precisely because God is no longer among you that you will experience disaster! The city will be destroyed and ploughed like a field, no one will know where the temple once was because of an overgrown thicket. It will be a place of curse—an abode for the wild animals of the forest.[68]

5.3. Community Relationship and Social Solidarity

While justice is an essential ingredient necessary for the creation and maintenance of a healthy, viable and flourishing covenant society, Micah's rhetoric reveals a society in which lack of justice resulted in fragmented covenant community relationship and unhealthy social solidarity. The social nature of the unfaithfulness of injustice is aptly demonstrated by a listing of its related transgressions: greed, economic piracy, and land confiscation (2:1–2, 8–9), wickedness and commercial corruption (6:10–12), and decadence, meanness, and fragmented family life (7:1–6). These contemptible moral aspects of the community's social relationship and solidarity are discussed below.

5.3.1. Greed, Exploitation and Oppression

The deterioration of moral values did not only cut across those who occupy leadership positions. The whole way of life in Micah's society was overtaken by greed which has been geared toward avid and unsatisfiable consumption, and it has become scandalous. In Micah's rhetoric, this is not an accidental mistake but deliberate, well-calculated and conscious acts of theft of land and dignity (2:1–

---

[67] Allen, "Micah's Social Concern," 28.
[68] Wolff, *Micah*, 108.

2). The substantial change in the economic life of Israel especially during the period of the divided kingdom in which classical prophets ministered obviously made life a bit complicated for them. Craig L. Blomberg identified several factors that affected the socioeconomic life of the people:

> The development of class distinctions under the monarchy, the appearance of a commercial, moneyed class and the growth of a patriciate who lived a life of luxury and self-indulgence and gave not a thought to the miseries of the poor who toiled for them.... Again, the loss of ancestral properties to wealthy aristocrats who bought up vast tracts of land forever altered the economic landscape and widened the gap between rich and poor. The concomitant and growing love of luxury, pretentiousness and ostentatiousness was in striking contrast to the simple unsophisticated and natural life, traditional to old pre-monarchical Israel.[69]

Remarkably, new economic opportunities and influx of wealth in the eighth century brought an increasing rate of oppression of peasants in several agricultural communities of ancient Judah. The concentration of property through land foreclosure and its resultant eviction and confiscation (cf. Deut 27:17; Prov 23:10–11), which were regarded as reprehensible, had become widespread in Micah's time. Earlier, Micah condemned the general sin of covenant unfaithfulness and idolatry in 1:5–7, but the specific transgressions of Israel which have both socioeconomic and theological implications are addressed in 2:2, 8–9. At the socioeconomic level, the rich and powerful land industrialists were trying to get richer at the expense of the poor through their uncontrollable and insatiable greed and thus were destroying the fabric of the Israelite community.

Interestingly, it is not immoral to be wealthy (cf. Prov 22:4); rather, it is scandalously reprehensible to notice that those who do not have much are deprived of what is rightfully theirs by those who are not bothered by their consciences. Micah situates exploitation and oppression of the poor as a fundamental layer in his comprehensive denunciation of the unfaithfulness of injustice. While poverty may be relatively defined and occasionally caused by natural disasters, famine or drought, most certainly the poor in Micah's rhetoric are victims of corruption and exploitation. For Micah, exploitation and oppression of the poor is a principal example of injustice and a clear manifestation of the tragedy of a morally and spiritually corrupt nation. Micah identified covetousness as the foundation of the greed of the people and consequently the forerunner to other sins such as plundering or robbery, grabbing and exploitation (2:2, 8–9). While this is not technically idolatry (1:5), it is obviously a kind of

---

[69] Craig L. Blomberg, *Neither Poverty nor Riches: A Biblical Theology of Material Possessions* (Leicester; England: Apollos, IVP, 1999), 69–70.

idolatry since covetousness reveals the intent of their hearts; their god was Mammon.[70]

Whatever was the method these land industrialists adopted in taking advantage of people's inheritance—lawful or unlawful, it was of no significance under torah's requirement. They were expected to remember so as to give dedicated attention to torah's requirement that "inheritance"[71] remain within the border of families with the intention of ensuring that everyone can own at least reasonable amounts of property.[72] The essential motive of the religiously encouraging law of inheritance was the sole intention of acting as a check upon a situation in the event of the loss of the stipendiary *paterfamilias,* and so there would be no danger that the rest of the family members would starve to death or fall into slavery and the bond of continuity of the family be destroyed (cf. Ruth 3:3, 5).[73] Micah's outrage reveals that several dishonest and unethical maneuvers were designed to concentrate wealth in the hands of few and privileged individuals. The influential (2:1; 7:3) and arrogant (2:3) exploited those who were less privileged. The ethical foundations of the upper-class exploitation of the peasants were rent capitalism—that is, "the paying of rent to one or several owners of the various factors of production,"[74] rather than compassionate commitment to Yahweh's concerns. Such capitalistic ideas made them not only morally reprehensible but theologically contemptible.

Theologically, rather than upholding Yahweh's ownership of the land (Lev 25:23) and the understanding that the Israelites living in covenant community were stewards of Yahweh's gift of land to Israel, they believed that it was the entitlement of anyone who had power and influence to take possession of it at any time.[75] Surprisingly, an interesting reversal is hinted in 2 Kgs 25:12, when Judah's elite are exiled. The failure of the people in their responsibility to recognize this sense of the conditionality of Yahweh's gift of the land to Israel is encapsulated in Micah's sentence of judgement. Distinctively, Micah remarks that all such persons who have been involved in the exploitation of the vulnerable in society would meet Yahweh's judgement and realize that they are without God (2:4–5). He employed the rhetorical tool of hyperbole to make his point; drawing a contrast between wealth and poverty, gain and loss, he directed his

---

[70] Dempster, *Micah*, 94.
[71] By ancient right, a person's "inheritance" (נחלה) belongs to him and it is the prerogative of the family (Lev 25:23–34; 1 Kgs 21:4); Waltke, *Minor Prophets*, 637.
[72] For Israel's property ethics, see Christopher J. H. Wright, *Old Testament Ethics for the People of God* (Leicester: InterVarsity 2004), 207; Wright, *God's People in God's Land: Family, Land, and Property in the Old Testament* (Grand Rapids: Eerdmans, 1990).
[73] Allen, "Micah's Social Concern," 24–25.
[74] Blomberg, *Neither Poverty nor Riches*, 73.
[75] Waltke, *Minor Prophets*, 635.

indictments to those who illegitimately acquired lands and who will be dispossessed of them. This shares obvious similarity with Amos 5 as Hemchan Gossai remarks, "Now, the 'fruitful earth' is no longer providing for the poor, the 'people of the land', but is taken over by the powerful.... The land, as a gift from Yahweh and as an element which is the right of every Israelite, now becomes the exclusive property of the rich."[76]

Yahweh's judgement on these coveters who have schemed in the night to plan and to exploit their neighbors will be the reduction of the rich and powerful to the level of the oppressed and marginalized that they have dispossessed by removing their means of economic survival. Accordingly, all their houses and fields will be given to a violent, heartless enemy who will drive them out of their land and home. They will become landless and homeless in the very precise sense of the word, as they are completely banished from Yahweh's assembly. Truly, there would be a reversal of fortune as the evil they devised will be returned on their own head.[77] However, it is not clear if such reversal includes the return of the exploited lands to their original owners.[78]

5.3.2. Wickedness and Commercial Corruption

Micah's oracle unit in the sixth chapter (6:9–16) makes a quick transition from the sphere of cult to culture, and from the temple to the marketplace. In this transition, one can observe the severance of interests and desires between Yahweh (6:8) and the people (6:10–12). Economic activities of trade and investment usually took place in the marketplace during the day and most people would visit for the purpose of making transactions and socializing with one another. Here, however, the prophetic voice criticizes a development in which the economic center has become so dreadful that neighbors practice cheating rather than compassionate love; personal gain which was founded on corruption flourished. Micah remarks that instead of walking humbly in the ways of Yahweh, traders walk in the statutes of Omri and the practices of the house of Ahab (6:16). Within the context of the oracle, these probably refer to "economic practices associated with these northern kings, 'a law-code of the individualistic

---

[76] Hemchan Gossai, *Justice, Righteousness and the Social Critique of the Eighth Century Prophets* (New York: Lang, 1993), 249.
[77] Dempster, *Micah*, 94.
[78] Hilary Marlow notes, the story of Naboth's vineyard in 1 Kgs 21 reflects a tradition in which an enforced annexation of land has serious consequences for King Ahab. Hilary Marlow, "Justice for Whom? Social and Environmental Ethics and the Hebrew Prophets," in *Ethical and Unethical in the Old Testament: God and Humans in Dialogue*, ed. Katharine J. Dell, LHBOTS 528 (New York: T&T Clark International, 2010), 112.

commercialism which now was displacing the ancient community economy of Israel's past'"[79]

Even ordinary commerce and trade, which were expected to be neutral, regularly turned into an atmosphere of seduction to sin. Normally, there were sanctions inscribed in the ancient Law codes that prohibited dishonest practices, falsehood, cheating, and plundering of neighbors (cf. Lev 19:35, 36; Deut 25:13–16), but it is apparently obvious that cheating was common, and deceits of commerce and trade were practiced with unrestricted liberty. Merchants or traders blatantly adopted unjust practices which perpetually made their houses treasure-troves of wealth. In Micah's rhetoric, this is obviously a false picture of reality. Ironically, their homes are havens of wickedness. Such wealth was acquired by dishonesty and sustained by violence.[80] Micah berates the presence of corrupt merchants or traders in Israel and speaks out against all forms of dishonest measures, fraudulent gains, deception and violence and all wickedness committed against the weak by the wealthy (6:12). Since the entire city was now infested with commercial corruption, and no doubt the responsibility for fraud and corruption was assigned to varying parties, between merchants from both city and country, each attempting to outshine the other in dishonest dealings, Micah's thus announced the enactment of the curses of the covenant (6:13–16) that are a verdict of destruction of the material benefits which are related to these commercial transactions.

Marlow remarks that the effects of "injustice manifest themselves in people as moral and physical sickness, and in the land as destruction and loss of fertility." The fraudulent and dishonest gains would guarantee no satisfactory enjoyment. Yahweh's verdict on such deceptive and violent, wicked behavior is to allow חלה (sickness) and שמם (desolation) "to afflict those who have presumed upon their wealth and status." This is not an abstract punishment but a physical one, affecting not only the people but the ultimate well-being of their land.[81] These people who are only interested in profits, luxury and extravagance will witness frustration and disappointments. These futility curses indicate that the quest for self-satisfaction and fulfillment at the expense of the poor and helpless will lead to unproductive and futile outcomes. Accordingly, Dempster summarizes the underlying theological idea of the futility curse and the ethical import of pointlessness of sin: "Whatever they try to do in the area of acquiring goods to satisfy their senses will not work: eating will not satisfy; saving will be impossible; planting seed will not return a harvest; the olive press will not yield oil; nor will the vat produce wine."[82]

---

[79] Allen, "Micah's Social Concern," 30.
[80] Dempster, *Micah*, 171.
[81] Marlow, "Justice for Whom?," 107.
[82] Dempster, *Micah*, 170.

5.3.3. Decadence, Meanness and Fragmented Family Life

At the heart of Micah's lament is the moral decadence that he witnessed in the beloved city which had lost its genuine spiritual uniqueness and was thus no longer a paradigm to the nations. Micah bemoaned his own frustration and disillusionment with Israel's situation probably in view of the expectation of coming judgement (7:4) and the social and moral conditions of the city which are completely abysmal.[83] His lamentable description of the state of society highlights once again how leaders of the judicial system which failed in their responsibility, to uphold the dignity of justice and of law and order, but succumbed to the temptation of replacing impartiality with self-centeredness. Their network of conspiracy perverted power into an unscrupulous and corrupt weapon for achieving personal ends. Consequently, the prevalent situation among the community members in general was the obvious spirit of heartless and mean individualism.[84] Micah's damming description of the disorganization of the social cohesiveness of the people in society is sketched out by Reimer:

> His oracles display a community not gathered with a common focus on the God of Zion, but fragmented by appetite and self-interest. It is a community which feeds off suffering brought about by injustice, rather than one which in its common struggle affirms equity and mercy. Its demeanour is not marked by joyful participation in redemption and freedom, but rather by loss, grief, and the ruin of its land and life within it. It is finally a society whose speech leads inevitably to violence, its troubled discourse tending towards breakdown of communication within the community, as well as between the community and its God.[85]

Regrettably, the lamentable phenomenon of strife among the people destroyed the strong social implications of race and religious devotion that bound them together as a covenant community. The viable circle of friendship and family faced psychological disequilibrium as intimacy could no longer guarantee faithfulness and reliability. In fact, the disintegration and fragmentation of family life, in Micah's striking commentary on the development of individualism, forces a man to go against his nature and outside the very core of the inner circles of interpersonal responsibility and familiarity—"friend-best friend-wife"—and keep his own suggestions and advices if he is not to encounter disloyalty and treachery.[86] This description of an extreme case of social disintegration in Micah's oracles clearly confirms the cultural degeneration on

---

[83] Dempster, *Micah*, 176.
[84] Allen, "Micah's Social Concern," 30–31.
[85] Reimer, "Prophet Micah and Political Society," 223–24.
[86] Allen, "Micah's Social Concern," 30.

account of corruption and moral deterioration. The social change, tension and distress in which Micah's oracles were literarily anchored reveal that family solidarity which was of primary significance within Israel could no longer be supported as "generations had become walled off from each other and had little mutual respect and understanding."[87] The cohesiveness of the entire family and household, which should stand united, structured and dependent upon the authority of the accepted hierarchy headed by the father of the family, now lack both individual and cooperate confidence.

5.4. Worship and Dedicated Lifestyle

Micah's concern for ethics is heartrendingly demonstrated in the description of the mutual relationship between worship and dedicated lifestyle. The oracle indicates a false understanding of worship; a dialogue with God that revolves around two spheres, the cult and culture.[88] As an essential domain of both private and public worship, the cult[89] plays a vital role in the religious life of ancient Israelite community.[90] Israel's cult is conceived as direct witness to and epitome of the dynamic practice of intimacy with Yahweh (in his very essence and character as sovereign and gracious). This dynamic relationship obviously becomes not only a necessary support for ethical intentions but a testimony about one who behaves in an ethical manner. Consequently, the prophetic polemics about the cult becomes very pointed when there is an imbalance in the divine-human relationship.[91] The rhetorical features that one finds in cult critical texts are those that compel the audience and/or readers to focus on the significance of the ethical behavior of ritual practitioners.[92] No doubt, there is obviously an inextricable relationship between the cult (worship) and culture (lifestyle). This relationship is described with different images by Claus Westermann:

---

[87] Allen, "Micah's Social Concern," 31.

[88] Dempster, *Micah*, 227.

[89] All forms of ritual activities, whether public or private, that are connected with homage to a deity, are treated under the term cult. The primary role of the cult is that of cultural transformation. See, Roland de Vaux, *Ancient Israel: Its Life and Institutions*, trans. John McHugh, Biblical Resource Series 3 (Grand Rapids: Eerdmans, 1997), 271.

[90] Walter Brueggemann, *Theology of the Old Testament: Testimony, Dispute, and Advocacy* (Minneapolis: Fortress, 1997), 650.

[91] Brueggemann, *Theology of the Old Testament*, 678.

[92] The term *ritual* is used to designate a recommended order for the performance of religious or devoted duties. In Old Testament scholarship, it is a general label for offerings, sacrifices and related activities. Bohdan Hrobon, *Ethical Dimension of the Cult in the Book of Isaiah*, BZAW 418 (Berlin: De Gruyter, 2010), 6, 10.

5. Ethical Burdens

The relevance of worship in Israel lies in its function as the focal point of the life of the people. What is decisive is not what happens in the isolated service, but rather what happens in worship for the whole people and the whole land. Therefore, the walk from the house to the service, and from the service back to the house, is an important factor of the service itself. What is brought into the service on these walks from the outside, and also what is taken back into everyday life from the service, are necessarily a part of the act of worship as well. Only in this way can worship be the center of the entire life of the people. Only in this way is criticism of worship also possible, as in the prophetic criticism of a worship which has become false.[93]

Employing different strategies and theological methodologies to the situations of their time, prophets such as Amos, Hosea and Isaiah speak with a vehemence of interest regarding the inseparable connection between cult (worship) and culture (ethics). Their criticisms do not categorically denounce cultic and/or ritual actions, the decency of the sacrifices, or even the devoutness with which the sacrifices are offered. Rather, these prophets enthusiastically criticize the absence of moral integrity in the lives of the worshippers (cf. Amos 5:21–24; 8:4–6; Hos 4:4–6; 6:1–6; Isa 1:10–17). They decried and denounced a superciliously blossoming and extravagant cult, such that was bereft of any sense of social obligations towards the weak and helpless within the society.[94] Thus they charged the people not only to perform rituals but to embody their performance of rituals with suitable, sustainable, healthy, merciful, and ethical attitudes toward one another. Such appropriate ethical behavior helps to define the cult/rituals as viable rather than outrageous.[95]

While these prophets are well known for their efforts to right the discrepancy in Israelite religion that focuses on the significance of rituals but diminished the necessity of morality, in their midst, however, is the obviously very persuasive Micah. A very stimulating concern of Micah's oracles is his classic definition of ethical religion: that which constitutes true worship. His definition of ethical religion sarcastically contrasts specific aspects of cultic service with dedicated lifestyle in society. Micah's literary analysis presents rituals as expressions of people's relationship with Yahweh (worship, offering and sacrifices) that do not impact positively on the horizontal dimension (social responsibility). This imbalance of relationship is poignantly addressed by Micah as his oracle switches from confrontation to reconciliation.

---

[93] Claus Westermann, *Elements of Old Testament Theology*, trans. Douglas W. Stott (Atlanta: John Knox, 1982), 79–80.
[94] Marrs, "Micah and a Theological Critique of Worship," 184.
[95] Theresa V. Lafferty, *The Prophetic Critique of the Priority of the Cult: A Study of Amos 5:21–24 and Isaiah 1:10–17* (Parkway: UMI Dissertation, 2010), 13.

Micah 6:6–8 presents two basic answers to the core question of how the individual should access Yahweh, especially when there is a dysfunction of relationship arising from violation of covenant requirements. The movement from where the people are to where Yahweh desires for them to be obviously requires a dramatic transformation of their perspective on the ritual and socio-ethical consequences of their covenant relationship with Yahweh. Micah 6:6–8 thus presents a transformation of the situation,[96] as the rhetorical "what" (מה) develops most clearly into the calm climactic religious instruction of 6:8. The insightful movement from creation (6:1b–2) to history (6:4–5) through cult (6:6–7) to ethics and theology (6:8) reaches comprehensively and collectively all aspects of Israel's life. This characteristic creativity of the combination of different elements in a distinctive manner shows what the basic issue is, at the core of Israel's faith. In light of the historical connections reflected in the literary expression of the emotional and interpersonal aspects of the covenant in the drama of the unit, Micah highlights what Israel must know about Yahweh; "He does not want the gifts of people—no matter how extraordinary, how ornate, how sacrificial."[97]

The social implications of Israel/Judah's covenant failures are due to lack of faithfulness, justice, and kindness. The people desire reconciliation, and they begin realistically and leisurely with qualitative and quantitative proposals that rapidly become impossibly large. Their proposal indicates a bankruptcy and distortion in the moral and theological spheres and, consequently the counter-proposal of 6:8 is offered as a solution. Obviously, gifts and sacrifices could be means of making atonement for sin (cf. Lev 4–5; 2 Sam 21:3; Ps 54:6), but Micah's critique indicates that these are an altogether complete misunderstanding of the place and purpose of sacrifice in the divine-human relationship. If rituals and sacrifices are not congruent with a life of faithfulness with God; rituals without ethical behavior permeating every aspect of life are worthless. Something much more than mere ritual performance is required. What is most essential in the divine-human relationship, that which truly defines an ethical religion, as Mic 6:6–8 makes clear, is not increasingly extravagant and cultic practice but personal duty and responsibility for fulfilling that duty in society. The theological and catechetical significance of the oracle's unit is captured by A. Vanlier Hunter:

> The good that Yahweh seeks in every person among his people is rooted in making justice and steadfast love the controlling interests in all of life, thereby fostering a relationship with Yahweh that is characterized by paying careful

---

[96] Marrs, "Micah and a Theological Critique of Worship," 199–200.
[97] Dempster, *Micah*, 163.

and judicious attention to honoring his claim on all of life. This is the offering Yahweh accepts.[98]

Micah's message is not a rejection of ritual but an insistence on maintaining the right priorities. A truly ethical religion such as Micah insists on must exhibit moral coherence and remarkable and dependable solidarity with God and humanity in social obligations. Most importantly, Mic 6:8 underscores the understanding that worship and lifestyle go hand in hand, at least in the sight of God. The fundamental requirement of Yahweh is that personal relationship with him must be manifested in responsible commitment to ethical living in society.

---

[98] A. Vanlier Hunter, *Seek the Lord! A Study of the Meaning and Function of the Exhortations in Amos, Hosea, Isaiah, Micah, and Zephaniah* (Baltimore: St. Mary's Seminary and University, 1982), 252.

6

MICAH'S ETHICAL THRUST FOR CONTEMPORARY SOCIOECONOMIC AND RELIGIOUS ENGAGEMENT

> If you're guided by a spirit of transparency, it forces you to operate with a spirit of ethics. Success comes from simplifying complex issues, address problems head on, be truthful and transparent. If you open yourself up to scrutiny, it forces you to a higher standard. I believe you should deliver on your promise. Promise responsibly.
>
> —Rodney Davis

This chapter attempts to explain from a theological viewpoint and thus formulate a generalized application of the ethical burdens of the previous chapter that echoes with similar concerns today. In some respects, such explanation and application may be seen as a simplification of ethical principles from a prophetic text who's *Sitz im Leben* is clearly difficult to determine more precisely. However, the impact of such echoes is succinctly captured by Amy-Jill Levine:

> The Bible offers numerous profound insights: that victims' voices must be heard; that perpetrators are also human beings made in the image and likeness of the divine; that violence impacts not only the victim and the perpetrator, but their families, their communities, even their descendants; that violence is not restricted to some other group but is in our own households; that responding to violence with more violence is not the answer; that there is no quick fix; that repentance is possible but that one also must take responsibility for one's own actions; that no one is immune to sin; that perfect justice is usually elusive.[1]

One must acknowledge that there are a number of pitfalls and challenges confronting contemporary ethical exegetes of the biblical text, namely, the interdisciplinary barriers of working with the Hebrew Bible itself, the challenges of

---

[1] Amy-Jill Levine, "Back Page Interview," in *The Church Times*, London, 15 July 2011, 39–40, quoted from Barton, *Ethics in Ancient Israel*, 6.

applying the text in a pluralistic, postmodern context and the difficulty of associating with an ancient and strange text as twenty-first century readers.[2] Notwithstanding, the significance of the biblical text for Christian ethical scholarship and moral theological reflection is noted by Emily Arndt:

> While biblical reading certainly involves personal and communal engagement and interpretative moments, exegetical work that takes advantage of the contributions of biblical scholars, modern and postmodern, can and should make an important contribution to the ethical appropriation of these texts. But beyond this, Christians *as* Christians have a basic imperative to be attentive readers, re-readers, and re-tellers of the biblical story. The Christian ethicist must consider what it means to our moral lives to be this kind of reader.[3]

Normatively, the chapter is hinged upon the basic and fundamental assumption that the biblical text is authoritatively commanding for the life of the church, not only within the scope of what happens in the isolated service of worshippers, but rather and very fundamentally, what happens in worship for the worshippers and the whole community as a nation. Thus, the scope of this application is relatively focused on the practice of faith within Christian communities and wider Nigerian society, where there is noticeably an undeniable experience of leadership failures, corruption, and exploitation of the poor and powerless, imbalance in administration of justice, and failure in the practice of true orthodoxy. Micah's structural socioeconomic and religious ideology and theology of resistance against oppression constitute a viable means of mediating ethical relevance for contemporary readers who are confronted with socioeconomic and religious contradictions in multidirectional paths.

6.1. Contemporary Christian Communities and Religious Leaders

In the last few decades of the twentieth Century, in view of the numerical growth of Christianity in the African continent, it is observed that Africa has not only ceased to be the dark continent as far as Christianity is concerned, but it is increasingly being acknowledged as one of the areas to which Christianity's center of gravity is drifting.[4] In his article written and posted on the *Washington Post* on May 20, 2015, Wes Granberg-Michaelson notes:

---

[2] Emily Arndt, *Demanding Our Attention: The Hebrew Bible as a Source for Christian Ethics* (Grand Rapids: Eerdmans, 2011), 21.

[3] Arndt, *Demanding our Attention*, 7.

[4] Wilbur O' Donovan, *Biblical Christianity in African Perspective* (Carlisle: Paternoster, 1995), 2; Tite Tienou, *The Theological Task of The church in Africa* (Achimota: African Christian, 1982), 49; John S. Mbiti has also noted that Nigeria has the largest number of Christians in Africa, and he predicted that by the end of the century, more than half of the

Religious convictions are growing and shifting geographically in several dramatic ways.... In 1980, more Christians were found in the global South than the North for the first time in 1,000 years. Today, the Christian community in Latin America and Africa, alone, account for 1 billion people. Over the past 100 years, Christians grew from less than 10 percent of Africa's population to its nearly 500 million today. One out of four Christians in the world presently is an Africa, and the Pew Research Center estimates that will grow to 40 percent by 2030.[5]

The overwhelming growth of Christianity in Africa confirms that most African nations have Christianity as their major religion.[6] The growth rate is occasioned by the supernatural orientation of African Christianity which places emphasis on God's active involvement in human life, on miracles, healing grace and prosperity as well as eternal life. The vibrantly outward religious life of the African Christians has led to the description of African Christianity as both a "mile long" and an "inch deep." This observation is both a complement and a criticism of African Christianity. As a complement, it indicates that African Christianity has witnessed an enormous growth in the past several decades. However, this growth in numbers has not been accompanied by spiritual depth and transformed lifestyle, thus the conclusion that African Christianity is only an inch deep.[7]

Most African nations are faced with the daily struggle of economic survival and the failure of government, and socioeconomic contradictions has presented a viable platform for the advent and sustenance of the controversial theology and gospel of Christian prosperity, popularly referred to as health-and-wealth gos-

---

population of Nigeria would be Christians. John S. Mbiti, *Bible and Theology in Africa Christianity* (Nairobi: Oxford University Press, 1986), 3.

[5] Wes Granberg-Michaelson, "Think Christianity Is Dying? No, Christianity Is Shifting Dramatically," *Washington Post*, May 20, 2015, https://www.washingtonpost.com/news/acts-of-faith/wp/2015/05/20/think-christianity-is-dying-no-christianity-is-shifting-dramatically/? See also Patrick Johnstone whose report on the steady growth of the number of Christians in Africa indicate a rise from 8 million (10 percent of the population) in 1900 to 275 million (57 percent of the population) in 1990. Patrick Johnstone, *Operation World* (Carlisle: OM, 1993), 37; Johnstone, *World Churches Handbook* (London: Christian Research, 1997), 15.

[6] A *Worldatlas* research indicates that "31 African nations have a Christian population that constitutes more than 50% of the national population of the country." Oishimaya Sen Nag, "African Countries Where Christianity Is the Largest Religion," September 20, 2017, https://www.worldatlas.com/articles/african-countries-with-christianity-as-the-religion-of-the-majority.html.

[7] Paul Kisau, "The Key to the African Heart: Rethinking Missionary Strategy in Africa," *AJET* 17.2 (1998): 93.

pel.⁸ In the *Encyclopaedia of Pentecostal and Charismatic Christianity,* Stanley M. Burgess notes that the prosperity gospel refers to, "Christian worldviews that emphasize an earthly life of health, wealth, and happiness as the divine, inalienable right of all who have faith in God and live in obedience to His commands."[9] While responding to the question on "Why is prosperity theology such an important issue to address for Africa," Conrad Mbewe said:

> We need to address prosperity theology here in Africa because it has replaced the true gospel of salvation with a kind of "gospel" that is no gospel at all. This is happening in what once were mainstream evangelical circles. Everywhere, especially on radio and television, almost all you hear is this message about how God in Christ wants us to be physically healthy and materially prosperous. You hardly ever hear sermons about sin and repentance. So salvation has now become deliverance from sickness and poverty. It is temporal rather than eternal. Prosperity theology is like the Arabian camel that gave the impression it simply wanted a little space in the tent, but now the whole of it is inside and the true gospel is outside. This erroneous teaching is filling churches across the continent with people who have no desire for true biblical salvation or godliness. Sadly, it's spreading like an uncontrollable bushfire.[10]

Interestingly, this observation is a suitable description of the Nigerian church,[11] which seems to be shifting grounds from a supernaturally oriented biblical Christianity that is committed to the ideals of social justice, service of the poor, honesty, integrity, and the fear of God. Today, these supernatural sensibilities that characterize Nigerian Christians and religious leaders have sadly collapsed into worldly obsessions and preoccupations. The recent economic recession in the country that is plagued by mismanagement (especially by her

---

[8] J. Kwabena Asamoah-Gyadu, *African Charismatics: Current Developments within Independent Pentecostalism in Ghana* (Leiden: Brill, 2005), 202; Jeff Atherstone, "Africa Infested by Health and Wealth Teaching," June 25, 2015, https://www.thegospelcoalition.org/article/africa-infested-by-health-and-wealth-teaching/; Collium Banda, "Empowering Hope? Jürgen Moltmann's Eschatological Challenge to Ecclesiological Responses in the Zimbabwean Context of Poverty" (PhD diss.; Stellenbosch: Stellenbosch University, 2016), 153.

[9] Stanley M. Burgess, ed., *Encyclopaedia of Pentecostal and Charismatic Christianity* (New York: Routledge, 2006), 393.

[10] Conrad Mbewe, "Prosperity Teaching Has Replaced True Gospel in Africa," June 25, 2015, https://www.thegospelcoalition.org/article/prosperity-teaching-has-replaced-true-gospel-in-africa/

[11] I am aware of the diversity of the Christian church or communities in Nigeria. No one can be so presumptuous as to claim to describe Christianity in Nigeria in the singular. However, my perception of the church bears the stamp of the part of the church I have experienced. The rest of Nigeria may not be too far from this description.

leaders) and mammoth corruption has given prominence to the flourishing of Christian denominations and churches and thus making her one of the most religious country in the world. Sadly, there is an unbelievable ungodliness and darkness in the practice of Christian faith as some religious leaders have become agents of injustice while a number of Christian communities have turned out to be centers of religious commercialization and consumption, religious profiteering, religious perversion, exploitation and inducement to poverty.

Most Nigerian health-and-wealth preachers take advantage of the poverty-stricken nature of the nation to spread their gospel. With strong emphasis, they teach their audience that it is an error for Christians to be poor and thus promise them "financial prosperity and perfect health. Anything less, they argue, is not God's will."[12] David Oyedepo, one of Nigeria's most celebrated gospel ministers and leader of Winners' Chapel, the single largest church in the world, remarks:

> I am redeemed to be enriched, so I will be an abuse to redemption if I don't actualize that dimension of my redemption.... I'd like you to say and believe this: 'I am saved to display his wealth! I am on the right side! I am not a goat! So wealth is my heritage, abundance is my birthright' Friend, you are saved to display his wealth on the earth! To clothe the naked, feed the hungry and attend to the sick! That's what you are sent to do! (Matt.25: 34–40).... Prosperity is our identity. If you don't demonstrate it, then you are a misfit in the kingdom.[13]

This ideology finds expression in contemporary Nigerian Christian culture and dominates the frontier of religious, socioeconomic, and institutional spheres. Certainly, the most anticipated objects of the prosperity theology are materialistic cravings such as wealth, healing, protection, and other miraculous expectations. What is very striking in the drama is that "the juicier the promises and claims, the more people it attracts, and the larger the crowd of people, the more money the preacher receives."[14] Although the obvious variations on the theme of self-help or motivation or simply entertainment are difficult to generalize, criticism of such ministers and ministries usually results in defensive pomposity or apparent reactions. It is in light of this observation that Micah's ethical concerns are applied to Christians and Christian religious leaders in Nigeria in the following directions.

---

[12] Moses Owojaiye, "Problems, Prospects and Effects of Health and Wealth Gospel in Nigeria (Part 1)," https://christianityinafrica.wordpress.com/2010/01/16/problems-prospects-and-effects-of-health-and-wealth-gospel-in-nigeria-part-1/

[13] David Oyedepo, *Understanding Financial Prosperity* (Ota: Dominion, 2005), 16–17.

[14] Goka Muele Mpigi, "The Prosperity Theology's Impact on the Contemporary Nigerian Church and Society," *SJER* 5.5 (2017): 34.

6.1.1. Living with the Fear of God and Trusting in His Sovereignty

Micah's message of the ethical concern of Yahweh's sovereignty and his commitment to the maintenance of justice in human life and history is a clear acknowledgement that emphasizes important realities that are of immense significance for Christians and Christian communities today. The sequence of judgement arising out of obvious violations of covenant obligations in Micah's oracles indicate a nation in which community members were living without the fear of God and the respect for his sovereignty. One of the saddest observations that validated the nation's unfaithfulness of injustice especially toward the less-privileged (such as robbery and exploitation, unjust commercial dealings, leadership and government that live in extravagance at the expense of the hard work of the people) was the disastrous, inauthentic and theological imagination and teachings of false prophets that created a fundamental tension between God's judgement and mercy (2:6–7; 3:11).

Micah's message underscores a fundamental connection between the key concepts of judgement and mercy; Yahweh's sovereign power to judge his people is balanced with Yahweh's sovereign mercy and grace (7:18–20). The sequence of judgement and salvation seeks to inspire fear and hope, two key notions that are put together in the closing cycle of the book's prophecy. In this sequence is a legal session in which Yahweh's people stand in trial before the sovereign ruler of the universe for turning aside from him and his ways and thus violating others (6:1–7:10). The failure of people to live up to the height of their responsibility for the love of justice, mercy and righteousness is inexcusable. Micah makes clear that Yahweh, although a God of love, is also a God of retribution who deals with His creatures' trespasses against His holiness because of His retributive justice. The transcendence of God is characteristically marked by both justice and love, and the obligation that God places on the life of humanity stresses Yahweh of fear, doing justice, the love of mercy, and an intimate daily walk with him.

Today, the proclamation of similar expressions: "God is on your side; don't worry; be happy; no weapon formed against you will prosper," without any sense of responsibility, have misguided many Christians and subverted the contagious message of the fear of God and of doing justice. Contrary to such theological perceptions and behavioral contrasts, the theological force of Yahweh's sovereignty underscores the need for people to live with the fear of God and be responsible to him for the treatment of others. When people are confronted with an understanding of the character of God and his word, they will be compelled to change their ways of life. The fear of God would restrain inhuman and unfaithful behavior in social interactions.

Micah's heartfelt and passionate plea for God's people to repent is a wake-up call to contemporary Christians and Christian communities in Nigeria where the unfaithfulness of injustice has fractured interpersonal relationship and community social solidarity. Micah makes clear that those who are rebellious and sinful and who have made it a habit to practice injustice will be judged (1:5) and will be answerable to God for what he expects of them (6:1–8). Consequently, the crucial invitation of the understanding of the theme of Yahweh's sovereignty and justice is to live with the fear of God and to trust in him. In the face of humanly unindictable injustice Christians and faith community members who live with the fear of God have no other recourse but to turn to him and it is to him that their appeal for strict judgement in both kind and degree is made and surrendered. Although the scale of people's indulgence to injustice is high, nevertheless the degree to which humanity will forever dwell in a torment and punishment of Yahweh's just recompense, as Micah's rhetoric indicates, should pull them out of their indifference regarding the extension of justice and kindness to others. While the principle of Yahweh's justice is clear, the understanding of Yahweh's sovereignty resulting in living daily with Yahweh's fear will potentially and enthusiastically stimulate in people right moral resolutions and healthy social order. That God reigns and remains the universal judge is ultimately a message of hope in a world of oppression and injustice.

6.1.2. Maintaining the Balance between Worship and Lifestyle

In the Old Testament, the tension that existed in the community of ancient Israel over the expected relationship between the worship of Yahweh and the attitude of those who worship him in community relationship and social solidarity is well articulated. Within the frame of the torah, service to God and moral attitudes are all equated as divinely commanded to be of unqualified significance (cf. Lev 26; Deut 4:25–28; 6:14–15; 7:1–5; 8:19–20; 11:16–17; 28:14). This concern is also reflected in a number of prophetic texts that describe Israel's moral landscape especially in terms of how morality and unfaithfulness of injustice directly affected her national destiny. While this apprehension is scarcely fixed, at least an essential concern can be noticed in the literary prophetic books in which the prophets are enthusiastically loud in their condemnation of worship (ritual) as it affects social ethics in community. In texts such as Amos 4:4–5; 5:21–24; Isa 1:11–17, faithful worshippers of Yahweh are encouraged not only to focus on legal cultic ritual requirements but to wholeheartedly comply with Yahweh's torah and concern or justice and appropriate social obligations in the context of relationships.[15]

---

[15] John Barton, "The Prophets and the Cult," in *Temple and Worship in Biblical Israel*, ed. John Day, Proceedings of the Oxford Old Testament Seminar (New York: T&T Clark, 2007), 111, 120; Daniel R. M. Carroll, "Failing the Vulnerable: The Prophet and

The sacrificial cultus and all other acts of worship are essential in the divine-human relationship, but the validity of these acts is undermined when unaccompanied by moral behavior and a sincere heart.[16] The offensive and completely unacceptable ritual acts of those who outlandishly worship Yahweh but only in name is captured by Amos:

> I hate, I despise your festive gatherings, and I will not take delight in your solemn assemblies. Even though you offer me your burnt offerings and your grain offerings, I will not accept them; and even the peace-offerings of your fatlings, I will not give attention. Take away from me the noise of your songs; I will not even listen to the melody of your harps. But let justice roll down like waters, and righteousness like an ever-flowing stream. (Amos 5:21–24; cf. Isa 1:11–17)

Within the essential boundaries of Yahweh's covenant grace, the powerful theological metaphor of Yahweh's covenant with Israel indicates that individual community members' uprightness and corporate compliance and responsibility (ritual/cultic actions) were to be the collective aspiration of the community.[17] Viable and functional cultic (worship) lifestyle must be complemented by actions of a suitable manner, actions that issue from righteousness. Consequently, in view of his increasingly and obviously heightened moral thoughtfulness, Micah pitched his tent with those who were determined to embody justice, tender mercy, and a humble walk with Yahweh.[18] Micah's oracles highlight the inextricable contradiction between the worship of God and covetousness and injustice. The proper relationship is well pictured in Mic 2–3 as Dempster notes:

> To worship Yahweh as the supreme God is to worship someone whose throne is founded on justice. In him all reality is perfectly integrated and proportioned, for after all he is the creator. His passion is justice. If something or person or force is elevated to the position of Yahweh and Yahweh is dethroned, this can only lead to injustice.... An essential problem is that when Yahweh is dethroned and replaced by an idol, a spiritual insufficiency is expressed in seeking more and more for the self. This is expressed in limitless coveting, which when acted out leads to proliferation of injustice.[19]

Social Care," *Transforming the World? The Gospel and Social Responsibility*, ed. Jamie A. Grant and Dewl A. Hughes (Grand Rapids: InterVasity, 2009), 42–45.

[16] Dempster, *Micah*, 229.

[17] Erhard S. Gerstenberger, "Non-Temple Psalms: The Cultic Setting Revisited," in *The Oxford Handbook of the Psalms*, ed. William P. Brown (Oxford: University, 2014), 343–44.

[18] James L. Crenshaw, *The Psalms: An Introduction* (Grand Rapids: Eerdmans, 2001), 165.

[19] Dempster, *Micah*, 254–55.

Micah's rhetoric presents essential proposals for Christians and contemporary faith communities on the nature of worship and the value of life lived in community of humanity, of attitudes towards neighbors and the objectives and impact of such human behaviors. There is truly a rhythm to a dedicated lifestyle and worship. What sustains viable community living is essentially a functional encounter with the life-giving God (who is committed to justice and kindness) and the embodiment of these values by the faithful worshippers in an effervescent living. Christians and contemporary faith communities are by Micah's ethical concern under demanding moral imperatives. Since the reputation of Yahweh (the God of Israel whom Christians worship) depends on actions of justice and kindness; Christians and faith communities must embody these ethical ideals of justice, kindness and social solidarity in accordance with Yahweh's instruction (Mic 6:8). Christian social solidarity with Yahweh in the community of humanity entails a stand against injustice and wickedness and those who practice evil, oppression, and deceit.[20]

While churches must continue to make their worship services vibrant proclamation of biblical texts, the correspondence between worship and dedicated lifestyle requires urgent evaluation. Like ancient Israel/Judah, contemporary faith communities may forget the call to ultimate sacrifice for God and consequently offer the wrong answers to questions regarding access to God within a context of true religion. They may be obsessed with extravagant and extreme performances of music, powerful sermons by distinguished charismatic and prophetic orators, extravagant gift offerings and donations, super Sunday commercials and susceptibility to the evils of empty religion. They might seem to be dwelling in the sacred realm where the name of God is adored and are separated from the concern for social justice, the weak and helpless. On the contrary, Micah's idea of fellowship and walking with God defines such form of extravagant worship divorced from the requirement of justice and the practice of reliable solidarity (חסד אהבת), as meaningless.

Micah's rhetoric regarding the correspondence between worship and dedicated lifestyle presents one of the starkest portraits of Christians and Christian communities not only in Nigeria but also the rest of Africa and the world generally. Christians living in Nigeria today have both a demanding responsibility to be faithful to God and at the same time be responsible and productive citizens in society. Contemporary Nigerian society offers a variety of opportunities and atmospheres for personal gains. There are often the demands of illegitimate accommodations and the danger of easily being captivated by the good material things of the world so that Christians become reluctant to risk their loss by standing up for what God requires of them. For example, one can observe op-

---

[20] John Kessler, *Old Testament Theology: Divine call and Human Response* (Waco, TX: Baylor University Press, 2013), 439.

portunity for deception, extortion, bribe, prejudice, mistreatment of the weak, helpless, poor and powerless, ingratiating oneself to unpleasant desires, and taking advantage of others in their moments of need. In the face of a corrupt and profane establishment—both private and public—they are to remain publicly devoted to God rather than relegating their faith to a private, personal sphere. Micah's call to seeking justice, loving kindness, and walking humbly with God is a reminder of what contemporary Christians and faith communities in Nigeria are called to embrace and embody. Christians and faith communities in Nigeria must know that overwhelmingly abundant rituals and sacrificial offerings will constitute worthless worship, which affect the moral conduct of worshippers in interpersonal relationship with one's neighbor. The lack of this is evidence of the absence of fruitful, viable relationship with God.

6.1.3. Pastoral Leadership and Prophetic Advocacy

In his attempt to deal with the unfaithfulness of injustice, Micah fought a perverted theology of super-grace with all his intellectual and rhetorical insights and capabilities.[21] He spoke passionately about the implications of the mercenary attitude of the dual Judean religious functionaries (prophets and priests) who were self-centered and self-serving in their leadership. Clearly, there is no doubt that Micah's observation and indictments make sense today. One of the saddest realities that Micah's denouncements highlight for the contemporary African religious landscape and for Christian communities in Nigeria is the pervasive presence of deceitful teachers, uninformed pastors, and fraudulent prophets. Generally, the reality of poverty and corruption in Africa has overwhelmingly resulted in compromised pastoral leadership and pulpit ministry in the Christian church.[22]

As it is today, one resides in a world and particularly a Nigeria of material and economic consciousness where life is almost measured in terms of economics with unprecedented material prosperity contrasting obvious abject material poverty, exploitation, corruption, and economic unrest. Consequently, as in Micah's time, religious leaders in faith communities have resorted to the use of business strategies that are appealing to advance their ministerial functions. These religious merchants whose priority is not limited to financial gains—it may include increase in social status, recognition, reputation, or other ad-

---

[21] Dempster, *Micah*, 96.

[22] See for example the insights of poverty and corruption in the research of Brett Younger, "Calorie Counting Ministers in a Starving World (Amos 5:14–24)," *RevExp* 110.2 (2013): 295–300; Noel Woodbridge and Willem Semmelink, "The Prophetic Witness of Amos and Its Relevance for Today's Church in African Countries for Promoting Social Justice in Democratic South Africa," *Conspectus* 16 (2013): 79–87.

vantages—adopt distortions, deceptions and all manner of exaggerations to promote religious loyalty and increase popular appeal in their religious messages and doctrines.[23] This trend is a direct manifestation of the spiritual materialism described by Al Chukwuma Okoli and Ahar Clement Uhembe as "commodification of spirituality in a consumeric society. In other words, spirituality is treated like every other commodity—it's something you pay for to gratify a certain need."[24] The degree of the infiltration of spiritual materialism in the religious landscape of the church in Nigeria has assumed the shape of a "commercialization of spiritual providence" and "materialization of religion."[25]

Reflecting concerns at the overwhelming presence of religious centers and Christian activities in Nigeria in the midst of the observable notoriety of poverty and corruption, Ben Kwashi notes: "This nation of Nigeria is blessed with every conceivable missionary church and para-church, and the number of prayer ministries is uncountable.... And what have we achieved?"[26] The pervasive religiosity of many Nigerians and the obviously material and socioeconomic crises of widespread poverty, disease, unemployment, illiteracy, and lack of general well-being have given rise to a situation described by the Nigerian literary genius, Wole Soyinka as that of "religious opportunism."[27] Similarly, Matthew Hassan Kukah a Nigerian religious leader who is also an assiduous advocate for social justice, true democracy, human dignity and national development, described the unfortunate trend as an atmosphere of "merchandizing of religion."[28] In his description, Kukah remarks:

> The ubiquity of religion has become a matter of worry and we need to pay attention to its implications. Today, Pentecostal pastors are busier than the men and women who run our polity as politicians or bankers. Pastors are scavenging for fortunes in the name of leading souls to God through the organization of

---

[23] Kenneth Baker, *The NIV Study Bible* (Grand Rapids: Zondervan, 1995), 1899; Adrian Rogers, "False Prophets: Their Method, Manner and Motives," http://www.oneplace.com/ministries/love-worthfinding/read/articles/false-prophets-theirmethod-manner-and-motive-14018.html; Lon Hetrick, "Selling the Gospel: The Christian Hype that Stifles Christian Hope," http://felixcheakam.com/77-selling-Jesus-at-a-discount.html.
[24] Al Chukwuma Okoli and Ahar Clement Uhembe, "Materialism and Commodification of the Sacred: A Political Economy of Spiritual Materialism in Nigeria," *ESJ* 10.14 (2014): 598.
[25] Okoli and Uhembe, "Materialism and Commodification of the Sacred," 601.
[26] Ben Kwashi, "The Christian and Corruption," in *Service with Integrity: The Christian in the Nigerian Project*, ed. Z. Chinne (Kaduna: ECWA Goodnews Church, 2008), 42.
[27] Wole Soyinka, *The Credo of Being and Nothingness* (Ibadan: Spectrum, 1991), 25.
[28] Matthew Hassan Kukah, *Religion, Culture and the Politics of Development* (Lagos: Centre for Black and African Arts and Civilisation, 2007), 38.

endless spiritual trade fairs called revivals and vigils aimed at indoctrinating ordinary citizens away from the culture of hard work and the need to develop a truly Christian ethic to wealth.[29]

Within the context of the Nigerian religious landscape, there are ample examples of religious leaders who have become stupendously rich, having numerous extravagant homes worth millions of naira, and the very best of automobiles and luxurious conveniences. Nigeria plays host to some of the world's most influential religious leaders and the world's largest church auditorium was recently dedicated in Abuja, the nation's capital.[30] The unprecedented Megachurches have become huge business-related enterprises and virtually corporate organizations in themselves. These Megachurches are established and managed by self-styled 'apostles' and prophets of faith who make use of these platforms to expand their influence and interests. Most often, the scandals that are associated with these religious ministers and their ministries are a legion of contradictions. Loose living, sexual infidelity and exploitation of minors, lies, embezzlement of funds, manipulation, financial exploitation, and spiritual abuse of parishioners, which are in short outrageous, feature prominently among such ministers as well as their ministries.[31] The phenomenon of cheap grace which is not inextricably connected with a message of responsibility is driving many gullible and uninformed worshippers to commit financial and moral misconducts so as to satisfy the demands of their self-styled prophets and church's expectations.

Granted that Micah's indictment bears the stamp of ancient Israel and Judah's religious self-consciousness and theocratic society that was rooted in social and historical realities,[32] reflection on Micah's indictment generates ethical concerns for pastoral leadership in the practice of religious faith within a context of socioeconomic and religious realities.

6.1.3.1. Religious Leaders with Sound Theological Balance

The challenge of Micah's colleagues (false prophets and priests) and the generality of the people was that of their emphasis on selective parts of biblical revelation. They were solely absorbed and at home with the doctrine of divine

---

[29] Kukah, *Religion, Culture and the Politics of Development*, 37–38.
[30] *Charisma* news published on 10:30AM EST December 7, 2018 that "the Glory Dome in Abuja, Nigeria can hold 100,000 people." The world's largest sanctuary is pastored by Dr Paul Enenche and his wife, Dr. Becky Enenche. "World's Largest Church Auditorium Dedicated in Nigeria." https://www.charismanews.com/world/74340-world-s-largest-church-auditorium-dedicated-in-nigeria.
[31] Dempster, *Micah*, 244.
[32] Allen, "Micah's Social Concern," 32.

election and blessing and the Zion theology. But they were not wholeheartedly passionate about the demanding responsibilities of election, blessings, and the Sinai tradition. These religious leaders failed to balance the covenant formulary: "I will be your God" with the consequence "you will be my people," as they emphasized only one side of the equation. According to Dempster, "heresy is usually not an outright rejection of the truth but its distortion through overemphasizing certain aspects and underemphasizing others."[33] Micah's sound theological debate indicates a rejection and total disregard of these spiritual leaders' message of cheap grace.

This fact of prophetic conflict in which Micah's colleagues in the prophetic profession were motivated solely by materialism and their one-sided theological narrative is a perennial problem in today's religious landscape that calls for greater emphasis on a wholistic understanding of Scriptures. The misappropriation of ministry position and authority for selfish interests usually involves a violation of principles of Bible interpretation.[34] This has become one of the escalating causes of exploitation and corruption in the country. Micah's confrontation of the distorted theological rationalization of his ministry colleagues suggests a genuine burden for theological balance on the part of religious leaders in Christian gospel ministry. Sound theological education and balance involves education in Christian life, education for ministry, Christian faith and equipping for the responsibilities of one's specific vocation in ministry and pastoral leadership in a congregation's life.[35] A compact and comprehensive statement of the scope of Christian education is:

> Education in the Christian sense includes all efforts and processes which help to bring children and adults into vital and saving experience of God revealed in Christ; to quicken the sense of God as a living reality, so that communion with Him in prayer and worship becomes a natural habit and principle of life, to establish attitudes and habits of Christ like living, human relations and to enlarge and deepen the understanding of the historic facts on which Christianity rests, and of the rich content of Christian experience, belief and doctrine.[36]

In order for spiritual leaders of the church in Nigeria to be effective advocates of social justice and the struggle for the liberation of the Nigerian people from the shackles of poverty and corruption, sound theological education is an urgent and remarkable requirement that cannot be inseparable from contemporary Christian missions. For Christianity in Nigeria to be a living experience of

---

[33] Dempster, *Micah*, 245.
[34] Abiodun Faleye Olukayode, "Religious Corruption: A Dilemma of the Nigeria State," *JSDA* 15.1 (2013): 174.
[35] Charles M. Wood, "An Invitation to Theological Study," *PJ* 42.2–3 (1989): 1–2.
[36] Bill Oldham, *Philosophy of Education* (New York: Abingdon, 1967), 4.

transformation, a transformative process of personal and communal engagement with the biblical text is crucial for a genuine redemptive mission within various ecclesial communities. The ministers (religious leaders) who are called to mediate the word to others can approach the text not merely as an historical record or even as a literary meditation of religious meaning for manipulative objectives, but as the word of God. Such an approach, rooted in faith, cannot bypass historical-critical exegesis and literary analysis. The special mission of the church in the world calls for specially trained men/women of God. These men/women must produce effective contextual hermeneutics that are true to the Scripture's message, and relevant for the culture and dilemma of the nation.

One understands the term "contextualization" to mean making concepts or ideas relevant to a given situation. In reference to the Christian practices, it is an effort to express the never changing word of God in ever-changing models for relevance.[37] With much of the nation going through socioeconomic contradictions of corruption, exploitation, poverty, suffering, health problems, et cetera, religious leaders in faith communities need sound theological education which can help them to serve people in various aspects of community development. They need training on how to effectively apply the biblical message to a changing and challenging moral culture and situation. Biblical interpretation in a cultural and cross-cultural context is a complex task involving the understanding of the receptor's culture and its world view and concerns, as well as a development of new ways of looking at the Bible's teachings that meet those concerns. Thus, Christian religious leaders need training in principles of interpretation and application to diverse cultures and situations. Critical interpretation of scriptures should be done in such ways that promote the culture of hard work with dignity, faithful stewardship, transparency, and accountability in the management of the nation's available corporate resources. Spiritual (religious) leaders of Christian communities in Nigeria must understand the fact that there are no simple answers to hard realities of life. Those who operate ministries without the pursuit of sound theological education and balance and whose ministries are divorced from issues of social justice, and real understanding of people and their problems in society, are ill prepared to be effective leaders of the church in the present reality. John Pobee in his book, *Towards Viable Theological Education* says:

> Authentic theology includes education of the ear to hear the cry of the people, of the heart to heed and to feel, of the tongue to speak to the weary and the broken a word that rebuilds them and kindles in them a fire of hope, and of the hands to work with the lowly to build a human world which the wealthy, the

---

[37] Tite Tienou, *The Theological Task of the Church in Africa* (Achimota: African Christian, 1990), 28.

mighty and the clever have shown themselves incapable of envisioning and fashioning.[38]

The necessity for sound theological education and balance for religious leaders must be considered as an urgent pursuit that will help to address and reduce the challenges of commercial and materialist spirituality that characterize most of contemporary Nigeria Christian communities' faith and practice.

6.1.3.2. Leaders with Great Moral Credentials

The realities of the leadership situation in many Christian communities in Nigeria today present one the best atmospheres for the application of Micah's leadership concern. In every society, there exist men who are appointed to certain privileged positions of leadership with the power of influence over others. The nature and direction of such influence obviously depend upon the content of the leaders' character. The more outstanding a leader is among his community, the more comprehensive is the circle and scope of his influence. Religious leaders are men of great religious influence and power. In order to maintain it as well as present a distinctive, compelling and attractive priestly profile in Christian communities and society, religious leaders must possess great moral credentials. The possession of deep and profound moral credentials marks them as Yahweh's messengers who are entrusted with the responsibility of making known divine revelations to Yahweh's faithful worshipers in Christian communities and society. Ministerial integrity is an eternal prerequisite for transformation; it promises productive and successful movement towards an ethical ministry that will stimulate confidence and reliability. Consequently, religious leaders have the responsibility of conducting themselves in a morally upright manner both in life and in ministry. They must faithfully demonstrate an unblemished and unmistakable soundness between words and actions.[39]

The desire to occupy such ministry positions in Christian communities must not be for the sake of being regarded as prominent, powerful and utterly sacrificing the rights and privileges of the people on the altar of greed. Such desire must be borne out of a genuine commitment to climb above self-centered ambition, a desire that will encourage confidence rather than thrusting people into the sphere of confusion and misery. Micah's indictment of Judah's charismatic and cultic leadership places a strong ethical caution on religious leaders at every level of ministry regarding the way and they consider their position and exercise their

---

[38] John Pobee, *Towards Viable Theological Education* (Geneva: WCC, 1997), 31.
[39] John MacArthur, *Rediscovering Pastoral Ministry* (Waco, TX: Word, 1995), 22; Christopher J. H. Wright, *Living as the People of God: The Relevance of Old Testament Ethics* (Leicester: Inter-Varsity, 1983), 204.

leadership influence. Micah underscores that the privilege and responsibility of ministry require men of sound and profound moral character that will consistently and reliably mediate Yahweh's word and fulfill ministerial functions (3:8). Since self-centeredness, greed and unrighteous ambition in leaders eventually lead to abuse of position and privilege; religious communities must look out for leadership qualities such as Micah's own attractive, brilliant, and shinning self-assessment (3:8). They must in line with Moses' counsel insist on leaders, "who fear [ירא] God, men of truth [אמת], those who hate [שנא] dishonest [בצע] gain" (Exod 18:21).

6.1.3.3. Uncompromised Prophetic Advocacy through Pulpit Ministry

In the Old Testament, the prophetic concern for oppression of the poor prioritizes the demand for justice. The classical prophets were nonconformists, relentlessly exposing and denouncing exploitation, corruption, and oppression in whatever shape and wherever they found it. They did not maintain the status quo in the name of religion. Filled with genuine spirituality and becoming informed advocates of socioeconomic justice, they proclaimed a prophetic message of "healing and wholeness of human relationships, of the well-being of creation, and of the covenant between Yahweh and Israel."[40] Amos for example, in no uncertain terms condemned the insensitivity and cruelty of the wealthy towards the poor: "they sold the righteous for money and the needy for a pair of sandals" (2:6), "oppress the poor and crush the needy" (4:1), and "tread upon the poor" (5:11) in their uncontrollable greed for gain.

It is despicable to note the tendency of the church and her leaders to undermine the human component in the community through unjust and unreasonable socioeconomic structures of livable human society and to defend the existing state of affairs, by not speaking out against matters of socioeconomic injustice and demanding social reforms but spiritualizing socioeconomic contradictions. Although it is difficult to deny that poverty, corruption and injustices are basically spiritual problems arising from the depravity of fallen humanity, one cannot just considers these issues as spiritual ones since human beings are responsible for the administration and implementation of economic structures.[41] Obaji M. Agbiji and Ignatius Swart have strongly observed that, "religious practitioners have often encouraged 'God-talk' that weakens the resolve of masses to rise up against unjust political and economic systems in Africa. Much of this

---

[40] John W. De Gruchy, *Christianity and Democracy: A Theology for a Just World Order* (Cambridge: Cambridge University Press, 1995), 44.
[41] Collium Banda, "Not Anointing, but Justice? A Critical Reflection on the Anointing of Pentecostal Prophets in a Context of Economic Injustice," *VE* 39.1 (2018): 5, a1870. https://doi.org/10.4102/ ve.v39i1.1870.

nonchalance with regard to public issues is initiated by the political elite and given impetus by religious leaders and by the faithful."[42] African Christian theology of the priesthood as unapologetically supernatural must stimulate and infuse religious leaders as basically social activists for justice and stewards of the mysteries of God. Like Micah, true spiritual leaders of the church in Nigeria (and in Africa and the world) must pay close attention to the voice of God and the demands of truth, honesty, and justice.

6.1.3.3.1. Advocacy that Gives Priority to Truth and Justice

Undoubtedly, the functionality and viability of a society depends on adherence to and maintenance of acceptable standards and ethical principles such as truthfulness, integrity, equity and justice, respect for human dignity, responsibility and accountability. The violation of these core moral values usually results in instability and disruption of society rather than stability and tranquility. Micah's struggle was against a different reading of Israel's narrative by theological leaders that justified crime and corruption. Micah's task was thus that of righting the situation by speaking the truth and advocating justice. One of his passionate responsibilities was his uncompromising announcements about sin and God's judgement. He made no mistake about his prophetic calling and consequently did not lower the standard of Yahweh's demand. He was bold to announce to Jacob its sin and to Israel its transgression. The fundamental definition and demonstration of his prophetic assignment occurs in the context of deceitful prophets who were misleading people by saying the opposite and who were under materialistic influence to announce what their audience desires (Mic 3:8; cf. 3:5–7).[43] These religious leaders lack the needed social consciousness and so could not have any sense of responsibility for the injustice and oppression perpetrated upon the common citizens by the wealthy and influential members of the nation.

Religious leaders of faith communities in Nigeria and Africa, regardless of the consequences, must be filled with the courage to live the profoundly different life demonstrated and encouraged by Micah. Micah spoke out courageously against rulers and the influential minorities for devising unjust and exploitative structures to deprive the poor and needy of their legitimate rights, denying the oppressed justice and exploiting widows and orphans (2:1–2; 3:1–4, 8; 6:10–16 cf. Isa 10:1–2). Contemporary religious leaders must be very sensitive to the lures of the moment and be certain that they do not create and promote a relax-

---

[42] Obaji M. Agbiji and Ignatius Swart, "Religion and Social Transformation in Africa: A Critical and Appreciative Perspective," *Scrip* 114.1(2015): 8. https://doi.org/10.7833/114-0-1115.

[43] Dempster, *Micah*, 245.

ing and entertaining kind of religion that does not certainly and completely inconvenience people or simply threatens their personal security. They must uncompromisingly speak the truth about sin and God's judgement not only to those who worship in their churches but also to those in power at different levels of national life. They cannot turn a blind eye and ear to officially sanctioned systems of injustices against the poor and marginalized in society. Genuine spiritual leaders of faith communities owe it a duty to listen for the voice of God and not the voice of the people. Listening carefully to the Scriptures will provide them the vision for understanding the world and the dynamics of their society and consequently demonstrating love for people and addressing contemporary situations.[44]

Micah's ethical concern reminds contemporary religious leaders and faith communities that any attempt to sacrifice the demands of truth and justice in favor of lies will obviously bring tragic ends. The uncompromising prophetic stances against injustice will not necessarily immune religious leaders against oppositions. Although Micah's message carried the force of divine authority, there are no clear indications that it had popular acceptance. Like Amos (cf. Amos 7:12–13), Micah's announcements were unacceptable in the sight of the false prophets and their followers (2:6–7). Religious leaders who will courageously take a stand against the unfaithfulness of injustices in society must be resilient as they will often find themselves standing alone and their messages unwelcomed.

6.1.3.3.2. Advocacy that Recovers and Develops Human Potential

Genuine prophetic advocacy declares God's word against everything that threatens God's agenda for humanity. It does not only announce the promises and claims of God for humanity but also practically point to new opportunities and possibilities. It employs the language of imagination by inviting people to visualize the God-intended era of possibilities and helping them to discern ways through which God would creatively use them.[45] The complacent attitude of many religious leaders in relinquishing their prophetic advocacy and thus spiritualizing current socioeconomic issues has resulted in the regression of the human potentials of people in Africa.[46] Today, many Nigerians have developed and are leaving with a disturbing passion and appetite for cheap wealth and ex-

---

[44] Dempster, *Micah*, 245.
[45] Dawn Ottoni Wilhelm, "God's Word in The World: Prophetic Preaching and the Gospel of Jesus Christ," in *Anabaptist Preaching: A Conversation Between Pulpit, Pew and Bible*, ed. David B. Greiser and Michael A. King (Telford: Cascadia, 2003), 77.
[46] Paul Gifford, *Christianity, Politics, and Public Life in Kenya* (New York: Columbia University Press, 2009), 250.

travagance without at the same time demonstrating the commensurate ethical hunger for hard work, honesty and responsible commitment to duties. This is partly due to the theology of cheap grace offered by many influential religious leaders. Dietrich Bonhoeffer describes the problem with the phenomenon of cheap grace in the church, which is simply an experience of the grace of God without an attendant change of attitude or lifestyle: "Cheap grace means the justification of sin without the justification of the sinner. Grace alone does everything, they say, and so everything can remain as it was before."[47] Micah dealt with this development that was easily complemented by ostentatious demonstration of religious power with abundance of expensive sacrifices and offerings. It was at home with socioeconomic exploitation and undermined the potential and well-being of the poor. There is no cheap grace without responsibility. In the New Testament, Paul's theology condemns those who would separate faith (grace) from the importance of a life path of hard work: "Never be lazy, but work hard and serve the Lord enthusiastically" (NLT, Rom 12:11; cf. 1 Cor 4:12; 9:6; Eph 4:28; 1 Thess 2:9; 4:11; 2 Thess 3:10–12).

Prophetic advocacy by religious leaders in Nigeria and Africa must make it a matter of urgent attention in their proclamation to quicken the poor in society not only to realize the uselessness of socioeconomic contradictions but also to present reliable means of dislodging and reducing, if not completely eradicating the unpleasant development. Consequently, the obvious tendency of contemporary religious leaders in faith communities and society to advocate faith and prayer religiously and uncritically without addressing political and socioeconomic structures has remained ineffective. Faith communities' members must be taught to understand as well as appreciate the fact that demonstrating confidence in religious leaders and the grace they carry without looking for ways of dislodging the socioeconomic structures of injustice is not an adequate solution to the problem. Consequently, Collium Banda notes,

> while seeking divine intervention remains important and necessary, it should not be employed to replace responsible actions that are geared towards fighting unjust systems ... behind economic injustice are human structures, human institutions, people, policies, practices, beliefs, attitudes, convictions and habits that need to be confronted, challenged, abandoned and transformed.[48]

In view of the lamentable socioeconomic injustices in Nigeria and Africa, religious leaders of faith communities "need to have the courage like Micah to call a spade a spade and to challenge their flocks to remember the costly grace

---

[47] Dietrich Bonhoeffer, *The Cost of Discipleship* (New York: Touchstone, 1995), 43.
[48] Banda, "Not Anointing, but Justice?," 5.

that necessitated the Son of God to die a gruesome death for human sin."[49] Although contemporarily pulpit ministry of some faith communities has helped to revive entrepreneurship among Christians, for Nigeria and indeed Africa to join the rest of the world and favorably compete in modern socioeconomic systems, "the greatest need is the development of transparent and accountable structures, systems, procedures and institutions to regulate all aspects of society."[50] The contemporary pulpits cannot afford to remain silent about current socioeconomic issues that are contradictory and obviously challenging. The Nigerian Christian pulpit must make informed and confident denouncements of national structures and policies that create undue hardships for citizens who are marginalized and held as economic hostages. The pulpit must teach and preach that miracles are not necessarily the answer; socioeconomic and political changes must come from citizens and Christians' hard work—from below, and not just by expecting miracles —from above. To achieve a better society, those who are sincere advocates of peace and justice cannot live in dread of the implications of censuring or peacefully challenging social injustice and the incompetence of those in power.

6.1.3.3.3. Advocacy that Censures Greed and Economic Idolatry

Very significant in the fight against current socioeconomic contradictions is prophetic advocacy that is committed to the worship of Yahweh and thus ready to denounce corruption, greed and economic idolatry. Micah's rhetoric indicates that greed and materialism were the basic problems of the spiritual and civil leaders of the nation: prophecy, administration of justice and teaching were driven by prosperity and bribes. Micah's response to the situation was his stimulating posture of being filled with the Spirit of God. This gave him not only the resolution and courage to speak the truth and describe the situation then and there, but the needed God-centered consciousness to say no to momentary attractions and enticements. Obviously, spiritual leaders who depend on Yahweh in a special manner will direct people to stay spiritually dependent. This could be the reason why genuine prophets shield away from materialism.[51] It is important to note that as a way of safeguarding the uncompromised prophetic advocacy of religious leaders in faith communities in Nigeria and elsewhere in the world, economic empowerment of religious leaders is vital. Prosperity and poverty both have their dangers: prosperity might lead to lack of dependence on God while poverty might lead to theft and consequently a violation of the cove-

---

[49] Dempster, *Micah*, 250.
[50] Paul Gifford, *Ghana's New Christianity: Pentecostalism in a Globalizing African Economy* (Bloomington: Indiana University Press, 2004), 197.
[51] Dempster, *Micah*, 246–47.

nant (cf. Prov 30:7–9). Dempster underscores the danger of materialism when he says, "The danger can be seen in the early days of Israel's history as a foreign prophet outside of Israel was motivated by wealth and would sell his blessings and curses to the highest bidder (Num 22–24)."[52]

Significantly, faith community members must reflect on the economic motivation for leadership. The effectiveness of prophetic advocacy in pulpit ministry rests on a number of factors, with the satisfaction of pastors or leaders' economic need serving as a key factor in safeguarding and nourishing the prophetic voice. Usually, when formal system of leadership opportunities, remunerations, and motivations make unethical practice subjectively gratifying, an individual has the rational tendency to act in a corrupt manner. Accordingly, Gary S. Becker remarks concerning the economists' usual analysis of choice is instructive: "a person commits an offense if the expected utility to him exceeds the utility he could get by using his time and other resources at other activities. Some persons become 'criminals', therefore, not because their basic motivation differs from that of other persons, but because their benefits and costs differ."[53] The salaries and social-welfare packages of those who occupy leadership positions in faith communities should not function as measures by which community members are saddled with undue responsibilities and thus prone to economic exploitation, as they remain the ones to bear the weight of their welfare economics. Truly, when leaders (usually few) seek the path of opportunities or privileges or benefits to the disadvantage of the good of all, in due course the life and welfare of society becomes a fertile ground for exploitation, corruption, violence, suffering, death and impediment to development.[54]

Support for priestly ministry was organized under the Law (Deut 18:1–8), and prophets were occasionally rewarded in appreciation of their service (1 Sam 9:7–8). However, to perform ministerial duties solely in the interest of financial or material gains results in mere professionalism or officialism and consequently religious commercialization and profiteering. Micah's anguish indicates that privilege and money without a sense of responsibility always corrupt the competence to see clearly, and to preach and teach truth without lowering standards.[55] He notes that the judges in the courts, the priests at the temple, and the prophets wherever they were found could all be secured with money in the form of bribes. Money became the idolatrous force that drove their lives so that they must covet it, and consequently this covetousness resulted in "cannibalism in the

---

[52] Dempster, *Micah*, 247; cf. 1 Sam 1–4 for the account of the corrupt sons of Eli and their material and sexual exploitation of Israel.
[53] Gary S. Becker, "Crime and Punishment: An Economic Approach," *JPE* 76.2 (1968): 176. https://www.journals.uchicago.edu/doi/abs/10.1086/259394.
[54] Dempster, *Micah*, 257.
[55] Smith-Christopher, *Micah*, 120.

courts, connivance among the prophets, and corruption of the priesthood."[56] If religious leaders occupy position of responsibility only to give privileged and favored treatments to those who bestow special and particular material benefits on them, disregard, take for granted the less privileged because of their social and economic standing and manipulate the word of God in their preaching, teaching and counseling ministry, it must be noted that such are a disgrace to God and they will ultimately be disgraced by God.

Today, the attempt to lower the standard of God's demand on people through the religious functions of preaching, teaching, and counselling has resulted in gathering, creating and maintaining faith communities that are peopled with strong, worldly, and materialistic consciousness. As one can observe in many faith communities, there is an extraordinary spectacle of religious programmes with large attendance of people, programmes designed to cater to fleshly desire, sensual appetites, and human pride.[57] Contemporary popular religious passwords such as "sow a seed to proceed," "envelop to develop," "quality seed begets quality harvest," are used by religious leaders to invite people as merchants in exchange deals with God for some material benefits. It is regrettable to note that such strategy designed only to seek the fulfilment of fleshly desires has left so much economic idolatry in religious communities and enfeebled their evangelistic witness and transformative impact on society. Micah offers spiritual leaders and faith communities of every age several important lessons. Essentially, spiritual leaders of faith communities must endeavor to intentionally incarnate the truth of godliness resulting in material contentment; they must have God as their ultimate treasure and not their treasury. This deliberate incarnation of godliness will infuse them with spiritual power resulting in dependence on God who is the true source of life and thus they will be able to confidently denounce greed, corruption, and economic idolatry. Faith communities are expected to stand in solidarity with the poor and marginalized majority in society. However, a situation in which religious leaders of faith communities are living in luxury and affluence whilst many of their followers are living in abject poverty requires self-criticism. A self-critical assessment of religious leaders' negative conduct will help them to prophetically denounce the luxury and greed of many corporate entrepreneurs, and national leaders who engage in such key roles that result in the impoverishment of people particularly in Nigeria and Africa in general.[58] If God and his provisions are not sufficient and satisfactory for human desires both in life and ministry, there is definitely an internal

---

[56] Dempster, *Micah*, 255.
[57] John MacArthur, *Ashamed of the Gospel: When the Church Becomes Like the World* (Wheaton: Crossway, 1993), 17.
[58] Agbiji and Swart, "Religion and Social Transformation in Africa," 14.

problem which will result to an external one in society; namely, covetousness that will lead to injustice.

6.2. The Wider Society and Socioeconomic Realities

The second sphere of the application of the ethical concerns of Micah's oracles is the wider Nigerian-African society. There is a massive national out-cry of people who are seeking ways of approaching and combating poverty, corruption, and exploitation in the Nigerian society. Since religious ideologies (as they are in the book of Micah) are invariably shaped by historical and socioeconomic contexts within which they emerge, Micah's ethical demands cannot be overlooked as they are uniquely and equally significant to the Nigerian context within which the phenomena of socioeconomic contradictions emerge.

Micah's oracles bear witness to actions in a given political, socioeconomic and religious context and with a critical, well-crafted understanding of the various ideologies and theologies of the past and present. These traditions are constantly being evangelically reinterpreted with the goal of presenting imaginative alternatives that are existentially possible. On the one hand, religious leaders and faith communities stand in solidarity with God and operate ministries in their context of socioeconomic contradictions with resentment, compassion, solidarity, and creative interpretation of Scriptures in view of the time. However, on the other, society generally is involved in the crisis. Consequently, ethical formulation cannot be removed from the life of people in society and society in general. A positive and transformed attitude is needed from those in society at different levels so as to strengthen the dignity of the drive at renewal and national transformation. Given the reality of widespread poverty, exploitation, corruption, and obvious failure of leadership in Nigeria, how can Micah's ethical concerns be contextualized and appropriated? Insights from Micah's ethical concerns regarding societal and leadership problems in his time and context generate the following resources for the contemporary Nigerian context with its socioeconomic realities.

6.2.1. Inspiring Governance, Accountable Leadership, and Transparency

In the Old Testament, ancient Israel was governed by elected or chosen, decentralized authorities. Whilst the Mosaic Law provides a set of norms that serves as Israel's distinctive wisdom (cf. Deut 4:8), prior to the institution of the monarchy (Deut 17:14–20), there was a "centralized ethical/legal canon" whose interpretation and enforcement was the responsibility of "community elders (heads of extended families) gathered typically at the administrative/judicial 'common' of the time, the main gate into and out of the city ('elders at the gate').[59] The particular administrative responsibilities of these elders at the gate are those of ensuring that society is characterized by righteousness and justice. They were to be guided by benevolent ethical norms especially towards the poor and needy (Job 29:7–17; cf. Exod 23:2–3, 6–8).

During the period of the divided kingdom in which Israel was ruled by a monarchy, the implementation of a bureaucratic structure led the classical prophets to unequivocally announce that the administration of justice was the supreme responsibility of Israel's ruling class. Consequently, James L. Mays remarks: "When the prophets spoke of justice, they frequently addressed specific groups whom they called 'officials', 'chiefs or heads', 'leaders', 'elders', all titles for persons who had roles of authority and power in the social and administrative structure of Judah and Israel."[60] That the prophets (with particular reference to Micah in this study) indicted the judicial (court officials) and religious (prophets and priests) authorities with a catalogue of misdemeanor indicates a degree of uninspiring governance, unaccountable leadership and lack of transparency. This is very pointed in the observation of Bruce C. Birch: "At every level those in leadership have failed to serve justice and righteousness. Their loyalties have been turned from God to the lure of wealth and power. From rulers and nobles to prophet and priest—at every level the covenant has been forgotten and corruption is evident."[61] Micah's lamentation at the failure of Israel's leaders within the context of historical and socioeconomic realities is sadly and painfully similar to the Nigerian context (as well as other African nations) where elected national leaders and politicians have failed to live up to the heights of their responsibility. Here and now, the obvious pitfalls of governing officials that Micah addressed within the historical and socioeconomic contexts of ancient Israel are widespread reality in Nigeria.

Efficient and inspiring governance implies the fair, just and effective administration of power and influence by those in a government position on behalf of citizens. It is a government that requires power and resource-sharing in the best interests of the people, with adequate consultation of citizens toward effective decision-making. Such a system of governance guarantees mutual trust, respect, and confidence for both the people and the leaders. Uninspiring leadership is characterized by oppression of the people and treating them as subjects and secondary rather than fellow citizens. Responsible leaders in good and in-

---

[59] Edd S. Noell, "Land Grabs, Unjust Exchange, and Bribes: Economic Opportunism and the Rights of the Poor in Ancient Israel," *SWJT* 59.2 (2017): 190.

[60] James L. Mays, "Justice: Perspectives from the Prophetic Tradition," *Int* 37.1 (1983): 9.

[61] Bruce C. Birch, *Let Justice Roll Down: The Old Testament, Ethics, and the Christian Life* (Louisville: Westminster John Knox, 1991), 265.

spiring governance consider themselves as those who elected to serve and not to oppressively dominate the people.

In Nigeria today, this democratic framework of inspiring governance and leadership appears to be obscure as government exists for itself and not for the people. The existing national political structure and system maintains a very high degree of irresponsibility and lack of accountability to the electorate. This lack of accountability and transparency is manifestly reflected in the prioritization of the maintenance of an extremely large cabinet with a substantial percentage of the current national budget vote on salaries and overheads of public officials: "Personnel costs will take 40% of the projected revenue for 2019, estimated at N2.29 trillion."[62] In a recent article that decries the current national budget, Comfort Oseghale notes:

> It is a known fact that most of the recurrent expenses in Nigeria's budget are used to fund the most mundane of activities.... Nigeria's inability to prioritize its needs and allocate resources accordingly through the years, has finally accorded us the unenviable rank of the world's poverty capital ... Instead of fixing key infrastructure and making sure public systems work, and by so doing, attract foreign investments, it is worrisome that the government is more concerned with bloated recurrent expenses for running ministries, departments and agencies of government, most of whom don't expend the budget on the activities they are meant for.[63]

This development has not only led to inequitable distribution of wealth as it favors only the rich, but has increased greed and corruption, and grants excessive influence and power to those in leadership position. Sadly, quality health services and education which are expected to be affordable and accessible to all are being exceptionally underfunded and their competence completely restrained. Quality education and health are now the exclusive preserve and reserve of the rich elite. The obvious implications are the suffering of people as their dignity and well-being are constantly being compromised. If contemporary Nigeria (and Africa in general) is to be reoriented/reeducated along the principles and paths of equality, justice, freedom, and equity in political and socioeconomic relationships of all citizens in Nigeria, national leaders at every level of government must seek to maintain a high degree of integrity, responsibility, transparency, and accountability in the administration of national resources, opportunities, rewards, and statuses for the benefit of all. They must

---

[62] Aderemi Ojekunle, "A Look at the Key Figures in Nigeria's 2019 Budget," December 20, 2018, https://www.pulse.ng/bi/finance/a-look-at-the-key-figures-in-nigerias-2019-budget/yj8pvqs.

[63] Comfort Oseghale, "Nigeria's Bloated Recurrent Expenditure," December 27, 2018, https://shipsandports.com.ng/nigerias-bloated-recurrent-expenditure/.

personally and collectively make a conscious effort and practical commitment to these moral virtues as their primary goal and responsibility.

6.2.2. Preventing Abuse through Just Civil Rule and Economic Policies

Perhaps one of the most solemn ethical messages from Micah for contemporary Nigerian society is that of the protection and prevention of abuse of the poor and marginalized through just civil rule and economic policies. Protection and prevention of abuse of the rights of the poor and marginalized was a unique moral leadership prize worth seeking by Israel's leadership within the ancient world as demonstrated by the Pentateuch as well as both wisdom and prophetic literature.[64] But as Micah's oracles (and other prophets) indicate, several arbitrary elements such as economic piracy and land confiscation (2:1–5), dishonest business practices and economic coercion (6:10–12), and other corrupt practices by officials and judges (7:3–4) weakened the standards of honesty and transparency governing human and material rights as well as commercial deals reflected in the Pentateuch (Exod 20:15, 17; Lev 19:35; Deut 19:14; 27:17), Wisdom (Prov 29:7; Job 36:6) and prophetic literature (Isa 5:8; 10:2; Jer 5:28; Hos 12:7–8; Amos 8:5–6; Hab 2:9).

While the poor in ancient Israel faced severe economic duress due to socio-economic changes that occurred during the period of Israel's divided kingdom between 800–600 BCE,[65] Micah specifically notes that economic pressure on the poor occurs through the wealthy urban land magnates forming private royal connections with the assistance of judicial and government officials of Israel and Judah (Mic 2:2). He verbally describes a cruel confiscation of the economic assets of the poor as an illegal action of those in power.[66] Noell expounds this economic disadvantage thus:

> The rights of the poor are violated when a landowner, merchant or lender leverages their economic advantage over a poor Israelite who is a tenant on the land, a farmer selling his crop, a consumer buying grain, or a borrower of basic foodstuffs. These rights are trampled by landowners and merchants who have the backing of the civil government. We find here the phenomenon of judicial malpractice for 'the mortgaging of and foreclosure upon family lands, members, and property involved court action.'[67]

---

[64] Christopher J. H. Wright, *Old Testament Ethics for the People of God* (Downers Grove: InterVasity, 2004), 313. See also, Craig M. Gay, "Poverty," in *The Oxford Handbook of Christianity and Economics* (Oxford: Oxford University Press, 2014), 620–36.
[65] Noell, "Land Grabs, Unjust Exchange, and Bribes," 191.
[66] Waltke, *Commentary on Micah*, 95–96.
[67] Noell, "Land Grabs, Unjust Exchange, and Bribes," 194.

Micah's attack on unjust economic exchanges (6:10–11) was most pointedly an unlawful period, in which there is lack of or biased implementation of the rule of law in view of covenant stipulation. This development finds expression in a number of prophetic complaints concerning false weights and balances (cf. Hos 12:7–8; Amos 8:5–6) resulting in lack of reliable commitment and solidarity in economic exchanges especially by the poor.[68]

Micah's message places an urgent demand on government functionaries in Nigeria about the significance of respecting human life, preventing abuse, and protecting the weak and vulnerable in society. As it is today, the need for justice in Nigeria is desperately an urgent concern for rejuvenated and efficient leadership, not only at a religious level but also in socioeconomic and political contexts. Nigerians long for voices of liberation in the judiciary, and of wisdom and passion in government to help them find just and unbiased paths into a future of growing and viable economic proportion and tranquility. Too many are they whose innocence and ignorance prevented them from comprehending the corrupt nature and moral failure of those in leadership who have taken advantage of them and thus increase economic inequalities and dislocations. When people are marginalized or taken advantage of in society, truly the value of their lives is diminished. Reflection on Micah's ethical concern thus calls for stricter measures for dealing with corrupt people by exposing and rooting them out of society. The development and enforcement of dynamic institutional measures will serve to constrain the economic advantages of the wealthy, distribute social trust more widely and promote socioeconomic rights of the poor and across society in general.

6.2.3. Commitment to the Ideals of Healthy and Viable Community Living

The spectrum of socioeconomic and religious realities reflected in Micah's oracles indicates why the book's ethical message is such an enduring and stimulating one, for inviting people to an embodiment of and commitment to the ideals of healthy and viable community living. The oracle units are filled with great moral diction concerning covenant fidelity that finds primary reality in the moral character, sensitivity, and action of Yahweh. Yahweh's faithfulness to Israel is directly grounded in the festive understanding of shared responsibility and loyal commitment to the requirements of the covenant at Sinai. The mani-

---

[68] For the use of illegal and dishonest measures to gain wealth and defrauding the poor see, Gary V. Smith, *Hosea, Amos, Micah*, The NIV Application Commentary (Grand Rapids: Zondervan, 2001), 556; John H. Walton, Victor H. Matthews, and Mark W. Chavalas, *The IVP Bible Background Commentary: Old Testament* (Downers Grove: Inter-Varsity, 2000), 786; J. Gordon McConville, *Deuteronomy* (Leicester: Apollos, 2002), 372.

fest demonstration of Yahweh's faithfulness find expression in Israel's saving events described by Micah (6:3–4; cf. Hos 11:1–2; Amos 3:1–2). Because Yahweh has demonstrated the paired qualities of justice and righteousness to Israel, Israel has the moral obligation to embody these same moral qualities in life and community social relationships. Micah's oracles are an obvious reflection of a community that failed to embody covenant obligations. The violation of prescribed legal illustrations of primary responsibilities such as those of the Decalogue was disregarded (cf. Deut 1:17; 17:8–11).

Sadly, the fundamental regard for virtue and disapproval of evil so as to give attention to the welfare of marginalized and most vulnerable individuals was ignored. Although they were expected to know justice (both by experience and practice), they hate good and love evil (3:1–2). Micah observes significant disparity between the principles of the covenant for viable community living especially in the equitable distribution of available basic resources and the unevenness and fragmentation that marked the socioeconomic sphere of their lived contexts (Mic 2:1–2). James L. Mays aptly describes the structural shift that undermined Israel's covenant community living, "The shift of the primary social good, land, from the function of support to that of capital; the reorientation of social goals from personal values to economic profit; the subordination of judicial process to the interests of the entrepreneur."[69] The extent to which the deficiency of moral value affected community living is seen also in the prophet's indictment of those who exploit and defraud by corrupt commercial dealings or the perversion of the processes of justice in the interest of the wealthy (6:11–12). The shattering of the moral fabric of their society; the collapse of the basic family structure (7:2–4) constitute both a result of societal collapse and a cause of it.

Micah's dynamic perspectives about viable community living are vital elements for creating a healthy viable community today. Viable community living must be a deliberate desire of community members and well supported commitment to covenant and a constitutional ethos of justice, honesty, integrity, and responsibility. Micah invites contemporary societies that are plagued by greed, exploitation, dishonesty, and corruption to a renewed sense of community. The oracles are essentially a call to the vital concern of honesty and justice required for a harmonious community relationship and experience. Practical and dedicated response to this invitation will help in the reduction if not complete elimination of the dreadful cancers of greed, wickedness, oppression, envy, jealousy, manipulation, and insincerity, that are undermining people's corporate existence and experience of growth and development. Nigerians must place justice, integrity, honesty, hard work and responsibility more prominently on the

---

[69] James Luther Mays, "Justice: Perspectives from the Prophets," in *Prophecy in Israel*, ed. David L. Petersen (Philadelphia: Fortress, 1987), 148.

agenda of national life both for citizens and leaders. Truly, strong, profound, and lasting commitment to God and the ideals of healthy community living can guarantee the well-being of a nation.

6.3. Injustice and National Development

Micah's oracles indicate the extent to which the unfaithfulness of injustice undermined society's peacefulness and well-being. The consequence of the unfaithfulness of injustice that Micah denounced in his oracles were obviously a result of the failure of Israel's leaders, who corrupted the political, socioeconomic and religious structures of their community, as well as disregarding the covenant principles that were expected to guide them. Rather than serving Yahweh's people in covenant fidelity, they pursued their selfish interest for materialistic gains. The rhetoric of the condemnation of injustice finds expression in society with repeated connection to the well-being of the land. While his comprehensive denunciations (cf. 3:1–12) are a typical representation of the severity of prophetic diatribe against Israel's ruling class, Yahweh's anger manifests most pointedly within "the context of the effect of judgment as punishment of society for ethical misdemeanours, a wrath that affects all of society and the eco-system too."[70] The basic and essential moral deduction from Micah's indictment for contemporary readers is that the prophetic denunciation demonstrates an insightful awareness of the problems that endanger the quality and fabric of human life, and all the more so, the likelihood of human survival. In Micah, the correlation between sin and judgement; that is, the experience of moral failures and national downfall is clear (3:12; 6:11–15): "The punishment is not abstract; it is physical, affecting not just the people but the well-being of their land, and is a direct reversal of the hopes and desires expressed in Ps 72."[71]

Since Micah's indictments of Israel/Judah at different levels are regarded as a prophetic channel of giving ethical significance to Israelite religion and a movement towards societal transformation,[72] the oracles are thus of considerable significance for Nigeria's (and other African nations) contemporary situation of various socioeconomic contradictions, corruption and exploitation that have undermined efficient governance, viable growth and development and national

---

[70] Katharine J. Dell, "Introduction," *Ethical and Unethical in the Old Testament: God and Humans in Dialogue*, ed. Katharine J. Dell (New York: T&T Clark International, 2010), 4.

[71] Marlow, "Justice for Whom?," 107.

[72] See Paul L. Redditt, "Wrath, Anger, Indignation," in *Westminster Theological Wordbook of the Bible*, ed. Donald Gowan (Louisville, KY: Westminster John Knox, 2003), 547–49; Walter Brueggemann, *Theology of the Old Testament. Testimony, Dispute, Advocacy* (Minneapolis: Fortress, 1997), 373–99.

transformation.[73] Within Nigeria's present democratic dispensation, the impact of corruption on the nation's transformation has been observed to include among others, inefficient governance, reduction of national wealth, weak service delivery, brain drain, insufficient infrastructural, and basic amenities (such as in the health, education and transportation sector), poor management of corporate enterprise and general moral decadence.[74]

Nigerians at every level of national life must know that the unfaithfulness of injustice not only has adverse effects on the poor and marginalized but obviously threatens the general well-being and prosperity of society, as it creates a fragmented and disorganized society in which social vices flourish. Consequently, Micah's oracles invite readers to reflect on the reality of cause and effect and thus, of the impact of their attitudes and behavior especially on those who are victims of exploitation and deprivation and society in general. Although the call for socioeconomic justice stemmed from different experiences and contexts, Micah's indictments are a stimulating invitation to contemporary readers' critical and serious self-reflection and evaluation of the impact of their actions on both human life and societal well-being.

---

[73] For readings on corruption and development in Nigeria, see Bello Ibrahim and Ahmad Hassan Ahmad, "The Impact of Corruption on National Development in Nigeria," *IJSRMS* 2.1 (2017): 13–23; Tolu Lawal, and Abe Oluwatoyin, "National Development in Nigeria: Issues, Challenges and Prospects," *JPAPR* 3.9 (2011): 237–41; Arinze Ngwube and Chuka Okoli, "The Role of the Economic Financial Crime Commission in the Fight against Corruption in Nigeria," *JSSS* 4.1 (2013): 92–107.

[74] Ibrahim and Ahmad, "The Impact of Corruption on National Development in Nigeria," 20; Ibrahim K. Mikail, "Corruption and National Development in Nigeria's Fourth Republic," *JORIND* 10.3 (2012): 227.

7

CONCLUSION

> There may be times when we are powerless to prevent injustice, but there must never be a time when we fail to protest.
> —Elie Wiesel

This study addressed political, socioeconomic, and religious circumstances that called forth Micah's prophetic oracles and how the literary prophetic discourse dealt with socioeconomic injustice and worship within the context of community relationship, national experience, and orientation. The book's superscription, which, of course, functions as the initial part of the prophet's curriculum vitae, provides information that hints at a particular nexus of political, socioeconomic, and religious realities. The book presents readers with several social distinctions along with a comprehensive and scathing critique of how changing domestic dynamics had induced manifold and widespread abuses. The substantial change in the economic life of Israel especially during the period of the divided Kingdom in which classical prophets ministered obviously made life complicated for them. The concentration of property through land foreclosure and its resultant eviction and confiscation (cf. Deut 27:17; Prov 23:10–11), which was regarded as reprehensible, had become widespread in Micah's time. Consequently, Micah found his prophetic call in Yahweh's transcendence and in the cry of oppression from the poor and marginalized.

Applying the ethical principles of Yahweh's sovereignty, justice and human responsibility, Micah rose to the challenge and categorically condemned religious activities and distorted theological discussion in the face of massive injustice. Remarkably, the literary text is poignantly filled with comprehensive accusations predominantly targeted at those who occupied positions of power and influence. Although Micah condemned the general sin of covenant unfaithfulness and idolatry (1:5–7), the specific transgressions of perversion of justice in the interest of materialism by those in leadership positions, whether administrative (3:1, 9, 11; 7:3) or religious (3:5, 11), the manner in which the wealthy had abused their position of influence (2:1–2, 8–9; 6:11–12) and the direct consequences of such violations, constitute the primary focus of this project. The deterioration of moral values did not only cut across those who occupy a leadership position but also meant that the whole way of life in Micah's society was that of greed which has been geared toward avid and unsatisfiable consumption and has become particularly scandalous. A spectrum of the society in Jerusalem had accumulated large estates and vast resources for themselves, and their insatiable greed was given approval by a corrupt judicial and religious system. The poor are seen as victims of the transgression of oppression and injustice (2:2; 3:1–3; 6:12) while the violation of covenantal responsibility is made obvious by idolatry (1:7; 5:13–14) and subjugation of the poor (2:2, 6–9; 3:1–3, 9). Micah decries the manner in which the less privileged in his community were treated by the wealthy, the hijacking of Israel's covenant, and the collusion of the leaders in the transgression that he saw. The ethical foundation of the upper-class exploitation of the peasants/poor was rent capitalism rather than compassionate commitment to Yahweh's concerns. Such capitalistic ideas made them not only morally reprehensible but theologically contemptible.

The study hermeneutically examined the literary portrayal of the unfaithfulness of injustice in the socioeconomic and religious layers in the book of Micah. Essentially, this chain of tradition (from the eighth century prophetic character, Micah) and the literary paradigm of preserving Micah's oracle of denunciation of unfaithfulness of injustice serve to situate the book's relevance beyond the original community or communities of readers to transhistorical readers with similar structural socioeconomic ideologies and a theology of resistance against oppression. The exploration examined essential ethical thrusts of Micah's prophetic discourse that encompasses various aspects of prophetic imagination in the book of Micah, namely: exploitation, leadership, prophetic advocacy, and exemplary living that balances worship and lifestyle with a view to transforming individuals, faith communities and communities and nations. In this project, the ethical thrusts of the examined oracle units provided a basis for making contemporary ethical demands upon Christian communities and the larger human society.

Micah presents several features that became the foundation upon which socioeconomic and religious transgressions were practiced. The development of an agrarian economy which suffered from insufficiently defined or prescribed economic rights, covenant unfaithfulness, inequality, corruption, exploitation and other measures adopted by the wealthy to obtain from public authorities severe economic privileges over the poor and disenfranchised underscores Micah's emphasis on the dark side of human life in society. This prophetic description exposes various degrees of exploitation and corruption with a momentum that moves from calling national leaders, wealthy land magnates and merchants who

7. Conclusion

engaged in crooked lending and commercial practices to listen, so as to embrace the demands of justice.

The intensity of the literary parallel between the prophet's description of the activities of judicial and religious leaders and those in which one lives in a contemporary African (Nigerian) context is chronically unrelenting. Such striking parallels form the basis of moving from a universal and normative description of ethical principles to a contextualized application of the ethical issues arising from the texts. These parallels when re-read by a contemporary African reader in a context of socioeconomic and religious contradictions generate viable and fruitful alternatives for addressing leadership failures, greed, exploitation, corruption, and inequality and consequently contributing to the creation and maintenance of a healthy viable community at different levels of national life.

In so doing, the study observes that among several institutional and national problems that have hindered sustainable growth and development generally in Africa and especially in Nigeria is the corruption factor, which is grounded on a poor and unproductive culture and orientation of irresponsible and unaccountable leadership and citizens. While many Nigerians seek support in religion and religious activities in the face of corrupt leadership and failed national governance, the quest for socioeconomic recovery has turned many religious organizations and faith communities to be centers of exploitation where teeming congregants are manipulated through distorted theological rationalization. Consequently, there are obviously complementary trajectories of socioeconomic contradictions in comparison with religious growth in Nigeria. In dealing with this thorn in the flesh, the project advocates that Christians and Christian Communities in Nigeria must as matter of necessity, make deliberate commitment to living with the fear of God and trusting in his sovereignty and endeavoring to maintain a healthy balance between worship and lifestyle. Religious leaders of faith communities like Micah must demonstrate great moral credentials in life and ministry, give priority to sound theological interpretation of the scriptures, and become solidly uncompromising in their prophetic advocacy. While faith and prayer prescriptions are important in the quest for growth and development, prophetic advocacy of religious leaders must give priority to truth and justice, censure greed and economic idolatry, and seek to recover and develop human potentials.

The oracles invite readers to the urgent and compelling ethical demands of addressing socioeconomic, religious, leadership and societal structures that make life complicated for people in society. They invite contemporary Christians and faith communities as public witness in a challenging moral culture to respond faithfully to the moral uncertainty created by unprecedented problems of socioeconomic and religious contradictions. The oracles are of stimulating impetus for Nigerians and her leaders to the values of good governance, responsible leadership, and transparency, of protecting and preventing abuse through just civil rule and economic policies, and for inviting people generally to unconditional commitment to the ideals of healthy and viable community living. To attain sustainable growth and development, leaders and citizens at various levels must embody charismatic enthusiasm, thoughtful leadership, and devotion to honest work.

Micah's charismatic enthusiasm for the nexus between socioeconomic and religious justice in society and fruitfulness and sustainable growth and stability in national life indicates his fundamental ethical concern and belief in a divinely established world order. Such an instituted world order places a demand on people and thus does not absolve them of their responsibilities. The neglect of justice and righteousness results in societal dislocation, disequilibrium, and clearly serious negative impressions on the poor, and marginalized. Consequently, thoughtful reflection on Micah's ethical thrust will hold human beings, especially those who occupy positions of influence and power, to be accountable for societal breakdown. The inspiring and stimulating motivation from Micah's ethical thrust for contemporary reflection and application is the development of a visionary, holistic approach, an organized socioeconomic equity and transparency framework by policy makers and the characteristic embodiment and demonstration of the virtues of honesty, integrity, and hard work at every level of life.

BIBLIOGRAPHY

Abogunrin, Samuel O. "The Community of Goods in the Early Church and the Distribution of National Wealth." *AJBS* 1.2 (1986): 74–94.

Achenbach, Reinhard. "'A Prophet like Moses' (Deut 18:15)—'No Prophet like Moses' (Deut 34:10): Some Observations on the Relation between the Pentateuch and the Latter Prophets." Pages 435–58 in *The Pentateuch: International Perspectives on Current Research*. Edited by Thomas B. Dozeman, Konrad Schmid and Baruch J. Schwartz. Tubingen: Mohr Seibeck, 2011.

———. "The Protection of *Personae Miserae* in Ancient Israelite Law and Wisdom and in the Ostracon from Khirbet Qeiyafa." *Semitica* 54 (2012): 93–125.

ActionAid Nigeria. "Corruption and Poverty in Nigeria: A Report." Abuja: Nigeria. 2015. http://www.actionaid.org/nigeria/publications/poverty-and-corruption-nigeria.

Adamo, David T. "The Task and Distinctiveness of African Biblical Hermeneutics." *OTE* 28.1 (2015): 31–52. http://dx.doi.org/10.17159/2312-3621/2015/v28n1a4

———. "What Is African Biblical Hermeneutics?" *JBT* 13.1 (2015): 59–72.

Agbiji, Obaji M., and Ignatius Swart. "Religion and Social Transformation in Africa: A Critical and Appreciative Perspective." *Scriptura* 114.1 (2015): 1–20. https://doi.org/10.7833/ 114-0-1115.

Aharoni, Yohanan. *The Land of the Bible: A Historical Geography*. Philadelphia: Westminster John Knox, 1979.

Alfaro, Juan I. *Justice and Loyalty: A Commentary on the Book of Micah*. Grand Rapids: Eerdmans, 1989.

———. *Micah: Justice and Loyalty*. Grand Rapids: Eerdmans, 1996.

Allen, Leslie C. *The Books of Joel, Obadiah, Jonah and Micah*. NICOT. Grand Rapids: Eerdmans, 1976.

———. "Micah's Social Concern." *Vox Evangelica* 8 (1973): 22–32.

Andersen, Francis I., and David N. Freedman. *Micah: A New Translation with Introduction and Commentary*. AB 24E. New York: Doubleday, 2000.

Anderson, Bernhard W. *The Eighth Century Prophets: Amos, Hosea, Isaiah, Micah.* Philadelphia: Fortress, 1978.

Andersson, Staffan, and Paul M. Heywood. "The Politics of Perception: Use and Abuse of Transparency International's Approach to Measuring Corruption." *PSt* 57.4 (2009): 746–67. https://doi.org/10.1111/j.1467-9248.2008.00758.x.

Arndt, Emily. *Demanding our Attention: The Hebrew Bible as a Source for Christian Ethics.* Grand Rapids: Eerdmans, 2011.

Asamoah-Gyadu, J. Kwabena. *African Charismatics: Current Developments within Independent Pentecostalism in Ghana.* Leiden: Brill, 2005.

Atherstone, Jeff. "Africa Infested by Health and Wealth Teaching." June 25, 2015. https://www.thegospelcoalition.org/article/africa-infested-by-health-and-wealth-teaching/.

Avalos, Hector. *The End of Biblical Studies.* Amherst: Prometheus Books, 2007.

Baker, Kenneth. *The NIV Study Bible.* Grand Rapids: Zondervan, 1995.

Banda, Collium. "Empowering Hope? Jürgen Moltmann's Eschatological Challenge to Ecclesiological Responses in the Zimbabwean Context of Poverty." PhD diss. Stellenbosch: Stellenbosch University, 2016.

———. "Not Anointing, but Justice? A Critical Reflection on the Anointing of Pentecostal Prophets in a Context of Economic Injustice." *Verbum et Ecclesia* 39.1 (2018): 1–11, a1870. https://doi.org/10.4102/ve.v39i1.1870.

Barker, Kenneth L. "A Literary Analysis of the Book of Micah." *BibSac* 155 (1998): 437–48.

Barton, John. *Ethics in Ancient Israel.* Oxford: Oxford University Press, 2014.

———. "The Prophets and the Cult." Pages 111–22 in *Temple and Worship in Biblical Israel.* Edited by John Day. Proceedings of the Oxford Old Testament Seminar. New York: T&T Clark, 2007.

———. *Understanding Old Testament Ethics: Approaches and Explorations.* Louisville: Westminster John Knox, 2003.

Becker, Gary S. "Crime and Punishment: An Economic Approach." *Journal of Political Economy* 76.2 (1968): 169–217. https://www.journals.uchicago.edu/doi/abs/10.1086/259394.

Beentjes, Pancratius C. "Constructs of Prophets and Prophecy in the Book of Chronicles." Pages 21–40 in *Constructs of Prophecy in the Former and Latter Prophets and Other Texts.* Edited by Lester L. Grabbe and Martti Nissinen. Vol. 4. Atlanta: Society of Biblical Literature, 2011.

Ben Zvi, Ehud. "The Concept of Prophetic Books." Pages 73–95 in *The Production of Prophecy: Constructing Prophecy and Prophets in Yehud.* Edited by Diana V. Edelman and Ehud Ben Zvi. London: Equinox, 2009.

———. *Micah.* Forms of the Old Testament Literature 21B. Grand Rapids: Eerdmans, 2000.

———. "Reconstructing the Intellectual Discourse of Ancient Yehud." *StRel* 39.1 (2010): 7–23.

Berges, Ulrich. "The Book of Isaiah as Isaiah's Book: The Latest Developments in the Research of the Prophets." *OTE* 23.3 (2010): 549–73.

Berković, Danijel. "Aspects and Modalities of God's Presence in the Old Testament." KAIROS - *EJT* 3.1 (2009): 51–72.

Birch, Bruce C. "Divine Character and the Formation of Moral Community in the Book of Exodus." Pages 119–35 in *The Bible in Ethics: The Second Sheffield Colloquium*. Edited by John W. Rogerson, Margaret Davies, and M. Daniel Carroll R. JSOTSup 207. Sheffield: Sheffield Academic, 1995.

———. *Let Justice Roll Down: The Old Testament, Ethics, and the Christian Life*. Louisville: Westminster John Knox, 1991.

Blenkinsopp, Joseph. *A History of Prophecy in Israel*. Louisville: Westminster John Knox, 1996.

Block, Daniel I. "Empowered by the Spirit of God: The Holy Spirit in the Historigraphic Writings of the Old Testament." *SBJT* 1.1 (1997): 41–52.

Blomberg, Craig L. *Neither Poverty nor Riches: A Biblical Theology of Material Possessions*. Leicester, England: Apollos, IVP, 1999.

Bonhoeffer, Dietrich. *The Cost of Discipleship*. New York: Touchstone, 1995.

Bright, John. *A History of Israel*. Philadelphia: Westminster, 1981.

Brueggemann, Walter. "Crisis-Evoked, Crisis-Resolving Speech." *BTB* 24.3 (1994):95–105.

———. *An Introduction to the Old Testament: The Canon and Christian Imagination*. Louisville, KY: Westminster John Knox, 2003.

———. *Reverberations of Faith: A Theological Handbook of Old Testament Themes*. Louisville: Westminster John Knox, 2002.

———. *Theology of the Old Testament: Testimony, Dispute, and Advocacy*. Minneapolis: Fortress, 1997.

———. "Walk Humbly with Your God: Micah 6:8." *JP* 33 (2010): 14–19.

Burgess, Stanley M. *Encyclopaedia of Pentecostal and Charismatic Christianity*. New York: Routledge, 2006.

Carr, David M. *An Introduction to the Old Testament: Sacred Texts and Imperial Contexts of the Hebrew Bible*. Chichester: Wiley & Sons, 2010.

Carroll, Daniel R. M. "Ethics." Pages 185–93 in *Dictionary of the Old Testament Prophets*. Edited by Mark J. Boda and Jordan G. McConville. Downers Grove: InterVarsity, 2012.

———. "Failing the Vulnerable: The Prophet and Social Care." Pages 33–47 in *Transforming the World? The Gospel and Social Responsibility*. Edited by Jamie A. Grant and Dewl A. Hughes. Grand Rapids: IVP, 2009.

———. "A Passion for Justice and the Conflicted Self: Lessons from the Book of Micah." *Journal of Psychology and Christianity* 25.2 (2006): 169–76.

Chaney, Marvin L. "The Political Economy of Peasant Poverty: What the Eighth-Century Prophets Presumed but Did Not State." *JRSSup 10 (2014)*: 34–60.

Chang, Dongshin Don. *Phinehas, the Sons of Zadok, and Melchizedek: Priestly Covenant in Late Second Temple Texts*. LSTS 90. New York: Bloomsbury T&T Clark, 2016.

Chisholm, Robert B., Jr. *Handbook on the Prophets*. Grand Rapids: Baker Academic, 2002.

Clark, Gordon R. *The Word Hesed in the Hebrew Bible*. JSOTSup 157. Sheffield: Sheffield Academic, 1993.

Coomber, Matthew J. M. "Caught in the Crossfire? Economic Injustice and Prophetic Motivation in Eighth-Century Judah." *BibInt* 19 (2011): 396–432.

Counet, P. Chatelion, and Ulrich Berges. *One Text, A Thousand Methods: Studies in Memory of Sjef van Tilborg*. BibInt 71. Leiden: Brill, 2005.

Crenshaw, James L. *The Psalms: An Introduction*. Grand Rapids: Eerdmans, 2001.

Cuffey, Kenneth H. "The Coherence of Micah: A Review of Proposals and a New Interpretation." DPhil. diss., Drew University, 1987.

Davies, Paul R. "Ethics and the Old Testament." Pages 164–73 in *The Bible in Ethics: The Second Sheffield Colloquium*. Edited by John W. Rogerson, Margaret Davies, and M. Daniel Carroll R. JSOTSup 207. Sheffield: Sheffield Academic, 1995.

Dawes, Stephen B. "Walking Humbly: Micah 6:8 Revisited." *SJT* 41.3 (1988): 331–39.

Day, John. "Asherah." *ABD* 1:483–87.

De Gruchy, John W. *Christianity and Democracy: A Theology for a Just World Order*. Cambridge: Cambridge University Press, 1995.

De Jong, Matthijs J. "The Fallacy of 'True and False' in Prophecy Illustrated by Jer. 28:8–9." *JHS* 12.10 (2012): 1–31.

———. *Isaiah among the Ancient Near Eastern Prophets: A Comparative Study of the Earliest Stages of the Isaiah Tradition and the Neo-Assyrian Prophets*. VTSup 117. Leiden: Brill, 2007.

De Vaux, Roland. *Ancient Israel: Its Life and Institutions*. Translated by John McHugh. Biblical Resource Series 3. Grand Rapids: Eerdmans, 1997.

Dell, Katharine J. "Introduction." Pages 1–8 in *Ethical and Unethical in the Old Testament: God and Humans in Dialogue*. Edited by Katharine J. Dell. New York: T&T Clark International, 2010.

Dempsey, Carol J. "Micah 2–3: Literary Artistry, Ethical Message, and Some Considerations about the Image of Yahweh and Micah." *JSOT* 85 (1999): 117–28.

Dempster, Stephen G. *Micah*. The Two Horizons Old Testament Commentary. Grand Rapids: Eerdmans, 2017.

Deng, Lual A. *Rethinking African Development: Towards a Framework for Social Integration and Ecological Harmony*. Asmara: Africa World, 1998.

Driver, Samuel R. *An Introduction to the Literature of the Old Testament.* New York: Scribner's Sons, 1913.

Edelman, Diana V. "From Prophets to Prophetic Books: The Fixing of the Divine Word." Pages 29–54 in *The Production of Prophecy: Constructing Prophecy and Prophets in Yehud.* Edited by Diana V. Edelman and Ehud Ben Zvi. London: Equinox, 2009.

Ehrlich, Carl S. *The Philistine in Transition: A History from ca. 1000–730 B.C.E.* Leiden: Brill, 1996.

Frevel, Christian. "Leadership and Conflict: Modelling the Charisma of Numbers." Pages 89–114 in *Debating Authority: Concepts of Leadership in the Pentateuch and the Former Prophets.* Edited by Katharina Pyschny and Sarah Schulz. Berlin: De Gruyter, 2018. https://doi.org/10.1515/9783110543391-001.

———. "Orientierung! Grundfragen einer Ethik des Alten Testaments." Pages 9–57 in *Mehr als Zehn Worte? Zur Bedeutung des Alten Testaments in ethischen Fragen.* Edited by Christian Frevel. Quaestiones disputatae 273. Freiburg: Herder, 2015.

Friedman, Hershey H. "Messages from the Ancient Prophets: Lessons for Today." *IJHSS* 1.20 (2011): 297–305.

Gay, Craig M. "Poverty." Pages 620–36 in *The Oxford Handbook of Christianity and Economics.* Oxford: Oxford University Press, 2014.

Gerstenberger, Erhard S. "Non-Temple Psalms: The Cultic Setting Revisited." Pages 338–49 in *The Oxford Handbook of the Psalms.* Edited by William P. Brown. Oxford: University Press, 2014.

———. "The Woe Oracle of the Prophets." *JBL* 81 (1962): 249–63.

Gifford, Paul. *Christianity, Politics, and Public Life in Kenya.* New York: Columbia University Press, 2009.

———. *Ghana's New Christianity: Pentecostalism in a Globalizing African Economy.* Bloomington: Indiana University Press, 2004.

Glenny, W. Edward. *Micah: A Commentary Based on Micah in Codex Vaticanus.* Leiden: Brill, 2015.

Gorman, Michael J. *Elements of Biblical Exegesis: A Basic Guide for Students and Ministers.* Peabody, MA: Hendrickson, 2008.

Gossai, Hemchan. *Justice, Righteousness and the Social Critique of the Eighth Century Prophets.* New York: Lang, 1993.

Gottwald, Norman K. "Social Class as an Analytic and Hermeneutical Category in Biblical Studies." *JBL* 112 (1993): 3–22.

Gowan, Donald E. *Theology of the Prophetic Books: The Death and Resurrection of Israel.* Louisville: Westminster John Knox, 1998.

Granberg-Michaelson, Wes. "Think Christianity Is Dying? No, Christianity Is Shifting Dramatically." *Washington Post.* May 20, 2015.

https://www.washingtonpost.com/news/acts-of-faith/wp/2015/05/20/think-christianity-is-dying-no-christianity-is-shifting-dramatically/?

Groenewald, Alphonso. "Ethics of the Psalms: Psalm 16 within the Context of Psalms 15–24." *Journal for Semitics* 18.2 (2009): 421–33.

Groenewald, Alphonso. *Psalm 69: Its Structure, Redaction and Composition*. Munster: LIT Verlag, 2003.

Hasker, William. "The Problem of Evil in Process Theism and Classical Free Will Theism." *Progress Studies* 29.2 (2000): 194–208.

Hasson, Nir. "Seal Impression with King Hezekiah's Name Discovered in Jerusalem." *Haaretz*. December 2, 2015. https://www.haaretz.com/archaeology/.premium-king-hezekiah-bulla-found-in-jerusalem-1.5429555.

Heschel, Abraham J. *The Prophets*. New York: Perennial Classics, 2001.

Hetrick, Lon. "Selling the Gospel: The Christian Hype that Stifles Christian Hope." http://felixcheakam.com/77-selling-Jesus-at-a-discount.html.

Hillers, Delbert R. *Micah: A Commentary on the Book of the Prophet Micah*. Philadelphia: Fortress, 1984.

Holladay, William L. *A Concise Hebrew and Aramaic Lexicon of the Old Testament*. Leiden: Brill, 2000.

Honeycutt, Roy L. "Amos and Contemporary Issues." *RevExp* 63 (1966): 441–57.

House, Paul R. *Old Testament Theology*. Downers Grove, IL: InterVarsity, 1998.

Hrobon, Bohdan. *Ethical Dimension of the Cult in the Book of Isaiah*. BZAW 418. Berlin: De Gruyter, 2010.

Huber, Robert V., Robert M. Grant, and Tracey Grant-Starter. *Who Is Who in the Bible*. Pleasantville, NY: Reader's Digest, 1994.

Huffmon, Herbert B. "A Company of Prophets: Mari, Assyria, Israel." Pages 47–70 in *Prophecy in Its Ancient Near Eastern context: Mesopotamian, Biblical, and Arabian Perspectives*. Edited by Martti Nissinen. SemeiaSt 13. Atlanta: Society of Biblical Literature, 2000.

———. "Covenant Lawsuit in the Prophets." *JBL* 78 (1959): 285–95.

Hunter, A. Vanlier. *Seek the Lord! A Study of the Meaning and Function of the Exhortations in Amos, Hosea, Isaiah, Micah, and Zephaniah*. Baltimore: Saint Mary's Seminary and University, 1982.

Hyman, Ronald T. "Questions and Response in Micah 6:6–8." *JBQ 33*.3 (2005): 157–65.

Ibrahim, Bello, and Ahmad Hassan Ahmad. "The Impact of Corruption on National Development in Nigeria." *IJSRSSMS* 2.1 (2017): 13–23.

Jacobs, Mignon R. *The Conceptual Coherence of the Book of Micah*. JSOTSup 322. Sheffield: Sheffield Academic, 2001.

―――. "Micah." Pages 276–81 in *Theological Interpretation of the Old Testament: A Book-by-Book Survey*. Edited by Kevin J. Vanhoozer. Grand Rapids: Baker Academic, 2008.
Jenkins, Philip. *The New Faces of Christianity: Believing the Bible in the Global South*. Oxford: Oxford University Press, 2008.
Jenkins, Willis. *The Future of Ethics: Sustainability, Social Justice, and Religious Creativity*. Washington, DC: Georgetown University Press, 2013.
Jensen, Joseph. *Ethical Dimensions of the Prophets*. Collegeville: Liturgical, 2006.
Jenson, Philip P. *Obadiah, Jonah, Micah: A Theological Commentary*. LHBOTS 496. New York: T&T Clark, 2008.
Jeppesen, Knud. "New Aspects of Micah Research." *JSOT* 8 (1978): 3–32.
Johnson, Elliott E. *Expository Hermeneutics: An Introduction*. Grand Rapids: Academic Books, 1990.
Johnstone, Patrick. *Operation World*. Carlisle: OM, 1993.
―――. *World Churches Handbook*. London: Christian Research, 1997.
Kaiser, Walter C., Jr. *A History of Israel*. Nashville: Broadman & Holman, 1998.
Kaiser, Otto. *Isaiah 1–12: A Commentary*. London: SCM, 1972.
Kazeem, Yomi. "Nigeria Has Become the Poverty Capital of the World." June 25, 2018. https://qz.com/africa/1313380/nigerias-has-the-highest-rate-of-extreme-poverty-globally/.
Keil, Carl Friedrich. *The Twelve Minor Prophets*. Translated by James Martin. Biblical Commentary on the Old Testament. 2 vols. Grand Rapids: Eerdmans, 1949.
Kessler, John. *Old Testament Theology: Divine call and Human Response*. Waco, TX: Baylor University Press, 2013.
King, Philip J. *Amos, Hosea, Micah: An Archaeological Commentary*. Philadelphia: Westminster, 1988.
Kisau, Paul. "The Key to the African Heart: Rethinking Missionary Strategy in Africa." *AJET* 17.2 (1998): 92–98.
Kukah, Matthew Hassan. *Religion, Culture and the Politics of Development*. Lagos: Centre for Black and African Arts and Civilisation, 2007.
Kwashi, Ben. "The Christian and Corruption." Pages 29–53 in *Service with Integrity: The Christian in the Nigerian Project*. Edited by Z. Chinne. Kaduna: The ECWA Goodnews Church, 2008.
Lafferty, Theresa V. *The Prophetic Critique of the Priority of the Cult: A Study of Amos 5:21–24 and Isaiah 1:10–17*. Parkway: UMI Dissertation, 2010.
Laney, J. Carl. "The Role of the Prophets in God's Case against Israel." *BSac* 138 (1981): 313–25.
Lawal, Tolu, and Abe Oluwatoyin. "National Development in Nigeria: Issues, Challenges and Prospects." *JPAPR* 3.9 (2011): 237–41.

Leuchter, Mark A. "The Priesthood in Ancient Israel." *BTB* 40.2 (2010): 100–10. https://journals.sagepub.com/doi/10.1177/0146107910364344.

Levine, Amy-Jill. "Back Page Interview." *The Church Times*. London. 15 July 2011.

Lindblom, Johannes. *Prophecy in Ancient Israel*. Oxford: Blackwell, 1962.

Lipschits, Oded, Omer Sergi, and Ido Koch. "Royal Judahite Jar Handles: Reconsidering the Chronology of the lmlk Stamp Impressions." *Tel Aviv* 37.1 (2010): 3–32. https://doi.org/10.1179/033443510x12632070179306.

Longman, Tremper III, and David Garland. *The Expositor's Bible Commentary*. Nashville, TN: Zondervan, 2008.

Longman, Tremper III, and Raymond B. Dillard. *An Introduction to the Old Testament*. Grand Rapids: Zondervan, 2006.

MacArthur, John. *Ashamed of the Gospel: When the Church Becomes Like the World*. Wheaton: Crossway Books, 1993.

———. *Rediscovering Pastoral Ministry*. Waco, TX: Word, 1995.

Malchow, Bruce V. "The Rural Prophet: Micah." *CurTM* 7 (1980): 48–52.

Mansueto, Anthony. "From Historical Criticism to Historical Materialism." Paper presented at Graduate Theological Union, Berkeley, CA, 1983.

March, W. Eugene. "Prophecy." Pages 143–57 in *Old Testament Form Criticism*. Edited by John H. Hayes. San Antonio: Trinity University Press, 1974.

Marlow, Hilary. "Justice for Whom? Social and Environmental Ethics and the Hebrew Prophets." Pages 103–21 in *Ethical and Unethical in the Old Testament: God and Humans in Dialogue*. Edited by Katharine J. Dell. LHBOTS 528. New York: T&T Clark International, 2010.

Marrs, Rick R. "Micah and a Theological Critique of Worship." Pages 184–203 in *Worship and the Hebrew Bible: Essays in Honour of John T. Willis*. Edited by M. Patrick Graham, Richard R. Marrs and Steven L. McKenzie. JSOTSup. 284. Sheffield: Sheffield Academic, 1999.

Marshall, Chris. "Divine Justice as Restorative Justice." Center for Christian Ethics (2012): 11–19.

Mason, Rex. *Micah, Nahum, and Obadiah*. New York: T&T Clark International, 2004.

Matthews, Victor H. *Social World of the Hebrew Prophets*. Peabody, MA: Hendrickson, 2001.

Mays, James L. "Justice: Perspectives from the Prophets." *Prophecy in Israel: Search for an Identity*. Edited by David L. Petersen. Philadelphia: Fortress, 1987.

———. "Justice: Perspectives from the Prophetic Tradition." *Int* 37.1 (1983): 5–17.

Mays, James L. *Micah: A Commentary*. OTL. Philadelphia: Westminster, 1976.

Mbewe, Conrad. "Prosperity Teaching Has Replaced True Gospel in Africa." June 25, 2015. https://www.thegospelcoalition.org/article/prosperity-teaching-has-replaced-true-gospel-in-africa/

Mbiti, John S. *Bible and Theology in Africa Christianity*. Nairobi: Oxford University Press, 1986.

McComiskey, Thomas Edward. "Micah." In *Daniel-Minor Prophets*. Edited by Frank E. Gaebelein and Richard P. Polcyn. 12 vols. The Expositor's Bible Commentary. Grand Rapids: Zondervan, 1985.

———. *The Minor Prophets*. Vol. 2. Grand Rapids: Baker, 1993.

McConville, J. Gordon. *Deuteronomy*. Apollos Old Testament Commentary. Leicester: Apollos, 2002.

McKane, William. *Micah: Introduction and Commentary*. Edinburgh: T&T Clark, 1998.

McKeating, Henry. *The Books of Amos, Hosea, Micah*. Cambridge: Cambridge University Press, 1971.

———. "Sanctions against Adultery in Ancient Israelite Society, with Some Reflections on Methodology in the Study of Old Testament Ethics." *JSOT* 11 (1979): 57–72.

McKeown, James. "Land." Pages 487–49 in *Dictionary of the Old Testament: Pentateuch*. Edited by T. Desmond Alexander and David W. Baker. Downers Grove: Inter-Varsity, 2003.

Mickelsen, Berkeley A. *Interpreting the Bible*. Grand Rapids: Eerdmans, 1963.

Mikail, Ibrahim Kawuley. "Corruption and National Development in Nigeria's Fourth Republic." *JORIND* 10.3 (2012): 227–33.

Millard, Alan R. "Sennacherib's Attack on Hezekiah." *TynBul* 36 (1985): 61–77.

Miller, Patrick D. *They Cried to the Lord: The Form and Theology of Biblical Prayer*. Minneapolis: Augsburg, 1994.

Mitchell, Eric A. "Micah—The Man and His Times." *SWJT* 46 (2003): 57–76.

Moberly, R. Walter L. 2008. "In God We Trust? The Challenge of the Prophets." *ExAud* 24:18–33.

Mosala, Itumeleng J. *Biblical Hermeneutics and Black Theology in South Africa*. Grand Rapids, MI: Eerdmans, 1989.

Mott, Stephen Charles. *A Christian Perspective on Political Thought*. Oxford: Oxford University Press, 1993.

Motyer, John A. *The Prophecy of Isaiah*. Leicester: Inter-Varsity, 1993.

Mpigi, Goka Muele. "The Prosperity Theology's Impact on the Contemporary Nigerian Church and Society." *SJER* 5.5 (2017): 34–43.

Na'aman, Nadav. *Ancient Israel and Its Neighbors: Interaction and Counteraction*. Winona Lake: Eisenbrauns, 2005.

———. "Hezekiah's Fortified Cities and the *LMLK* Stamps." *BASOR* 261 (1986): 5–21.

Nag, Oishimaya Sen. "African Countries Where Christianity Is the Largest Religion." (September 20, 2017. https://www.worldatlas.com/articles/african-countries-with-christianity-as-the-religion-of-the-majority.html.

Ngwube, Arinze, and Chuka Okoli. "The Role of the Economic Financial Crime Commission in the Fight against Corruption in Nigeria." *JSSS* 4.1 (2013): 92–107.

Noell, Edd S. "Land Grabs, Unjust Exchange, and Bribes: Economic Opportunism and the Rights of the Poor in Ancient Israel." *SWJT* 59.2 (2017): 183–99.

Nogalski, James D. *The Book of the Twelve: Micah-Malachi*. Macon, GA: Smyth & Helwys, 2011.

———. "Micah 7:8–20: Re-evaluating the Identity of the Enemy." Pages 125–42 in *The Bible as a Human Witness to Divine Revelation: Hearing the Word of God Through Historically Dissimilar Traditions*. Edited by Randall Heskett and Brian Irwin. LHBOTS 469. New York: Continuum, 2010.

O'Brien, Julia M. *Challenging Prophetic Metaphors: Theology and Ideology in the Prophets*. Louisville: Westminster John Knox, 2008.

———. *Micah*. Wisdom Commentary 37. Collegeville, MI: Michael Glazier Book, 2015.

O'Donovan, Wilbur. *Biblical Christianity in African Perspective*. Carlisle: Paternoster, 1995.

Oded, Bustenay. "Judah and the Exiles." Pages 435–88 in *Israelite and Judean History*. Edited by John H. Hayes and J. Maxwell Miller. London: SCM, 1990.

Ojekunle, Aderemi. "A Look at the Key Figures in Nigeria's 2019 Budget." December 20, 2018. https://www.pulse.ng/bi/finance/a-look-at-the-key-figures-in-nigerias-2019-budget/yj8pvqs.

Okoli, Al Chukwuma, and Ahar Clement Uhembe. "Materialism and Commodification of the Sacred: A Political Economy of Spiritual Materialism in Nigeria." *ESJ* 10.14 (2014): 595–606.

Oldham, Bill. *Philosophy of Education*. New York: Abingdon, 1967.

Olukayode, Abiodun Faleye. "Religious Corruption: A Delimma of the Nigeria State." *JSDA* 15.1 (2013): 170–85.

Olyan, Saul M. "Ben Sira's Relationship to the Priesthood." *HTR* 80 (1987): 261–86.

Osborne, Grant R. *The Hermeneutical Spiral: A Comprehensive Introduction to Biblical Interpretation*. Downers Grove: Inter-Varsity Press, 1997.

Oseghale, Comfort. "Nigeria's Bloated Recurrent Expenditure." December 27, 2018. https://shipsandports.com.ng/nigerias-bloated-recurrent-expenditure/.

Otto, Eckart. "Human Rights: The Influence of the Hebrew Bible." *JNS* 25.1 (1999): 1–20.

———. "Myth and Hebrew Ethics in the Psalms." Pages 26–37 in *Psalms and Mythology*. Edited by Dirk J. Human. LHBOTS 462. London: T&T Clark, 2007.

———. "Of Aims and Methods in Hebrew Bible Ethics." *Semeia* 66 (1995): 161–72.

———. *Theologische Ethik des Alten Testaments*. Stuttgart, Berlin, Cologne: Kohlhammer, 1994.

Owojaiye, Moses. "Problems, Prospects and Effects of Health and Wealth Gospel in Nigeria (Part 1)." https://christianityinafrica.wordpress.com/2010/01/16/problems-prospects-and-effects-of-health-and-wealth-gospel-in-nigeria-part-1/.

Oyedepo, David. *Understanding Financial Prosperity*. Ota: Dominion, 2005.

Pawson, David. *Unlocking the Bible: A Unique Overview of the Whole Bible*. London: Collins, 2003.

Pfeiffer, Charlse F., and Everett F. Harrison. *The Wycliffe Bible Commentary*. Chicago: Moody, 1990.

Pierce, Timothy M. "Micah as a Case Study for Preaching and Teaching the Prophets." *SWJT* 46.1 (2003): 77–94.

Pobee, John. *Towards Viable Theological Education*. Geneva: WCC Publications, 1997.

Premnath, Devadasan N. "Amos and Hosea: Sociohistorical Background and Prophetic Critique." *Word & World* 28.2 (2008): 125–32.

———. *Eighth-Century Prophets: A Social Analysis*. Saint Louis: Chalice, 2003.

Preuss, Horst D. *Old Testament Theology*. Louisville: Westminster John Knox, 1996.

Provan, Iain, V. Philips Long, and Tremper Longman III. *A Biblical History of Israel*. Louisville: Westminster John Knox, 2003.

Pyschny, Katharina and Sarah Schulz. "Debating Authority—Concepts of Leadership in the Pentateuch and the Former Prophets: An Introduction." Pages 1–16 in *Debating Authority: Concepts of Leadership in the Pentateuch and the Former Prophets*. Edited by Katharina Pyschny and Sarah Schulz. Berlin: De Gruyter, 2018. https://doi.org/10.1515/9783110543391-001.

Rad, Gerhard von. *Old Testament Theology*. London: Oliver & Boyd 1962.

Rainey, Anson F. "The Chronicler and His Sources—Historical and Geographical." Pages 30–72 in *The Chronicler as Historian*. Edited by M. Patrick Graham, Kenneth G. Hoglund, and Steven L. McKenzie. JSOTSup 238. Sheffield: Sheffield Academic, 1997.

Redditt, Paul L. "Wrath, Anger, Indignation." *Westminster Theological Wordbook of the Bible*. Edited by Donald Gowan. Louisville, KY: Westminster John Knox, 2003.

Reimer, David J. "The Prophet Micah and Political Society." Pages 203–24 in *Thus Speaks Ishtar of Arbela: Prophecy in Israel, Assyria, and Egypt in the Neo-Assyrian Period.* Edited by Robert P. Gordon and Hans M. Barstad. Winona Lake, IN: Eisenbrauns, 2013.

Rendtorff, Rolf. *The Canonical Hebrew Bible: A Theology of the Old Testament.* Translated by David E. Orton. Tools for Biblical Study 7. Leiden: Deo, 2005.

Richelle, Matthieu. "The Structure and Theology of Micah 4–5: A New Approach." *VT* 62 (2012): 232–47.

Rogers, Adrian. "False Prophets: Their Method, Manner and Motives." http://www.oneplace.com/ministries/love-worthfinding/read/articles/false-prophets-theirmethod-manner-and-motive-14018.html.

Ross, Allen P. "Proverbs." *The Expositor's Bible Commentary.* 12 vols. Edited by Frank E. Gaebelein. Grand Rapids: Zondervan, 1991.

Routledge, Robin L. *Old Testament Theology: A Thematic Approach.* Apollos: Inter-Vasirty, 2008.

Schart, Aaron. *Die Entstehung des des Zwölfprophetenbuchs: Neubearbeitungen von Amos im Rahmen schriftenuebergreifender Redaktionsprozesse.* BZAW 260. Berlin: de Gruyter, 1998.

Schofield, Alison, and James C. Vanderkam. "Were the Hasmoneans Zadokites?" *JBL* 124 (2005): 73–87.

Shaw, Charles S. *The Speeches of Micah: A Rhetorical-Historical Analysis.* JSOTSup 145. Sheffield: JSOT, 1993.

Simundson, Daniel J. *Hosea, Joel, Amos, Obadiah, Jonah, Micah.* Abingdon Old Testament Commentaries. Nashville: Abingdon, 2005.

Sloane, Andrew. *At Home in a Strange Land: Using the Old Testament in Christian Ethics.* Peabody, MA: Hendrickson, 2008.

Smith, Gary V. *Hosea, Amos, Micah.* The NIV Application Commentary. Grand Rapids: Zondervan, 2001.

Smith, Ralph L. *Micah-Malachi: Word Biblical Commentary 32.* Waco, TX: Word, 1984.

Smith-Christopher, Daniel L. *Micah: A Commentary.* OTL. Louisville: Westminster John Knox, 2015.

Snoek, Hans. "Key Concepts in the Dialogue between African and European Biblical Scholars." Pages 85–104 in *African and European Readers of the Bible in Dialogue.* Studies of Religion in Africa 32. Leiden: Brill, 2008.

Soyinka, Wole. *The Credo of Being and Nothingness.* Ibadan: Spectrum, 1991.

Steck, Odil Hannes. *The Prophetic Books and Their Theological Witness.* Translated by James. D. Nogalski. Saint Louis: Chalice, 2000.

Sweeney, Marvin A. *The Twelve Prophets: Micah, Nahum, Habakkuk, Zephaniah, Haggai, Zechariah, Malachi.* Berit Olam. Collegeville: Liturgical, 2000.

Sweeney, Marvin A. *Isaiah 1–39 with Introduction to Prophetic Literature.* FOTL 16. Grand Rapids: Eerdmans, 1996.

Tate, Randolph W. *Biblical Interpretation: An Integrated Approach.* Grand Rapids, MI: Baker Academic, 2008.

Tiemeyer, Lena-Sofia. *Priestly Rites and Prophetic Rage: Post-exilic Prophetic Critique of the Priesthood.* FAT 2/19. Tubingen: Mohr Siebeck, 2006.

Tienou, Tite. *The Theological Task of the Church in Africa.* Achimota: African Christian, 1982.

Townsend, Peter. "What Is Poverty? An Historical Perspective." Page 5–6 in *UNDP: What Is Poverty? Concepts and Measures.* Brasilia: International Poverty Center, 2006.

Troxel, Ronald L. *Prophetic Literature: From Oracle to Books.* Chichester, West Sussex: Wiley-Blackwell, 2012.

Udoekpo, Michael U. *Rethinking the Prophetic Critique of Amos 5 for Contemporary Nigeria and the USA.* Eugene, OR: Wipf & Stock, 2017.

Ukpong, Justin S. "Developments in Biblical Interpretation in Modern Africa: Historical and Hermeneutical Directions." Pages 11–28 in *The Bible in Africa: Transactions, Trajectories, and Trends.* Edited by Gerald O. West and Musa W. Dube. Leiden: Brill, 2000.

Van der Toorn, Karel. *Scribal Culture and the Making of the Hebrew Bible.* London: Harvard University Press, 2007.

Van der Woude, Adam S. *Micaha. De Prediking van het Oude Testament.* Nijkerk: Callenbach, 1976.

Wagenaar, Jan A. *Judgement and Salvation: The composition and Redaction of Micah 2–5.* VTSup 85. Leiden: Brill, 2001.

Waltke, Bruce K. *The Book of Proverbs, Chapters 1–15.* NICOT. Grand Rapids: Eerdmans, 2004.

———. *A Commentary on Micah.* Grand Rapids: Eerdmans, 2007.

———. "Micah." Pages 591–764 in *The Minor Prophets: An Exegetical and Expositional Commentary.* Edited by Thomas Edward McComiskey. Grand Rapids: Bakers, 1998.

———. *Obadiah, Jonah, and Micah.* Edited by Donald J. Wiseman. Tyndale Old Testament Commentaries. Downers Grove: Inter-Varsity, 2009.

Walton, John H., Victor H. Matthews, and Mark W. Chavalas. *The IVP Bible Background Commentary Old Testament.* Downers Grove: Inter-Varsity, 2000.

Watson, Paul L. "Form Criticism and an Exegesis of Micah 6:1–8." *RQ* 7.1 (1963): 61–72.

Weingart, Kristin. "Wie Samaria so auch Jerusalem: Umfang und Pragmatik einer frühen Micha-Komposition." *VT* 69.3 (2019): 460–80. https://doi.org/10.1163/15685330–123413.

Wendland, Ernst R. "A Discourse Structural Overview of the Prophecy of Micah." *The Bible Translator* 69.2 (2018): 277–93. https://journals.sagepub.com/doi/10.1177/2051677018785213.

Wessels, Wilhelm. "YHWH, the God of New Beginnings: Micah's Testimony." *HvTSt* 69.1(2013): 1–8. art. #1960, 8 pages. http://dx.doi.org/10.4102/hts.v69i1.1960.

West, Gerald O. "Do Two Walk Together? Walking with the Other through Contextual Bible Study." *ATR* 93.3 (2011): 431–49.

———. "Locating 'Contextual Bible Study' within Biblical Liberation Hermeneutics and Intercultural Biblical Hermeneutics," *HTS* 70/1 (2014): 1, art. #2641, 10 pages. http://dx.doi.org/10.4102/hts.v70i1.2641.

———. "Exegesis Seeking Appropriation; Appropriation Seeking Exegesis: Rereading 2 Samuel 13:1–22 in Search of Redemptive Masculinities." *VE* 34.2 (2013):1, art. #761, 6 pages. http://dx.doi. org/10.4102/ve.v34i2.761.

Westermann, Claus. *Basic Forms of Prophetic Speech*. Translated by Hugh C. White. Louisville, KY: Westminster John Knox, 1991.

———. *Elements of Old Testament Theology*. Translated by Douglas W. Stott. Atlanta: John Knox 1982.

Wilhelm, Dawn Ottoni. "God's Word in The World: Prophetic Preaching and the Gospel of Jesus Christ." Pages 76–93 in *Anabaptist Preaching: A Conversation Between Pulpit, Pew and Bible*. Edited by David B. Greiser and Michael A. King. Telford: Cascadia, 2003.

Willis, John T. "Fundamental Issues in Contemporary Micah Studies." *RQ* 13 (1970): 77–90.

Wolff, Hans Walter. *Micah: A Commentary*. Continental Commentaries. Translated by Gary Stansell. Minneapolis: Augsburg, 1990.

———. *Micah the Prophet*. Translated by Ralph Gehrke. Philadelphia: Augsburg Fortress, 1981.

———. "Micah and the Moreshite-The Prophet and His Background." Pages 77–84 in *Israelite Wisdom: Theological and Literary Essays in Honor of Samuel Terrien*. Edited by John Gammie et al. Missoula: Scholars, 1978.

Wood, Charles M. "An Invitation to Theological Study." *PJ* 42.2–3 (1989): 1–2.

Woodbridge, Noel and Willem Semmelink. "The Prophetic Witness of Amos and Its Relevance for Today's Church in African Countries for Promoting Social Justice in Democratic South Africa." *Conspectus* 16 (2013): 79–100.

Wright, Christopher J. H. *God's People in God's Land: Family, Land, and Property in the Old Testament*. Grand Rapids: Eerdmans, 1990.

———. *Living as the People of God: The Relevance of Old Testament Ethics*. Leicester: Inter-Varsity, 1983.

———. *Old Testament Ethics for the People of God*. Leicester: Inter-Varsity, 2006.

Younger, Brett. "Calorie Counting Ministers in a Starving World (Amos 5:14–24)." *RevExp* 110.2 (2013): 295–300.

Zapff, Burkard M. "The Book of Micah–The Theological Center of the Book of the Twelve?" Pages 129–46 in *Perspectives on the Formation of the Book of the Twelve Methodological Foundations—Redactional Processes—istorical Insights*. Edited by Rainer Albertz, James D. Nogalski and Jakob Wöhrle. BZAW 433. Berlin: de Gruyter, 2012.

Zimmerli, Walther. "From Prophetic Word to Prophetic Book." Pages 419–42 in *The Place Is Too Small for Us: The Israelite Prophets in Recent Scholarship*. Edited by Robert P. Gordon. Winona Lake: Eisenbrauns, 1995.

MODERN AUTHORS INDEX

Abogunrin, Samuel O.   1–2, 173
Achenbach, Reinhard   62, 123, 173
Adamo, David T.   10, 173
Agbiji, Obaji M.   154–55, 160, 173
Aharoni, Yohanan   21, 173
Ahmad, Ahmad H.   168, 178
Albertz, Rainer   37, 187
Alexander, Desmond   51, 181
Alfaro, Juan I.   3, 19, 30, 51, 73–74, 119, 173
Allen, Leslie C.   40, 44, 46, 75, 117, 127–28, 130, 132–34, 150, 173
Andersen, Francis I.   20, 39–41, 44–45, 56–57, 59–63, 65, 70, 72, 78–81, 87–89, 92–94, 99, 102–3, 105, 108, 173
Anderson, Bernhard W.   30, 174
Andersson, Staffan   2, 174
Arndt, Emily   111, 140, 174
Asamoah-Gyadu, Kwabena J.   142, 174
Atherstone, Jeff   142, 174
Avalos, Hector   111, 174
Baker, David W.   51, 181
Baker, Kenneth   149, 174
Banda, Collium   142, 154, 157, 174
Barker, Kenneth L.   45, 174
Barstad, Hans M.   23, 119, 184

Barton, John   30, 111, 113–15, 139, 145, 174
Becker, Gary S.   159, 174
Beentjes, Pancratius C.   122, 174
Ben Zvi, Ehud   13–14, 35–36, 38, 48–49, 55–56, 62, 64, 66, 78–80, 83, 92–95, 102, 107, 119, 174, 177
Berges, Ulrich   9, 35, 175, 176
Berković, Danijel   87, 175
Birch, Bruce C.   112, 162, 175
Blenkinsopp, Joseph   19, 51, 175
Block, Daniel I.   122, 175
Blomberg, Craig L.   129–30, 175
Boda, Mark J.   114, 175
Bonhoeffer, Dietrich   157, 175
Bright, John   25, 29, 31, 175
Brueggemann, Walter   90–91, 116, 134, 167, 175
Burgess, Stanley M.   142, 175
Carr, David M.   22, 25, 39–40, 118, 175
Carroll, Daniel R.M.   29, 34, 54, 112–14, 117–18, 145, 175
Chaney, Marvin L.   29–30, 32, 175
Chang, Dongshin D.   124, 176
Chavalas, Mark W.   21–22, 165, 185
Chisholm, Robert B.   84, 176
Clark, Gordon R.   18, 176

Coomber, Matthew J. M. 30–31, 176
Counet, Chatelion P. 9, 176
Crenshaw, James L. 146, 176
Cuffey, Kenneth H. 40, 176
Davies, Margaret 112–13, 175, 176
Davies, Paul R. 112, 176
Dawes, Stephen B. 91, 176
Day, John 26, 145, 174, 176
De Gruchy, John W. 154, 176
De Jong, Matthijs J. 123–24, 176
De Vaux, Roland 67, 134, 176
Dell, Katharine J. 131, 167, 176, 180
Dempsey, Carol J. 20, 54, 176
Dempster, Stephen G. 18–21, 23–26, 28–29, 33–34, 38, 41, 43–44, 46–48, 55, 57–58, 60, 62–64, 66–68, 72, 78, 80–81, 83, 87–88, 90, 95–96, 101, 105–6, 117, 121, 126, 130–34, 136, 146, 148, 150–51, 155–56, 158–60, 176
Deng, Lual A. 2, 176
Dillard, Raymond B. 41, 46, 180
Dozeman, Thomas B. 123, 173
Driver, Samuel R. 22–23, 177
Dube, Musa W. x, 13, 185
Edelman, Diana V. 35–36, 174, 177
Ehrlich, Carl S. 21, 177
Freedman, David N. 20, 39–41, 44–45, 56–57, 59–63, 65, 70, 72, 78–81, 87–89, 92–94, 99, 102–3, 105, 108, 173
Frevel, Christian vii, ix, 112, 119–21, 177
Friedman, Hershey H. 117, 177
Gaebelein, Frank E. 45, 94, 181, 184
Gammie, John 19, 186
Garland, David 88–89, 180
Gay, Craig M. 164, 177

Gerstenberger, Erhard S. 49, 146, 177
Gifford, Paul 156, 158, 177
Glenny, Edward W. 102, 177
Gordon, Robert P. 23, 41, 119, 183, 186
Gorman, Michael J. 9, 177
Gossai, Hemchan 131, 177
Gottwald, Norman K. 31, 47, 177
Gowan, Donald E. 24, 167, 177, 183
Grabbe, Lester L. 122, 174
Graham, Patrick M. 21, 86, 180, 183
Granberg-Michaelson, Wes 140–41, 177
Grant, Jamie A. 146, 175
Grant, Robert M. 22, 25, 178
Grant-Starter, Tracey 22, 25, 178
Greiser, David B. 156, 186
Groenewald, Alphonso x, 9, 14, 114, 178
Harrison, Everett F. 41, 183
Hasker, William 115, 178
Hasson, Nir 34, 178
Hayes, John H. 27, 49, 180, 182
Heschel, Abraham J. 25, 178
Hetrick, Lon 149, 178
Heywood, Paul M. 2, 174
Hillers, Delbert R. 18, 34, 54, 56–57, 62, 65, 68, 74, 76, 84–85, 88, 91–92, 95, 97, 99–100, 102–4, 107, 118, 178
Hoglund, Kenneth G. 21, 183
Holladay, William L. 50, 178
Honeycutt, Roy L. 16, 178
House, Paul R. 16, 178
Hrobon, Bohdan 125, 134, 178
Huber, Robert V. 22, 25, 178
Huffmon, Herbert B. 79, 83, 122, 178
Hughes, Dewl A. 146, 175
Human, Dirk J. x, 113, 183

Hunter, A. Vanlier 136–37, 178
Hyman, Ronald T. 79–80, 89, 91, 178
Ibrahim, Bello 168, 178
Jacobs, Mignon R. 34, 40, 54, 60, 66, 178–79
Jenkins, Philip 10, 179
Jenkins, Willis 5, 179
Jensen, Joseph 113, 179
Jenson, Philip P. 22, 48, 56–59, 61–62, 64–65, 67–71, 75, 78, 84, 86–88, 90–91, 94, 96–102, 104, 106–8, 179
Jeppesen, Knud 44, 179
Johnson, Elliott E. 14, 179
Johnstone, Patrick 141, 179
Kaiser, Otto 32, 179
Kaiser, Walter C. 26–27, 179
Kazeem, Yomi 1, 179
Keil, Carl Friedrich 41, 179
Kessler, John 87, 147, 179
King, Michael A. 156, 186
King, Philip J. 21, 179
Kisau, Paul 141, 179
Kukah, Matthew H. 149–50, 179
Kwashi, Ben 149, 179
Lafferty, Theresa V. 135, 179
Laney, J. Carl 79, 81, 179
Lawal, Tolu 168, 179
Leuchter, Mark A. 124–25, 180
Levine, Amy-Jill 139, 180
Lindblom, Johannes 122, 180
Lipschits, Oded 22, 29, 180
Long, Philips V. 24, 183
Longman, Tremper III 24, 41, 46, 88–89, 180, 183
MacArthur, John 153, 160, 180
Malchow, Bruce V. 19, 32, 180
Mansueto, Anthony 6, 180
March, Eugene W. 49, 180
Marlow, Hilary 131–32, 167, 180

Marrs, Richard R. 86, 180
Marrs, Rick R. 86, 135–36, 180
Marshall, Chris 116–17, 180
Mason, Rex 25, 37, 180
Matthews, Victor H. 21–22, 122, 165, 180, 185
Mays, James L. 17–18, 20, 22, 24, 32, 46, 55, 57–59, 61, 68, 71–72, 74–76, 78, 81–82, 84, 86–93, 95–100, 102, 108, 162, 166, 180
Mbewe, Conrad 142, 181
Mbiti, John S. 140–41, 181
McComiskey, Thomas E. 40–41, 45, 181, 185
McConville, Gordan J. 114, 165, 175, 181
McKane, William 81, 181
McKeating, Henry 32, 112, 181
McKenzie, Steven L. 21, 86, 180, 183
McKeown, James 51, 53, 181
Mickelsen, Berkeley A. 8, 181
Mikail, Ibrahim K. 168, 181
Millard, Alan R. 27, 181
Miller, Maxwell J. 27, 182
Miller, Patrick D. 87, 181
Mitchell, Eric A. 19, 181
Moberly, R. Walter L. 34, 54, 181
Mosala, Itumeleng J. 6–8, 11–12, 38–39, 181
Mott, Stephen C. 116, 181
Motyer, John A. 27, 181
Mpigi, Goka M. 143, 181
Na'aman, Nadav 27, 105, 181
Nag, Oishimaya S. 141, 182
Ngwube, Arinze 168, 182
Nissinen, Martti 122–23, 174, 178
Noell, Edd S. 162, 164, 182
Nogalski, James D. 23, 35, 37–38, 46, 49–51, 53–54, 70, 72, 76, 79,

97, 100– 101, 105–6, 127, 182, 184, 186
O'Brien, Julia M. 36–37, 182
O'Donovan, Wilbur 140, 182
Oded, Bustenay 27, 182
Ojekunle, Aderemi 163, 182
Okoli, Al Chukwuma 149, 182
Okoli, Chuka 168, 182
Oldham, Bill 151, 182
Olukayode, Abiodun F. 151, 182
Oluwatoyin, Abe 168, 179
Olyan, Saul M. 124, 182
Orton, David E. 123, 184
Osborne, Grant R. 7, 182
Oseghale, Comfort 163, 182
Otto, Eckart 113–15, 182–83
Owojaiye, Moses 143, 183
Oyedepo, David 143, 183
Pawson, David 19, 183
Pfeiffer, Charlse F. 41, 183
Pierce, Timothy M. 45, 79, 183
Pobee, John 152–53, 183
Polcyn, Richard P. 45, 181
Premnath, Devadasan N. 23, 31–32, 183
Preuss, Horst D. 123, 183
Provan, Iain 24, 183
Pyschny, Katharina ix, 119, 177, 183
Rad, Gerhard von 75, 183
Rainey, Anson F. 21, 183
Redditt, Paul L. 167, 183
Reimer, David J. 23, 34, 119, 133, 184
Rendtorff, Rolf 123, 184
Richelle, Matthieu 40, 184
Rogers, Adrian 149, 184
Rogerson, John W. 112–13, 175–76
Ross, Allen P. 94, 184
Routledge, Robin L. 123, 184
Schart, Aaron x, 39, 184
Schmid, Konrad 123, 173

Schofield, Alison 124, 184
Schulz, Sarah 119, 177, 183
Schwartz, Baruch J. 123, 173
Semmelink, Willem 148, 186
Shaw, Charles S. 4, 46, 184
Simundson, Daniel J. 40, 78, 184
Sloane, Andrew 111, 113, 184
Smith, Gary V. 165, 184
Smith, Ralph L. 19, 32, 184
Smith-Christopher 22, 29, 40, 44–45, 68, 72, 74, 159, 184
Snoek, Hans 8, 184
Soyinka, Wole 149, 184
Stansell, Gary 19, 186
Steck, Odil Hannes 35, 184
Swart, Ignatius 154–55, 160, 173
Sweeney, Marvin A. 48, 55, 106, 184–85
Tate, Randolph W. 7–9, 185
Tiemeyer, Lena-Sofia 125, 185
Tienou, Tite 140, 152, 185
Townsend, Peter 2, 185
Troxel, Ronald L. 35, 185
Udoekpo, Michael U. 16, 185
Uhembe, Ahar C. 149, 182
Ukpong, Justin S. 12, 185
Van der Toorn, Karel 122, 185
Van der Woude, Adam S. 44, 185
Vanderkam, James C. 124, 184
Vanhoozer, Kevin J. 34, 54, 179
Wagenaar, Jan A. 44, 185
Waltke, Bruce K. 19, 41–42, 44, 46, 50–53, 58, 66–67, 69–70, 72–73, 80, 82–83, 94, 96, 98–100, 107, 130, 164, 185
Walton, John H. 21–22, 165, 185
Watson, Paul L. 78, 80, 185
Weingart, Kristin 27–28, 185
Wendland, Ernst R. 43–44, 186
Wessels, Wilhelm ix, 45, 186
West, Gerald O. ii, x, 10–11, 13, 185–86

Westermann, Claus 48–49, 134–135, 186
Wilhelm, Dawn O. 156, 186
Willis, John T. 44, 186
Wöhrle, Jakob 37, 187
Wolff, Hans W. 18–19, 44, 54, 71, 78, 80, 82, 96, 128, 185–86
Wood, Charles M. 151, 186
Woodbridge, Noel 148, 186
Wright, Christopher J. H. 67, 113, 116–17, 130, 153, 164, 186
Younger, Brett 148, 187
Zapff, Burkard M. 37, 187
Zimmerli, Walther 41, 187

ANCIENT SOURCES INDEX

Hebrew Bible/Old Testament

Genesis
2:8	53
3:15	20
3:23–24	53
4:10	84
9:25	108
12:1–3	20
15:8	86
16:5	107
32:3–21	87
39:12	61
42:27	96
42:28	96
43:12–18	96
43:21	96
44:1	96
44:11	96
49:17	70

Exodus
3	122
3:16	120
3:18	120
4:20	94
4:29	120
5:8	69
5:15	69
6:7	91
12:21	120, 154
13:2	88
15:20	84
17:5–6	120
18	120–121
18:12	120
18:13–26	67–68
18:27	67–68
18:21	121, 154
18:22	121
19:7	120
20:12	108
20:15	164
20:16	97
20:17	51, 164
20:1–17	113
20:22–23:33	113
21:15	108
21:17	108
22:21–22	62, 76
22:25–26	61, 64
22:26–27	61
22:28	88
23:2–3	162
23:6–8	76, 162
23:10–19	86
24:1	120
24:9	120
24:13	120
28:40–43	124
29:1–9	88, 124
32:9	76

33:3	75–76	12:6–8	72
33:5	75–76	14:4	76
34:6–7	59	14:44	76
34:9	75	18:1–4	124
34:18–26	86–87, 88	18:20–21	75
		21:6–9	26
Leviticus		21:8, 9	70
1:4	88	21:21–24	62
2:1	88	22:28	84
4:15	120	22–24	85, 159
4–5	136	23:7	96
9:1	120	25:1	85
9:3	88	26:52–57	51
10:11	75	26:55–56	54
10:10–11	125	27:7	51
13:45	73	28–29	87
17–26	113	35:33	64
18:21	88	36:1–12	51
18:24–28	64		
19:9–10	103	Deuteronomy	
19:17	104	1:9–18	68
19:35–36	95, 96, 132, 164	1:13–17	120, 121, 166
20:2–5	88	1:15–18	67
20:9	108	2:5	53
22:23	88	2:9	53
22:27	88	2:19	53
23:4–44	87	4:6	101, 161
23:22	103	4:8	101, 161
25:10	51	4:25–28	145
25:23	53, 130	5:6–21	113
25:23–34	130	5:21	51
26	145	5:25	93
26:25	99	6:14–15	145
26:26	99	6:15	76
26:33	53	7:1–5	145
26:34	98	7:18	84
		7:21	76
Number		8:19–20	145
6:24–26	69	10:12–13	90
11	120, 121	10:17–18	90
11:16	121	10:18	61
11:20	76	11:16–17	145
12:6	122	12–26	113

12:9	64	34:10	122–23, 173
12:31	88		
13:6	70	Joshua	
13:17	107	3:1	85
16:1–17	87	3:10	76
16:18–19	121	4:19	85
17:8–13	75, 125, 127, 166	12–22	53
17:14–20	161	14–15	54
18:1–8	124, 159	14:2	54
18:10	72, 88	15:44	21
18:14	72, 88	18–20	54
18:15	122, 123, 173	18–22	54
19:14	62, 164	18:11	54
21:18–19	108	19:51	54
21:18–21	108		
21:23	64	Judges	
22:1–4	104	4:5	121
23:5–6	85	5:4	57
24:13	61	8:34	84
24:12–13	64	10:11–14	79
24:17–18	62	11:30–40	88
24:19–21	103		
25:13–16	95, 96, 132	Ruth	
27:17	129, 164, 169	1	108
27:18	70	1:9	64
28:1–14	71, 145	3:3	130
28:18	99	3:5	130
28:39	99		
28:40	99	1 Samuel	
28:41	99	1–4	159
28:49–68	53	4:3	76
28:54	107	6:2	86
28:56	107	9:7–8	71, 159
28:58	94	10:6	65
30–31	99	13:11	84
30:9	88	15:23	72
31:17–18	69	26:18	84
32:1–43	79		
32:7	84	2 Samuel	
32:15	108	12	76
33:10	125	13:1–22	11
33:30	75	15	108
38–40	99	15:2	121

21:3	86, 136	8:27	100
		9:7–9	101
23:1–3	122	10:11	101
24:23	88	10:18	101
		15–19	24
1 Kings		15:37	24
1:2	107	16	28
1:7	124	16:2–4	33, 88
2:26–27	124	16:3	33, 88
3:4	88	16:5–9	25
8:56	64	16:10–18	33
8:63	88	17:17	72, 88
13:30	49	18:4	26
14:3	71	18:4–5	25, 28
14:22–23	28	18:13	27
16:24	100	18:13–14	27
16:25	100	18:15–16	27
16:25–33	100	19:35–37	27
16:31	101	20:20	26
18	101	21:6	88
18:12	65	21:13	101
21	97, 100, 101, 131	22:19	102
21:1–3	51	23:10	88
21:4	130	25:12	130
21:16–20	48		
22	56	1 Chronicles	
22:6–7	123	24	124
22:21	65	29	124
22:22	65		
22:51–53	101	2 Chronicles	
		11:8	21
2 Kings		11:5–12	21
2:9	65	13:2	17
2:16	65	13:18	75
3:1–3	101	14:9–12	21
3:11	123	14:20	75
3:27	88	16:7–8	75
4:42	71	17:7–9	125
6:8–12	123	26:18	124
6:26	69	27:3–7	24
8:5	69	27:5	24
8:7–9	71	27:7	24
8:18	100	28–30	26

28:3	33	6:10	72
28:24–25	33	7:8	87
29–32	25	10:9	104
29:3–19	26	12–14	62
29:20–36	26	15–24	114, 178
29:21	124	15:1–5	79, 80
30:26	26	16	114, 178
31	25	18:17	87
31:1	26	22:5	72
31:19	124	24:3–4	79
32:2–4	26	24:3–6	80
32:4, 30	26	29	93
32:5	26	33:5	117
35:14	124	34:14	68
		44:7	72
Ezra		45:7	68
2	37	46:5	76
7:10	125	46:8	102
10:39	124	48	76
		50	79
Nehemiah		51:18	88
1:11	94	54:4	89
8:1–8	125	54:6	136
8:11	125	55:14	107
9:32	123	57:7	87
12:44–47	124	61:6	94
		68:8	57
Job		68:19	87
3:18	94	69	9, 14, 178
6:20	72	72	167
19:3	72	72:2–4	62
21:10	99	74:4	95
22:6	61	77:12	59
24:2–4	62	78:7	59
26:3	93	84	76
29:7–17	162	86:11	94
29:16	116	87	76
33:27	74	89:14	91
36:6	164	95:2	87
42:2	116	97:10	68
		106:7	84
Psalm		114:1–2	58
1	59	119:52	84

143:5	84	20:20	108
144:7	87	21:15	90
145:14	87	22:4	129
146:7	90	22:14	96
146:8	87	22:28	62
		23:10–11	62, 129, 169
Proverbs		24:15	104
1:7	93	24:23	121
1:11	104	29:7	164
1:22	68	30:7–9	159
2:7	59, 93		
2:17	107	Ecclesiastes	
2:18	74	2:8	63
2:21	59, 93		
3:21	93, 94	Song of Songs	
5:3	57	4:11	57
5:20	107	5:5	57
8:14	93, 94	7:7	63
8:36	68		
9:10	93	Isaiah	
10:9	74	1–12	32, 179
11:1	96	1–39	48, 185
11:3	59, 94	1:1	19, 22, 72, 95
11:6	59, 94	1:2	41
11:11	59, 94	1:2–3	79
11:27	68	1:10	41, 125
12:2	68	1:10–17	135, 179
14:9	59	1:11–17	117, 145, 146
14:11	59	1:15	69
14:29	59	1:17	68, 90
14:35	72	1:21–23	68, 90
15:25	62	1:23	39
15:33	93	1:26	68, 90
16:10	72	2:1	19
16:11	96	3:2	39
16:28	107	3:7	61
17:9	107	3:14	39
17:23	121	4:1	61
18:1	93	5:1–7	80, 104
18:5	121	5:4	83
19:10	63	5:7	68
20:10	96	5:23	68
20:23	96	5:8	164

5:8–18	30	30:9	125
5:8–10	39	30:12	75
5:9	49	30:32	94
5:13	49	31:1	75
5:20	90	31:4–5	39
5:23	39	33:14–16	79, 80
5:24	49	34:11–17	76
5:29	99	37:3	106
6:1	19	37:9–13	27
7	25	41:29	65
7:1–2	25	46:9–18	116
7:3–14	25	52:4	51
7:26	125	54:3	98
8:16	125	58:4	87
8:17	69	58:6	116
8:18	39	58:9	69
8:20	125	59:19	94
9:15	65		
10:1–2	30, 155,	Jeremiah	
10:2	39, 164	1:2	72
10:3	106	2:2–37	79
10:5	94	2:26	123
10:24	94	5:13	65
10:20	75	5:28	164
12:6	76	6:4	71
13:21–22	76	6:14	71
14:5	94	6:15	58
14:13	95	6:17	106
14:32	39	7:2	126
20	26	7:6	62
20:2–3	123	7:31	88
22:8–11	26	8:11–12	58
24:12	102	11:2	95
27:9	72	11:11	69
28	56	12:11	98
28:2–4	49	13:1–11	123
28:7	39, 123	13:21	107
28:7–13	39	14:9	76
28:9–10	39	14:10–14	88
28:16–17	39	14:14	65
28:17	126–27	14:21	108
29:5–8	39	18:18	125
30:3–5	49	19:5	88

19:8	102	16:63	58
19:13	64	21:2	57
20:11	58	21:21	72
21:12	116	22:5	64
22:3	117	22:15	64
22:13–17	74	24:13	64
22:15–16	62, 117	24:17	73
22:18	49	24:22	73
23:1–6	44	26:5	104
23:16	71	28:16	97
23:13	70	33:2	106
23:32	70	33:6	106
25:9	102	33:7	106
25:18	102	36:25	64
26:2	126	36:29	64
26:17–18	20	39:24	64
26:17–19	27	40:46	124
26:18	37, 44	43:19	124
26:28	17	44:15–31	124
27:9	72	44:23	125
28	56, 71	45:10	95
28:8–9	176	48:11	124
29:18	102		
30:22	91	Daniel	
33:21	124	4:34–35	116
36:5–6	126		
47:7	94	Hosea	
50:39	76	1:1	28, 72
51:37	102	1:9	91
		4:1	41, 91
Lamentations		4:4–5	126
3:1	94	4:4–6	135
4:13	87	4:5	56
		4:10	99
Ezekiel		5:6	99
1:3	72	5:10	62
3:17	106	6:1–6	135
4:1–6	123	6:9	62
7:23	97	8:7	99
7:26	123, 125	9:7	57
11:5	122	9:7–8	56
13:2	123	9:8	106
13:10	71	9:11	99

9:12	99	8:5–6	164–165
9:12–13	99		
9:16	99	9:3	70
11:1–2	166	9:10	57
12:7	51		
12:7–8	164, 165	Obadiah	
12:8	96	1:1	72
12:10	122		
		Jonah	
Joel		1:1	72
1:1	72	3:6	61
1:2	41		
2:27	76	Micah	
3:9	71	1	63, 118
4:6	95	1–2	40
4:18	57	1–3	37, 39–40, 92
		1–5	40, 44
Amos		1:1 vii, 17, 19–21, 23, 28–29, 46, 72, 88, 92–93	
1:1	28, 72	1:1–7	43
2:6	65, 154	1:2	41, 43, 77
2:12	57	1:2–4	117
3:1	41, 52	1:2–7	25, 29, 42, 44
3:1–2	166	1:2–8	24
3:12	52	1:2–16	47
4:1	154	1:2–2:13	40, 42, 45
4:4–5	145	1:2–3:12	41, 117
4:11	154	1:3–7	48
5	16, 131, 184	1:5–7 28, 33, 92, 101, 117, 129, 169	
5:7	51		
5:10–17	51	1:5 18, 28, 33, 39, 89, 100–101, 117, 129, 145	
5:11	99–100		
5:14–15	90	1:5–3:12	28
5:14–24	187	1:6	19
5:19	79	1:6–7	18
5:21–25 117, 135, 145–146, 148, 179		1:6–16	18
7:10–17	56	1:7	23, 25, 170
7:12–13	57, 156,	1:8	19
7:13	126	1:8–16	26, 28, 42–44, 48, 117
7:14	123	1:9	20, 28
7:16	57	1:14	20, 23
8:4–6	135	1:14–15	21
8:5	95–96	1:16	19, 63

2	70
2–3	20, 54, 102, 146, 176
2–5	44, 185
2:1	19–20, 22, 49–50, 52, 130
2:1–2	30, 32, 49, 52, 55, 57, 128, 155, 166, 170
2:1–3	18, 39
2:1–4	19
2:1–5	v, x, 3, 15, 42, 44, 47–48, 54–55, 59, 70, 118, 164
2:1–11	3, 42, 47
2:1–13	43, 48
2:2	20, 33, 37, 48–50, 53, 129, 164, 170
2:2–3	122
2:2–4	19, 37
2:3	19, 49, 52–53, 59, 76, 93, 98, 130
2:3–5	49, 52, 57, 59
2:4	38, 53
2:4–5	20, 49, 130
2:5	53, 59
2:6	56, 59, 66, 127, 154
2:6–7	55, 144, 156
2:6–9	170
2:6–11	v, 3, 15, 18, 33–34, 42, 44, 47, 55, 66, 70
2:7	55–56, 58–59
2:8	22, 33, 62, 64
2:8–9	18, 62, 128–29, 170
2:8–11	55–56, 60
2:9	x, 20, 33, 55, 62–64
2:10	20, 38, 64
2:11	39, 55, 65–66
2:12–13	38, 40–42, 44–45, 66
3	40–41, 66, 93
3:1	17, 19, 22, 41, 43, 46, 67, 74, 77, 90, 122
3:1–2	166
3:1–3	18, 67, 169–70
3:1–4	33, 41–42, 66, 70, 73, 120, 155
3:1–4:8	40, 45
3:1–5:15	42
3:1–12	v, x, 3, 42–43, 66, 119–120, 167
3:2	20, 67–68, 70
3:2–3	33, 71, 105
3:3	20, 69
3:3–8	34
3:4	59, 67, 69, 127–28
3:5	19, 70, 76, 93, 169
3:5–6	20
3:5–7	x, 15, 42, 66, 69, 122, 126, 155
3:5–8	18, 39, 44, 70
3:6	72, 98
3:6–7	70, 72
3:7	72, 128
3:8	19, 42, 89, 122, 126, 154–55
3:9	20, 22, 33, 74, 122, 169–70
3:9–10	70
3:9–11	122
3:9–12	15, 27–28, 39, 41–42, 44, 66, 73, 126
3:10	33
3:11	x, 15, 18, 22, 33–34, 39, 42, 44, 56, 66, 69–71, 73–75, 103, 122–23, 127, 144, 155, 169
3:12	x, 19–20, 39, 76, 93, 127–28, 167
4–5	40, 184
4–7	37, 40
4:1	154
4:1–4	44
4:1–5:15	41–42, 117
4:1–7	43
4:1–8	45
4:1–13	42
4:1–15	44
4:3	19
4:3–4	100
4:4	19
4:6–7	41
4:6–8	44

Ancient Sources Index

4:8–14	43	6:6–7	33, 81, 85–86, 127, 136
4:9–10	20	6:6–8	x, 15, 18, 34, 45, 79–81, 84–85, 89, 91, 136, 178
4:9–5:14	40, 45		
4:10	38	6:7	33
4:11–13	45	6:7–8	92
4:12	19	6:8	vii, 81, 86, 89–92, 94, 101, 106, 117, 126, 131, 136–37
4:13	45		
5:1	42	6:9	92–94
5:1–8	43	6:9–15	103
5:1–14	45	6:9–16	v, 15, 29, 41–44, 92, 131
5:1–15	42	6:10–11	165
5:2–9	98	6:10–12	92, 95, 104, 128, 131, 164
5:4	23		
5:5–6	45	6:10–13	103
5:6–7	41	6:10–16	155
5:6–8	20	6:11–12	166, 170
5:7	19	6:11–15	167
5:8	19	6:12	33, 106, 132, 170
5:9–14	43	6:13	92, 98
5:10–15	45	6:13–15	96, 98
5:11	154	6:13–16	97, 103, 132
5:13–14	170	6:14–15	98, 100, 103, 145
5:13–15	33	6:15	19, 98, 103
6–7	40, 44, 77	6:15–16	45
6:1	19, 41, 77, 81, 93	6:16	91–92, 100–101, 131
6:1–2	43, 79, 82, 136	7:1	19, 103
6:1–3	80	7:1–2	18, 103, 109
6:1–5	45, 81–82, 86	7:1–3	105
6:1–7:6	117	7:1–6	v, x, 15, 42, 44, 102, 109, 128
6:1–7:7	40		
6:1–7:10	144	7:1–7	78
6:1–7:20	40–42, 45	7:1–8	43
6:1–8	v, 3, 42–43, 77–81, 145, 185	7:2	91, 103, 105
		7:2–4	103, 107, 109, 166
6:1–16	120	7:2–6	103, 122
6:2	81	7:3	33, 105, 109, 130, 169
6:3	77, 84, 86, 91	7:3–4	103, 105, 120, 164
6:3–4	83, 116	7:4	19, 109, 133
6:3–5	81–82, 86	7:5	107–8
6:4	23, 84	7:5–6	103, 106, 109
6:4–5	136	7:6	108
6:5	77, 83, 86, 91	7:7–20	42, 45
6:6	86	7:8–20	38, 40, 44, 78, 182

7:9–13	43	1:6–2:10	124
7:11	19	1:10	88
7:11–13	38	3:4	95
7:12	23	3:20	94
7:14–20	43		
7:15	23	**New Testament**	
7:17	38		
7:18	18, 41, 46, 89, 117	Matthew	
7:18–19	20	5:3–12	45
7:18–20	38. 45, 98, 144	25:34–40	143
7:20	20		

Romans
12:11   157

Nahum
1:1   72
3:6   108

1 Corinthians
4:12   157
9:6   157

Habakkuk
1:1   72
1:15–17   104
2:9   164
2:12   74
2:16   49

Ephesians
4:28   157

1 Thessalonians
2:9   157
4:11   157

Zephaniah
1:1   72
2:13–15   72
3:5   49
3:15   72
3:17   72

2 Thessalonians
3:10–12   157

Haggai
1:1   72
1:3–12   126
1:6   99

Zechariah
1:1   72
7:1–3   123
7:2–14   125
7:10   62

Malachi
1:1   72

www.ingramcontent.com/pod-product-compliance
Lightning Source LLC
Chambersburg PA
CBHW030826230426
43667CB00008B/1394